CONTEMPORARY
TRADE STRATEGIES
IN THE PHILIPPINES

Contemporary

Trade Strategies

in the Philippines

A Study in Marketing Anthropology

NORBERT DANNHAEUSER

RUTGERS UNIVERSITY PRESS

New Brunswick, New Jersey

The author gratefully acknowledges permission to include in chapters 6 and 8 of this book, his own material as it appears in the following articles.

"Commercial Relations Between Center and Periphery in North-Central Luzon: Detrimental Dependence or Generative Interdependence?" *Philippine Studies* 29(1981): 144–169. Reprinted by permission. Copyright © 1981 by the Ateneo de Manila University Press.

"Development of a Distribution Channel in the Philippines: From Channel Integration to Channel Fragmentation," *Human Organization* 38(1979):74–78. Reprinted by permission. Copyright © 1979 by the Society for Applied Anthropology.

"Evolution and Devolution of Downward Channel Integration in the Philippines," *Economic Development and Cultural Change* 29(1981):577–595. Reprinted by permission of The University of Chicago Press. Copyright © by The University of Chicago Press.

"Modernization of Distribution Channels and the Dependency Issue: Interregional Commerce in North-Central Luzon, Philippines," *Journal of Anthropological Research*, forthcoming. Reprinted by permission.

Library of Congress Cataloging in Publication Data

Dannhaeuser, Norbert, 1943–
Contemporary trade strategies in the Philippines.

Bibliography: p.
Includes index.
1. Marketing channels—Philippines—Case studies.
2. Economic anthropology—Philippines—Case studies.
I. Title.
HF5415.129.D36   381'.09599   82-5382
ISBN 0-8135-0950-5   AACR2

To H. A. D.

CONTENTS

MAPS AND TABLES

PREFACE

DURING THE PAST HALF-CENTURY the trade of consumer products in developing countries has changed phenomenally. The portion of consumer items derived from industry has expanded, and new marketing institutions responsible for their movement have spread. Yet anthropologists have been remiss in studying these changes. They have been more interested in marketplaces, commercial networks of peasant produce, and petty entrepreneurship. In fact, tradition has confined most of their work to the rural and poor urban sectors of developing countries. Also the fact that modern channel institutions (such as retail franchises, supermarkets, and mass advertising) are very familiar to anthropologists coming from a Western background, no doubt has convinced many that such trade channels are the proper preserve of business administration and marketing, not of anthropology.

What this position forgets, of course, is that modern commercial institutions and trade strategies are pervasive in many third world countries today and have affected them for some time. If anthropologists hope to continue to contribute to the understanding of these societies, therefore, they need to turn their attention to how industrial consumer products are distributed. This the present study hopes to do. Although writing from an anthropological perspective, I have used insights derived from marketing and related fields. I am convinced that marketing and anthropology have much to offer one another and that a subfield of marketing anthropology is a distinct possibility—hence, the subtitle of this book.

Spadework for this study began between 1969 and 1971 while I was conducting research on regional trade networks in Dagupan and its hinterland. This work was continued to 1974 when I realized that to understand commercial relations in Dagupan, the trade connections with Manila needed to be uncovered. Research on this took place in 1975–1976—six months in Manila and six months in Dagupan. Sponsorship came from the Ford Foundation Southeast Asia Fellowship Program, and a Fulbright-Hays Senior Lectureship provided additional support. I hereby gratefully acknowledge their assistance. The then director of the Philippine American Education Foundation in Manila, Professor Juan R. Francisco, was particularly helpful. So also were Professor Mary B. Hollnsteiner and the staff at the Institute of Philippine Culture, Ateneo de Manila University. As a visiting reasearch associate of the institute I enjoyed ready access to its facilities. I also want to acknowledge the help of James Hoyt (cultural attaché at the U.S. embassy). The American Historical Library in the embassy proved a treasure of information on the American period in the Philippines. The Ateneo Law and Business Administration Library, the Library of Business Administration at the University of the Philippines, the De La Salle Library, and the Philippine National Archives also gave me generous access to their material.

Special thanks go to Robin Ang, Lydia Chua, Linda Arenas, Anna Aquino, Jose Dy, Nestor Peralta, and Pepito Zabala in Dagupan. All of them proved invaluable friends and guides. The completion of this project would have been far more difficult without the help and company of Rebecca Hagey, Alan Smith, and Don Welty. It hardly needs to be mentioned that without the cooperation of hundreds of business operators and company employees in Manila and Dagupan this study would not have been possible. I collectively thank them here.

Professor James N. Anderson introduced me to the Philippines. To him and to Professor Jack M. Potter I owe much of my professional interests. To both of them I express my deep appreciation, as well as to Professors William G. Davis and Aram A. Yengoyan who made valuable comments on an earlier draft of this book.

My wife, Charlotte, greatly assisted in editing this work. But her most important contribution was in the field. She charmed into interviews many a hard-nosed businessman who at first had refused.

The ethnographic present spans 1975 to 1977 unless otherwise indicated. Occasionally pseudonyms are used in the text to protect the identity of individuals and firms.

Abbreviations used in the text:

ACCJ	*American Chamber of Commerce Journal*	*FEER*	*Far Eastern Economic Review*
BD	*Business Day*	*MT*	*Manila Times*
EM	*Economic Monitor*	*MH*	*Marketing Horizons*
		PDE	*Philippine Daily Express*

CONTEMPORARY TRADE STRATEGIES IN THE PHILIPPINES

Chapter 1

INTRODUCTION

THIS IS A STUDY of trade channels responsible for the distribution of industrial consumer goods in the Philippines. It traces their history over the past 80 years and describes how they are organized today. The evolution of different types of channels is compared, and the study examines what repercussions these systems of distribution have had upon local social and economic arrangements.

During the past century today's industrial societies experienced a fundamental change in the market channels through which commodities move from producers to consumers. Channels that in the late nineteenth century were fragmented—even in the United States—into many small and independent trade units and numerous trade levels, have matured barely a century later into a system in which large enterprises and channel integration are the norm. Producers gained control over retailers, large retailers moved into manufacturing, and wholesalers became successful retailers as well as producers (Bucklin 1972a). This shift is most apparent on the retail level where the independent Mom and Pop stores along country roads and the general store on Main Street have virtually been replaced by catalog-order houses, department stores, discount houses, supermarkets, retail chains, and cooperatives.

Throughout this period the goal of the channel members remained the same, namely to maximize sales and profits. It was in the twentieth century, however, that circumstances encouraged traders and producers to follow one particular strategy in order to reach that goal. This strategy stresses distribution at least as much as production, seeks to control the movement of products to consumers, and hopes to realize mass marketing by means of intensive advertising and penetration of foreign markets. One result of this has been the proliferation of the multinational enterprise which today enjoys a prominence in open economies it has not had since the days of colonial mercantilism in the seventeenth and eighteenth centuries.

By no means has this transformation been confined to Europe, the United States, and Japan. As the growth of multinationals implies, trade channels within less developed countries are subject to considerable pressures from the outside. Sears Roebuck in Mexico, Shell Oil stations in the Philippines, VW in Brazil, and Coke nearly worldwide attest to this. Also developments internal to these countries are important. Commercialization, urbanization, improved transportation, and spreading consumer demand, all help to change the formerly itinerant character of market activities—peddlers, rotating markets—into a stationary one. The store is challenging market vendors, and in some areas the manufacturer-controlled retail chain is troubling independent stores.

Anyone interested in analyzing modern market channels in a developing setting, as I am in this study, cannot do better than turn to the Philippines. Since the Spanish period this country has had an open economy subject to profound influences from the West and Japan. Methods of product distribution introduced from these societies have been experimented with more readily there than perhaps in any other country. Moreover, the most appropriate trade channels to examine are the ones organized around industrial consumer goods. Because of their close association with the capital-intensive and overseas sector, their distribution has been subject to a considerable amount of change.

This study begins with a historical sketch of industrial consumer goods distribution in the Philippines and continues with a more detailed examination of individual product channels. My aim is to employ both a historical and a synchronic perspective. The past, especially the last 50 or 60 years, is taken account of, and particular events as well as general processes that had a bearing on the evolution of distribution are considered. At the same time I devote much space to analyzing how distribution is organized today.

Studies of marketing have a tendency to concentrate on either the minute or the grand. Either an individual firm, single channel, or a community is scrutinized; or marketing behavior on the national or international level is the subject (Epstein 1975). I hope to bridge the anthropologists' proclivity for detail and the economists' prejudice for the aggregate by using the trade link between Manila and a medium-range commercial town to the north (Dagupan) as a convenient anchorage. This enables me to examine national and international developments that, by virtue of the dominant position of Manila, appear first in that city, and to trace them out into the provincial hinterland. My intention is to have sufficient regional awareness to take into account developments on the national level without losing sight of the empirical detail that is needed to trace their local manifestations.

Within this general framework I stress three themes. One is concerned with the types of channel organizations that exist. Among the possible classifications of distribution, the one I find most satisfactory relates channel structure to marketing strategy. Some suppliers in Manila follow active sales penetration into the provinces and establish branches or send out salesmen; others are more conservative in their approach and wait for customers to come by. Much of the book is devoted to showing whether trade channels are characterized by one or the other preference, how this becomes manifest in the channel organization, and whether these preferences correspond to the ethnic background of the traders.

Another theme is the direction of channel evolution between Manila and the provinces. The past few years saw students of marketing construct models designed to predict the evolution of product distribution. Naturally, most of these models have been derived from the past record of today's developed countries, and usually the assumption is that the evolution experienced there will be repeated in currently developing societies. I examine whether this assumption is appropriate for the Philippines.

In the last part of the book I turn to the third theme. It is concerned with the local consequences of downward channel penetration, the effect of modern marketing systems reaching out of Manila into the provinces. Do they complement, modify, or destroy traditional modes of distribution? Has their entrance enhanced the position of local traders or not? These questions relate to the current debate about international trade and the beneficial or exploitative effects of multinational firms upon developing countries.

A similar issue exists within such countries. Inside of virtually all developing societies large and aggressive enterprises extend their management of product distribution beyond the primary urban areas into the provincial frontiers. Many of these firms are likely to be branches, subsidiaries, or license holders of foreign concerns. In examining the local repercussions of Manila-based distribution channels, therefore, certain facets of the discussion surrounding international commerce and multinationals will prove relevant to this study.

A WORD ABOUT the research procedures employed for this study is in order. My overall aim was to combine extensive and intensive field techniques and to pursue follow-up work where opportunities allowed. Most of the work was conducted in English which is the lingua franca of the Philippine commercial community. In Dagupan a random sample of 252 neighborhood store operators was interviewed using a standard format. Nearly all medium- to large-scale merchants of the city were contacted, and 85 percent (180 out of 210) responded positively. In-depth interviews were administered, and in many cases repeat visits took place over the years. I also contacted key merchants in provincial towns surrounding Dagupan who had trade relations with the city. Most useful for the project were the many friends gained among the local traders. Because they allowed me to stay in their stores for long periods and permitted me to accompany them on their travels to Manila and to provincial customers, they enabled me to share the experience of being a merchant in the Dagupan-Manila region.

In Manila I combined library research with lengthy interviews of company managers engaged in product distribution in north-central Luzon. Fifty-five companies were covered in this fashion.

Chapter 2

THE AMERICAN PERIOD

The Philippines

WHEN IN 1898 the Americans took over the Philippines from Spain, the country was sparsely populated, physically and ethnically fragmented, and rebellious against colonial rule. It boasted some wealth in subsistence and cash crop agriculture, but little in the extractive and manufacturing industries. The provincial system of transportation was largely confined to shipping plus a small railroad on Luzon Island, and whatever urbanization had evolved centered in Manila, Cebu, and Iloilo. Add to this a shattered administration and an educational system that did not exist on the national level, and one has a country that, to say the least, appeared to promise limited potential for the future.

When in 1935 the commonwealth was proclaimed, conditions had changed. The population was in the middle of a long-term upward trend, reaching 16 million in 1939, up from eight million in 1903. Sophisticated forms of plantations and agricultural processing had become common. Mining, most notably of gold and copper, had expanded, keeping the more destructive effects of the Depression at arm's length. By this time a locally controlled and viable administration integrated the country; so also a network of roads, the extent of which was remarkable considering the fact that large-scale construction had begun only within the previous 20 years. Urbanization spread beyond the three traditional centers of

Manila, Cebu, and Iloilo, and American-oriented elementary education became the right of every child.

But not all had changed. The intervening three decades had little impact on industrial manufacturing. Except for a few enterprises in cigarettes, soft drinks, beer, shoes, and textiles, factory production in the Philippines was nonexistent. Cottage industry remained the prevailing mode, and the production of cash crops remained the main source of income. The Philippines continued to be a traditional agrarian society. Given this relatively static economic structure, what had happened to the domestic system of product distribution? Did it show a similar degree of conservatism or did it, alongside so many other facets of Philippine society of the day, experience rapid change?

Early Period

At the turn of the century the ethnic composition of trade was decidedly plural. On the top of the channel stood European and American merchants who controlled the large-scale import and export trade. These relied on the intermediary level of wholesaling, store retailing, and assembly which the Chinese dominated. In the words of the head of a European importing firm doing business in Manila at this time, "the [European] firms here, with very few exceptions, only sell in Manila and to the Chinese, who are the intermediaries for the provinces. . . . For importers and exporters it would not have been possible to do any work at all; in fact, the trade of the island, small as it is compared to what it might be, has depended entirely upon the Chinese, because . . . they sell to the men in the interior, and barter with the natives for produce in exchange for imports" (quoted in Wickberg 1965:68). Filipinos, insofar as they participated in commerce at all, confined their activities largely to the marketplace where they engaged in petty trade of goods derived from the peasantry.

This ethnic cleavage corresponded to the structure of distribution of the day. At the apex were several general-line trading houses active in the import and export business, such as Castel Brothers, Wolf and Sons, and Camaron Macaughlin. Below these existed the "large wholesaler of imported goods and export produce" (ibid.: 72), most of them Chinese. These sold to subwholesalers and retailers and bought from assemblers of produce. Some also maintained secret agents in the provinces who, through shops and stores, bought up items and retailed products for the "head" or employer (*cabecilla*) in Manila (ibid.). Aspects of this *cabecilla* system among the Chinese foreshadowed American-inspired franchising and branching that began to blossom half a century later.

On the retail level two competing institutions existed. One of these consisted of store outlets of various types: the small general goods store (*tienda de sari sari*), knickknack stores (*tienda de chucherias*), hardware stores (*tienda quincallera*), and the impressive urban bazaars (large general stores). The other consisted of the periodic market and the itinerant vendor. Before the mid-nineteenth century these markets virtually monopolized local and regional distribution. Since then permanent stores had made considerable headway, and the monopoly of the markets began to be confined to the local trade of peasant products.

In the parlance of modern marketing, by the turn of the century distribution of imported goods in the Philippines was vertically and horizontally fragmented. Enterprises were small, even in the import and export trade, and their internal organization was maintained by means of kin and ethnic ties. The small, independent store typified the system on the retail level. Aggressive marketing from Manila and its organizational implications hardly existed. Advertising was in limited use, and except for informal, often secret, methods, such as the *cabecilla* system, importers and others in Manila rarely developed ways to contact provincial consumers directly. Maximizing the movement of products into the provinces was a question that did not receive formal and organized attention.

Commonwealth Period

By the mid-thirties 400 importers and exporters were operating in the Philippines (mainly in Manila) as were 1,700 wholesalers and some 80,000 stationary retailers (U.S. Department of International Reference Service 1948).[1] The number of commercial units had expanded by a factor of two to three since the turn of the century. The value of domestic trade had also grown. The distribution of imported items, selling of native products to consumers, and buying produce for others added up to ₱660 million in 1913 and ₱1 billion in 1923 (Philippine Islands 1924). Infrastructure programs, the large expatriate community, bilateral trade with America, the growth of the population, and peasants entering commercial agriculture were responsible for this expansion. In the field of distribution, product specialization became popular among large trade firms. Thirty years before, the general-line trade houses dominated large-scale distribution; shortly before World War II this was changing. Their position began to be challenged by Bachrach Motors, Metro Drugs, Botica Boie (drugs), Radiowealth (radios), and other firms that helped establish new norms of specialization. The general-line trade houses, now exemplified by Pacific Commercial Company, Theo. H. Davies and Company, Elizalde and Company, and Macondray and Company, remained the largest in the business, but the field began to be crowded by those who handled a restricted set of products.

Despite the growing role of commerce and product specialization, in many ways distribution by the thirties had changed little from what it had been three decades before. Its ethnic composition, for instance, had remained basically the same. In 1924 the Commercial Handbook could state that "Chinese middlemen . . . often serve as the connecting link between American and European importers and exporters and the Filipino consumers and producers" (ibid. 1924:55). Concerning the upper end of the channel, a similar publication in 1927 pointed out that "the American and European firms ordinarily import directly. . . . A few of the larger Chinese firms also have been importing directly in recent years, but the bulk of the merchandise handled by the Chinese distributors is purchased through the importers or . . . through manufacturers' representatives, who are in most part American" (U.S. Department of Commerce 1927:99). The Euro-Americans continued to control the overseas trade, and the Chinese, many of them residing around the Divisoria market area in Manila, were in the jobbing and retailing business to a degree that they "probably control[led] 65% to 75% of the merchandise distributed" (ibid.). As before, Filipinos found themselves within the small-scale sector of marketplace exchange.

This overall stability in ethnic makeup, though, did not prevent changes in detail. European, especially British, interests dominated overseas trade up to 1914, when World War I temporarily eliminated their competition for the Americans. After that the Americans ruled supreme. A decade later a few large Chinese enterprises (such as Cheng Ban Yek and Company and Go Fay and Company) began to organize their own import business from the States, and several American and European firms, in turn, entered the Chinese domain and began to wholesale and retail on their own. At the same time the Japanese appeared. In 1931, 50 percent of the imported textiles came from Japan, and after the Manchurian incident, when the Japanese faced a boycott from the Chinese in the Philippines, their bazaars began to spread in Manila and elsewhere (Hartendorp 1952).

Filipinos, finally, were not idle. They entered into store trade (pharmacy, gifts, school supplies) in greater numbers than ever before. Symptomatic of this was the rising call by Filipinos to restrict the Chinese hold over commerce and the spate of articles that appeared in the *Philippine Journal of Commerce* giving advice to prospective Filipino entrepreneurs on how to begin and be successful in the *sari-sari* or small-scale neighborhood store business. These developments, however, failed to alter the ethnic plurality of distribution in the Philippines. It remained essentially tripartite with Filipinos in small-scale buy-and-sell, Chinese in more substantial retailing and wholesaling, and Euro-Americans oriented toward overseas sources and outlets.

The structure of distribution channels in the Philippines also proved conservative. The fragmented nature of the channel had if anything been intensified in the intervening period because of the growth in the number of traders and the trend toward product specialization. The following statement made in 1927 about retail trade could just as well have been written 30 years before: "There are a few fairly large stores in some of the more important towns, but by far the most important factors in the retail distribution system of the Philippines are the numerous tiendas, or small general stores, located throughout the islands. These are supplemented by the población markets, which are found in nearly all towns, and by the Chinese bazaars. . . . These three classes of establishments, the tiendas, bazaars, and markets, account for the bulk of the retail sales" (U.S. Department of Commerce 1927:102–103). In Manila experiments in department-store management were made, but the American-owned Heacock's on Escolta (the main business street) remained the only really successful attempt. Large import-export houses, the complex wholesale and subwholesale level, and the fragmented retail structure had survived the intervening years.

Yet, innovations that went beyond the confines of Manila and that had some radical implications for the future were not totally absent. These appeared when several substantial American Manila-based companies started to control distribution beyond their own trade level and began to push sales aggressively. A striking example is the Pacific Commercial Company (PCC) which at the time was the largest American company in the Philippines. Established in 1911, it flourished when the European competition was eliminated during World War I. By the thirties it averaged ₱40 million in sales per year and retained 1,000 employees (one-fifth of them Americans). Its chief activity was representing American companies in the Philippines. In 1923 it had exclusive licensing agreements with more than 30 major concerns, among them Carnation Milk Products Company, H. J. Heinz and Company, Sherwin-Williams Company, GMC Trucks, Procter and Gamble Distributing Company, and International General Electric Company. It also exported hemp, sugar, cigars and cigarettes, rattan, and hats, and had its hand in processing by operating a metal sheet plant, a machine shop, a car repair shop, and several other establishments.

To accommodate all these activities the company was divided into import, export, finance, warehousing, traffic (it had its own trucking fleet until commercial transportation improved), and manufacturing departments. Far from being satisfied with Manila, Iloilo, and Cebu as most importer-distributors of the day were, "the company maintained offices in most of the large cities and towns in the Philippines and its salesmen [or 'field representatives' as they were already then known] covered every nook and corner of the country" (Hartendorp 1952:424). These offices were run as branch and residence agencies and supplied local dealers and bought goods from provincial producers and assemblers. PCC also had two subsidiaries, American Hardware and Plumbing Company and the International Cold Stores, which had their own retail outlets. Overseas offices were located in New York, San Francisco, Seattle, Sydney, and Kobe.

Given its size and extensive interests in product distribution, it is understandable that PCC was one of the first in the Philippines to create a publicity department and to turn to advertising beyond the practice current then of placing tiny notices in the local newspapers. In 1919 it was the largest advertiser in the Philippines. As Gleek rather grandiosely puts it, "its condensed milk advertising was credited with having saved the lives of countless children, while its advertisements for pumps promoted public health by preaching the dangers of polluted water" (Gleek 1975:45). At a time when the lack of active sales strategies by local merchants was bemoaned by American observers, personnel of PCC fanned out into the provinces beating the bushes for new customers. There is the case of the Luzon-Lagio plow. In the teens PCC had designed an iron plow similar to the wooden plow used by Filipinos. To distribute it the company advertised, passed out booklets and handbills to large numbers of farmers, and sent demonstrators into the rice districts who, with the aid of local officials and live demonstrations of the plow, tried to convince local buyers. After some five years of very intensive work, nearly 900 dealers in the country sold the Luzon-Lagio plows. American-style aggressive marketing started to penetrate the Philippines.

PCC did not stand alone; it was merely the epitome of a more widespread trend. Enterprises grew in size, shed their familial method of organization, emphasized internal specialization along functional lines, and began to accept marketing as a separate and formally defined activity. As I show in more detail in Chapter 6, Singer Sewing Machines already had its own distribution network throughout the islands in the second half of the nineteenth century. Others created theirs at the turn of the century. For example, three large general supply firms (North American Trading Company, American Commercial Company, and the Pacific and Oriental Trading Company) had licensed "agencies in every place of size throughout the Archipelago" (Bellairs 1902:198–199). These agencies, however, were not the same as the more elaborate branch offices of later years. Not until the twenties and thirties was it valid to state that "general importers or large business firms often take a great part in the distribution of their merchandise to consumers, and frequently the trade in the interior is virtually in their hands" (Philippine Islands 1924:55), and that "large distributors in Manila often have branches in the more important towns throughout the Provinces" (U.S. Department of Commerce 1927:99).

Instead of investing in provincial branches or assigning agencies, some firms began to send an employed, itinerant sales force into the field. Improvements in transportation made this an increasingly attractive choice. Ang Tibay, for instance, still a prominent footwear manufacturing company today, had a "corps of well-trained and experienced agents that distributed into different parts of the country" (Philippine Journal of Commerce 1937:8). They served wholesalers and were assigned to Luzon, to the Visayas (central Philippines), to Sulu and Mindanao in the south, and to Manila. Also the Philippine Manufacturing Company (groceries) started in 1920 to have its salesmen contact provincial wholesalers and retailers, whereas previously customers had to call on the salesmen in their offices.

The formal use of hired itinerant fieldmen in the Philippines was further developed in the twenties. It was then that Erlanger and Galinger, Inc. of Manila introduced "scientific salesmanship" into the country (Roxas 1968). Convinced that a salesman must know the product he sells before he can sell successfully, it initiated an elaborate course in salesmanship and follow-up training of field personnel. The need for this was especially pressing for E&G because the company dealt with office machinery which required technical handling. Others with less demanding products followed this lead only slowly, and for most the Chinese wholesalers in Divisoria continued to be the avenue through which their goods found their way into the provinces.

Some of these American-inspired innovations of market penetration were similar to channel organizations the Chinese had introduced a long time before. I have mentioned the *cabecilla* system, vestiges of which survived in the form of interlocking ownership arrangements between wholesalers and retailers. While the Chinese chose this organization to gain security and maintain an ethnic defense against outsiders, Americans used branching, field salesmen, licensing, and the like to create demand and for aggressive marketing. These new organizations existed in the open. Legally sanctioned, they were pushed by advertisements and written about, and were therefore very visible. Because of this publicity it is easy to overestimate the trend toward market integration during this period. It certainly was not sufficiently pervasive to change the fragmented nature of distribution in the Philippines, and the coming war forced a pause in even these hesitant developments. In keeping with its previous record, the leader of channel innovations proved to be politically the most astute. PCC liquidated itself a few months before the Japanese invasion.

Dagupan

During the period of American tutelage, Dagupan consolidated its position as the foremost trade center in north-central Luzon (see Map 1). It had not always occupied that position. Central Pangasinan in the nineteenth century had a mature, cyclical market system of which Dagupan was an important, but not dominant, member. It "apparently lacked the far-ranging peddlers that brought a measure of prosperity to nearby Binmaley and San Carlos" (Doeppers 1971:73). The town's future was not to lie with the horizontal exchange of peasant produce, but with the vertical movement of interprovincial trade. Warehousing, transportation, and eventually distribution through stores were to become its hallmark. Dagupan in the nineteenth century was an important center for the largely waterborne traffic of goods between the interior of Pangasinan and the Ilocano provinces to the northeast and (secondarily) Manila to the south. The town's location on the Lingayen Gulf at the mouth of the Pantal River, parts of which could be used as a harbor, secured it an advantage over other communities. But it was the coming of the railroad that finally made Dagupan.

Over the span of two decades the town was the head of the only convenient overland transportation link between the northern end of the Central Plain and Manila. The partial completion of the Manila-Dagupan Railroad by the British in 1894 assured it this position. This experience was sufficient to propel it far beyond other incipient urban centers of the region. Until the line was extended beyond Dagupan to just north of San Fernando (La

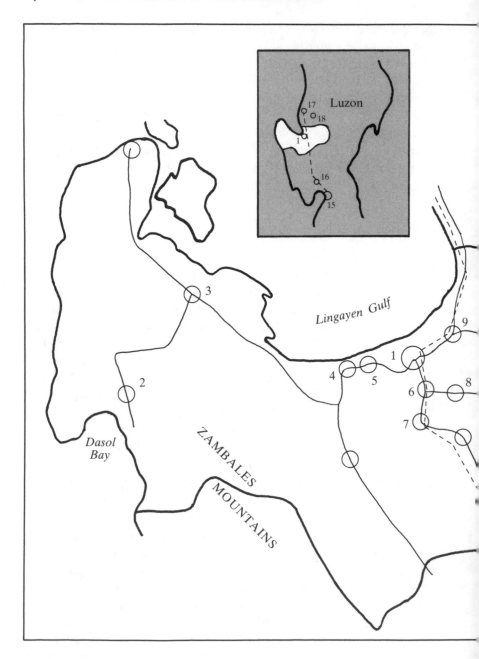

NORTH-CENTRAL LUZON AND PANGASINAN

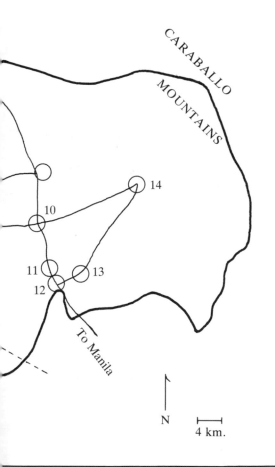

Legend

◯ : Major *población*
—— : Road
----- : Rail

CARABALLO MOUNTAINS

14

10

11 13

12

To Manila

N

4 km.

Union) in 1914, the town was the entrepôt of the flow of commodities between the Ilocos coast, Pangasinan, and Manila. Once the line was extended, Dagupan's position had been consolidated to such an extent that its size attracted newcomers and resources.

Commerce has always been important to Dagupan, much more than production. As Dagupeños untiringly like to point out, this is enshrined in its name, which is derived from *nandaragupan* (Pangasinan) or "old meeting place." Between the late nineteenth and early twentieth centuries its commercial function shifted from assembly of produce derived from its hinterland to the breaking and distribution of manufactured goods from Manila. In the mid- and late nineteenth century Pangasinan was the main rice-exporting province of the Philippines. Together with the Ilocano provinces, it was also a major supplier of tobacco for the Manila market. Dagupan at this time served as the center for transshipment of rice and tobacco intended for Manila, and warehouses along its riverbanks became a common sight. Distribution of imports was less important. Produce for local consumption entered the town's marketplace from its immediate hinterland. More suggestive of the future were the stores run by Europeans and Chinese that established themselves along what was already then the main business street. These sold hardware, dry goods, and general household items from Manila, and in keeping with the main function of Dagupan at that time, many of them skillfully combined this distribution with the purchase and transport of local produce to the south.

During the next 30 years several developments changed this commercial pattern. When the railroad was completed shipments between Dagupan and Manila were facilitated. The reputation of Dagupan as a commercial center improved, and many Chinese settled there in the nineties. These, together with the Americans who came shortly thereafter, helped absorb the growing flow of consumer goods from Manila. Demand for such products intensified in the teens when Dagupan served as the conduit of Manila-derived goods and equipment to be used in the construction of the hill station, Baguio, 50 kilometers to its northeast (Reed 1976). Concurrently, the town started to lose its role as the assembly point of produce for Manila. To cash in on the transportation of rice, it was decided in Manila to build a rail spur into the core of the rice-producing area of eastern Pangasinan. Once this was done, shipments of rice to Manila began to bypass Dagupan. The expansion of the road network in the Central Plain had the same effect. The coup de grace to Dagupan's assembly function came in the twenties when Pangasinan was replaced by the Cagayan Valley in northern Luzon as a major rice-exporting region.[2] By the commonwealth period Dagupan's merchants therefore had shifted away from assembly in favor of downward distribution.

The commercial prosperity of Dagupan did not suffer from this change. To act as the distributive center for Pangasinan at that time was to serve one of the largest provincial populations in the Philippines. This population was relatively wealthy because of its varied agricultural activities, and it had received perhaps more infrastructural investments from the colonial administration than any other province outside of Rizal. Demand for an increasing range of sophisticated products in the region was assured, and history and geography had admirably prepared Dagupan to serve that demand. During this period the city's functions diversified. A sizable copra factory was added to the city's marginal cottage industry, and what was to become the largest bus company in the Philippines, Pantranco, was initiated by some local Americans. A fishpond industry spread along the Lingayen Gulf, and Dagupan became a major trade center of *bangus* (milkfish). Higher educational and medical institutions were drawn to it, and until World War II the only bank in Pangasinan could be found in Dagupan. With the opening of several cinemas it also became the place for entertainment in the region. Between the 1890s and 1930s the city had prospered, and its position as the center of north-central Luzon was assured.

The Ethnic Factor

Records attest to the importance of Chinese in Dagupan since at least the second half of the nineteenth century when they introduced the large general store or bazaar (Doeppers 1971:74–75; Flormata 1901). During the period 1910–1915 they operated one dry goods and five general stores (there were also several Filipino and American-owned shops). The Chinese formed the center of commerce, and by the nineties they had acquired a very strong hold over the Manila-Dagupan trade.

In 1903 the town had 400 Chinese, more than any other community in Pangasinan. At that time the total population of Dagupan was 20,357. By 1939 the population had risen to 32,602, and the number of Chinese and Chinese mestizos stood at 900 (U.S. Bureau of the Census 1905, vol. 2; Philippine Commonwealth 1940–1943, vol. 1). Throughout this period Chinese dominated the store trade while Filipinos concentrated on petty buy-and-sell. The 1935 anniversary issue of one of the local weeklies offers some flavor of the ethnic cleavage that prevailed then. It names the town's substantial trade establishments, and of the 64 stores listed, 26 are Chinese (*Siliw* June 1935). This alone hardly suggests a monopolistic position for the Chinese, but they did control the larger establishments and the most important product lines. They operated virtually all hardware, dry goods, grocery, and bazaar stores. Only two Japanese challenged them in these fields and then only with commodities originating in Japan. Filipinos with stores handled more restricted lines, such as sports goods, arms, school supplies, musical instruments, drugs, and hats, some of which they obtained from local Chinese subwholesalers. The Chinese, in sum, continued to be responsible for the bulk of the distributive trade from Manila; yet Filipinos, as on the national level, were beginning to join in.

What about the Euro-Americans in Dagupan? The town had no equivalent positions available in import-export which were traditionally their preserve in Manila. Nor was there a sizable expatriate community remaining in Dagupan during the commonwealth period. From a peak of 50 or 60 Euro-Americans in the teens their number had dwindled to about 20 in the thirties. Some parallels with conditions in Manila, though, did exist. Whereas in Manila Euro-Americans maintained contact with Western overseas interests, in Dagupan some represented large Manila trade houses that had offices in the community. Instead of Chinese or Filipinos, Americans often operated the agencies and branches that "progressive" Manila businesses had opened in Dagupan.

Organization of Distribution

Turning to the structure of Manila-Dagupan distribution channels, some evidence suggests that the *cabecilla* system prevalent among the Chinese in the last half of the nineteenth century also extended into Dagupan. In the American period, however, only modified forms of it survived in the shape of joint ownerships, partnerships, commissioned agents, and family branching.[3] The *cabecilla* system was best suited to circumstances in which the Manila merchants were involved in both assembly and distribution. As these merchants shifted their attention to one or the other activity—in Dagupan usually to distribution—the payoff resulting from retaining store merchants as hired salesmen in the provinces diminished. Moreover, Chinese traders in Dagupan, who continued to combine distribution with assembly, had attained a position of sufficient strength that they did not need to tie themselves to a single outlet or source in Manila, let alone act as a hired representative. Various covert means of integration with Manila suppliers continued among the Chinese, as I show in more detail in Chapter 4, but these usually took a different form from the *cabecilla* system.

In the twenties and thirties the majority of merchants in Manila and Dagupan, whether Chinese or Filipinos, were independent traders. This was true both in the legal sense and in the sense that buyers could contact whichever suppliers they wished. The typical channel ran from importers to wholesalers in Manila's Divisoria. These resold to local subwholesalers or wholesaler-retailers who came from Dagupan. The latter provisioned the better-off consumers in the provincial town and passed goods on to vendors and dealers in the neighboring municipalities. The vertical channel was fragmented with some items passing through as many as six to seven levels before reaching their final destination.

The retail level was also atomized. The marketplace next to Dagupan's plaza started to attract permanent stall vendors, the empty interstices along the main business street were filled with a great variety of shops, and the *sari-sari* store was spreading in the residential districts of the *población* (urbanized center of the town; see Map 2). It hardly need be mentioned that, whether small or large, these enterprises were of the owner-operator type, boasted minimal internal division of labor, and were conservative in sell-

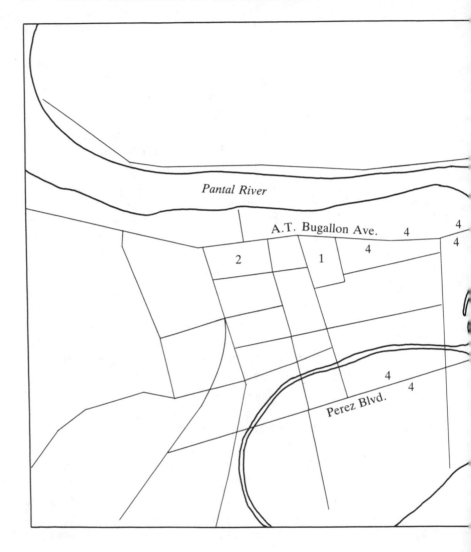

DAGUPAN *POBLACIÓN*

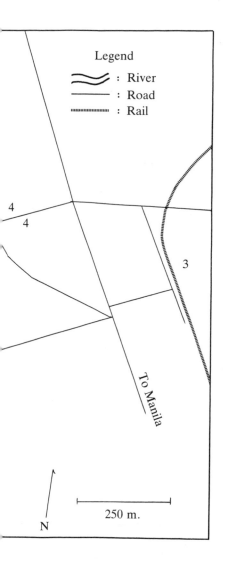

Legend

≈ : River

—— : Road

⊪⊪⊪⊪⊪ : Rail

4
4

3

To Manila

250 m.

N

KEY TO MAP 2

Marketplace 1
Plaza 2
Principal commercial
    zones 4
Railroad station 3

ing. Even the largest stores on the principal business street (now known as A. T. Bugallon Avenue) were located in wooden buildings with the owner's residence above the store and display restricted to a single ground-level room that faced the street. Innovations like the department store, which had already appeared in Manila, or display behind glass windows were far removed from conditions prevailing in Dagupan even in the thirties.

In most cases Dagupeños bought their supplies in Manila and transported them north by rail or (later) truck. Advertisements by Manila firms entered the city mostly in subdued form via local newspapers, which the bulk of the population did not read. Radio was yet to become a mass medium, and the cinema was used only sparingly for this purpose. The main exception to such conservatism in consumer promotion was the road shows that a few Manila companies organized in the thirties. If Manila firms pushed products aggressively, it was usually among Dagupan's merchants, not directly at the consumer level. This sales strategy was shared by Dagupeño traders. Some, especially Filipinos who relied on retail sales, dabbled in display, but most aggressive marketing, insofar as it was indulged in at all, was directed to other traders. Some of the town's large merchants maintained "rolling stores" or trucks that visited neighboring municipalities to deliver and take orders from local merchants.

Some innovations in marketing organization that were accepted in Manila had an impact in Dagupan. These took three forms. A growing number of company salesmen from Manila started to cover Dagupan, branch offices of Manila suppliers opened in the town, and licensing agreements with Dagupeño stores proliferated. By the thirties traveling company salesmen from Manila had become sufficiently numerous in Dagupan for one or two hotels to specialize in serving them. Twenty to 30 of them acted for their Manila principal(s) in more or less permanent capacity in Dagupan. Others made the city their jumping-off place for trade excursions to the north, so that by 1936 Dagupan was "the cross-road for salesmen who travel in Pangasinan, La Union, Ilocos Sur, Ilocos Norte" (Philippine Commonwealth 1936:265–266).

Of course, in themselves itinerant salesmen were nothing new. The growing tendency of the larger Manila distributors to hire them, organize them, and send them to medium-range centers like

Dagupan, however, was. The same can be said about branches. Wholesale branches in particular had existed for a long time, but the twenties and thirties witnessed an unprecedented rise of interest in them and a greater willingness to establish branches in the provinces even for retail purposes. The general trade houses Erlanger and Galinger and Getz and Brothers opened branches in Dagupan to sell office machinery and bicycles respectively. After having had an agency in the city for 20 years, Manila Trading and Supply Company, the exclusive distributor for Ford in the Philippines, upgraded it into a branch. Eventually the same was done by PCC, which, among its many other interests, represented GMC Trucks in the Philippines.

Instead of entering Dagupan's market by opening branches, several Manila companies resorted to contractual means to gain downward control. For example, PCC had appointed the largest hardware store in the town, Tan Co Co, to be its exclusive dealer of GMC Trucks in north-central Luzon before it opened its own branch outlet in Dagupan. Several local store merchants, such as the proprietor of City Grocery, received the right to distribute a particular brand of gasoline under license. These agreements with gasoline companies were not yet full franchises; Dagupan license holders could handle other, noncompeting goods. Tan Co Co remained a hardware store, and City Grocery was not turned into a gas station. However, the decision by Stanvac in 1939 to open a service station in Dagupan under a full franchise that allowed the dealer to be only in the car business, forebode the future world of franchising.

DURING THE AMERICAN PERIOD institutions distributing consumer goods in Manila and Dagupan experienced some change. Innovations that connected Manila suppliers directly to provincial retail outlets were introduced, the layout of some stores was modernized, and advertisements, together with promotions, were increasingly indulged in. Aggressive marketing, much cherished by the Americans, was making inroads in the Philippines. Also Filipino participation in medium-scale trade grew. But modernization was localized and experimental. The organization of distribution in the country remained basically fragmented, conservative, and divided into ethnic enclaves. More pronounced transformations of trade channels had to await the post-World War II period.

Chapter 3

INDEPENDENCE

The Philippines

Organization of Distribution

MORE THAN A GENERATION after the end of World War II, the Philippines has remained a producer of agricultural and mining products for export and an importer of manufactured goods. The country still has a long way to go before joining the ranks of Taiwan and South Korea.

Despite this continuity, the Philippines today is hardly a carbon copy of what it was 40 years ago. The threefold increase of its population, which now stands at 46 million (1980), by itself attests to this. Urbanization has progressed. The primary city, Manila, and the regional centers of Cebu, Iloilo, Davao, and Bacolod (Negros) are now joined by tertiary ones of considerable size: Cagayan de Oro (northern Mindanao), Tarlac (Tarlac), Angeles (Pampanga), Cabanatuan (Neuva Ecija), Legaspi (Albay), Dagupan, and so on. Urbanization has helped commerce, as did the steady rise until recently in the real income of urban and rural households.[1]

The number of commercial units and trade volume have also increased precipitously: wholesalers in 1972 numbered 12,000 and retailers 330,000 (up from 6,000 and 122,000 respectively in 1961). Total trade volume in 1969 was valued at ₱14 billion (₱6.5 billion in 1961) (Republic of the Philippines 1964–1965; 1973; 1975).

Moreover, the Philippine government started to interfere in the economy to an unprecedented degree. Gone are the days when the free-wheeling American entrepreneur (or Filipino, or Chinese) could invest in what he considered would promise the highest return without regard to restrictions on imports, local manufacture, and his ethnic background.

During this period merchants in the Philippines pushed actively for sales. By the mid- and late fifties the United States-derived notion of marketing was widely shared among at least the more prominent members of the commercial community, and its implications for sales organizations started to be implemented. Hints of this already existed before the war, but it was only now that the advantages of seeking sales aggressively and creating demand were generally accepted. Also the Japanese adopted this strategy and during the sixties began to challenge the heretofore paramount position of the United States in the import trade.

This diffusion of an active marketing strategy was enhanced by changes in the manufacturing sector. Earlier I said that the economic structure of the Philippines had changed but little since the prewar years. This is only true concerning its fundamental structure. Industry received a boost in the fifties when overseas and local interests, who formerly relied on imports of consumer products, decided to manufacture them in the country. Why this change of heart?

The immediate impetus came in 1948 when the newly independent government struggling with foreign exchange difficulties decided to limit its dollar losses by restricting imports. Once the first step was taken, it was easy to support the decision with new arguments, and soon the administration felt that the restrictions were necessary to protect and encourage local manufacture. Thus was born the era of import and exchange controls, which was to last in its original form for a decade and under various guises ever since. As the World Bank has put it, the decade of growth, 1950–1960, "resulted in the productive employment of surplus labor and capital, the creation and education of a new entrepreneurial class, and the setting of new national and social goals" (World Bank 1976:187), among which the most important was industrialization.

The only problem was that the manufacturing capacity created centered on the assembly of imported consumer goods, many of them luxury items. What the planners had not foreseen was "the tendency of capital to flow into the most profitable industries and that the act of restricting imports of non-essential consumption goods would raise the domestic prices of these goods sharply and thereby make their production the most profitable opportunity available" (Baldwin 1975:149). The finished components of these products were imported at an increasing rate. Until very recently the production of intermediate industrial commodities was neglected by policymakers and investors alike. Only in the late sixties and seventies did the government try to rectify the situation with the establishment of the Board of Investment (BOI), implementation of export incentives, and devaluation. For all intents and purposes, therefore, the Philippines is just as import dependent for its manufactured consumer goods today as before except that the assembly stage has been transferred to the country.

Another unforeseen result of import controls was that they did not just encourage Filipino entrepreneurs to enter into manufacturing. Virtually all major brand-name products started to be assembled by subsidiaries of overseas firms, by joint ventures, or by local companies under license. Products of firms like VW, GE, Colgate-Palmolive, Datsun, Matsushita, and Ford were "produced" in the Philippines under close foreign supervision.[2] In this respect import and exchange controls ironically encouraged foreign investments and tight foreign supervision over manufacturing. They also resulted in increasing control by foreigners, either directly or through licenses, over the distribution of the products now locally assembled. In this roundabout way the government policy of import controls stimulated the importation of active marketing strategies and ensured that these strategies experienced their earliest widespread application in the distribution of locally assembled cars, appliances, motorcycles, and similar foreign-derived goods.

These developments had a devastating effect upon the traditional general-line trade houses. Under the government control policy, import licenses were required which trade houses and smaller (Chinese) importers found difficult to obtain. The government preferred to grant them to industrial end users and large Filipino retailers. These would contact the trade houses and place orders for foreign goods. From acting as importers they became indentors, and "trading houses . . . were relegated to a somewhat passive position," the U. S. Department of Commerce lamented (1965:45). Some survived the fifties by doing this and representing foreign suppliers in the Philippines; others added manufacture or assembly, usually under license, to their repertoire.

With decontrol in the early sixties the situation improved only slightly for trade houses. They could again engage in importation, but so could smaller importers. Simultaneously, large local buyers (manufacturers and retailers) and foreign suppliers saw it was to their advantage to contact one another directly by sending their own representatives so as to avoid the middleman's commission. The market, therefore, had become far more competitive for trade houses than it was before the war. Many dropped unprofitable lines and retrenched by concentrating on one or another more restricted product mix. Today less than 10 general-line trade houses remain. They are still important, but far from being the channel leaders they once were. In each of the major commercial divisions (drugs, hardware, grocery, and so on) about 5 to 10 limited-line trade houses dominate distributing. There are also several distributive networks managed by manufacturers themselves (for instance, San Miguel Corporation) (Economic Development Foundation n.d.:50–57).

General-line trade houses have their uses. They reduce marketing costs to the foreign supplier, assure the customer of good advertising, and guarantee steady sales for established products. All too often, however, they prove too passive in selling—for example, they confine themselves to contacting wholesalers—and are reluctant to stock goods that have no ready market. In special cases trade houses hire salesmen at the request and expense of the principal whose products these salesmen will handle. But under these circumstances the principal might as well seek a more exclusive arrangement with a national distributor, or move into distribution himself. Many have done just that. Arrangements like those in which Foremost Traders Corporation, the exclusive seller of Dutch Baby Milk, markets it throughout the islands by means of a large sales force assigned only to that product, or in which Radiowealth sees to the distribution of its own appliance brand by means of retail branches and franchises, are common today. They are at least as noticeable as Macondray and Company, Inc., Connell Brothers Company (Phil.), Marsman and Company, Inc. and a few other trade houses who cling to the traditional pattern of representing a wide range of products to retailers and consumers.

This is not to say that the fragmented nature of distribution has disappeared in the Philippines. Rather, new channel systems that were only hinted at in the thirties have transformed the channel of entire product lines. Today it is common for Manila manufacturers to handle distribution of their own products to the subwholesale and retail or consumer level or to appoint a distributor to do so for them on an exclusive basis. Wholesale and retail branching is not rare anymore, and franchising has caught on to a degree that rivals the experience of this movement in the United States. Literally hundreds of company salesmen from Manila firms comb the provinces offering promotions, taking orders, and making deliveries, and mass media advertising reaches virtually all barrios of at least the lowland population. Certain symbols of commerce—the Petron station, Coke trucks, the DRB appliance dealership, the Wrigley dispensary in *sari-sari* stores—are as ubiquitous as formerly only the Singer sign was. In these, and many more cases, distribution has been rationalized and integrated down to retailers.

What does the distributive channel look like numerically in the Philippines? Next to the few general-line trade houses and the more specialized national distributors (there are about 200 of these) there exist a large number of importer-distributors (about 800 to 1,000) most of which are part of the traditional trading economy. Centered mainly in Manila's Divisoria market district, they are smaller than the national distributors. Each handles only a restricted product range, and their market coverage is less inclusive. Among them are found the regional wholesaler-distributors who confine their activity to a particular territory—Visayas, northern Luzon, and so on. In addition, there are 11,000 wholesalers who often double as retailers. These dominate distribution on the provincial and municipal level and serve as dealers for Manila suppliers. Finally, there is the amorphous group of retailers. Without counting hawkers and peddlers, they are divided into those who carry durable goods (41,300 in 1972) and those who concentrate on produce (including grocery—291,000) (Economic Development Foundation n.d.:50–57; Republic of the Philippines 1973). The former include independent stores, franchise outlets, and department stores; the latter range from *sari-sari* stores and market stalls to supermarkets.

Increasing market integration from the top down, therefore, has not eliminated the middle-range wholesalers, not to mention the multitude of small retail outlets. With the proliferation of the *sari-sari* stores (in 1961, 56 percent of all retail establishments were of this type, in 1972, 73 percent!) the retail level is more atomized than ever. Today national distributors who want to reach consumers must expect to contact 50,000 to 100,000 retailers who are scattered over the islands. No wonder that only large companies can afford to do so.

During the past three decades several new types of retail institutions have appeared in the Philippines. To appreciate the full extent of what has been called the retail revolution it is best to look at Greater Manila. As late as 1955 a geographer could write that the retail pattern of Manila consisted of three categories: marketplaces scattered throughout the city with the main wholesale center in Divisoria, retail stores lining the business streets, and the neighborhood or *sari-sari* stores everywhere (McIntyre 1955). Conditions seemed not to differ much from what they had been before the war. A more fine-grained analysis, however, would have revealed several new developments even then.

Escolta, which before the war was the main street for retailing consumer durables, in the fifties served the upper crust of Manileños, and mass retailing had shifted to the Quiapo and Santa Cruz districts to the east. There, a few large department stores (Good Earth Emporium, C.O.D., Sarmiento) and large specialty stores (Shoe Mart, National Book Store) had opened their doors. Supermarkets first appeared across the Pasig River to the south in Ermita district where most foreigners (Americans) could be found. Acme opened in 1948 and was heralded as the first modern supermarket in Asia patterned after the U.S. model.

Twenty years later, fashionable Escolta was dying, Quiapo and Santa Cruz were still buzzing but looked seedy, and Divisoria was increasingly challenged by other wholesale points in the city. Rapid suburbanization to the east and southeast of the city was aided by the flow of investments into real estate developments, and several large-scale shopping centers were created to serve the new business and residential communities. These were followed by the decidedly plush commercial centers and malls of Makati Supermarket, Greenhills, Harrison Plaza, and the like, which invited modern specialty shops and giant supermarkets and department stores to locate on their premises. Most of these retail outlets are independent, although they do have to conform to certain market-ing procedures (proper display and the like) to keep their priv-ileged location. Other firms form retail chains (Rustan, Queens, Shoe Mart) or try their hand at voluntary co-ops, such as Cash and Carry.[3] These new institutions, of course, are not confined to the commercial centers. In 1961, nine department stores and 11 super-markets with 20 or more employees each existed in the Philippines (nearly all in Manila); in 1972 their respective numbers had grown to 34 and 21 (Republic of the Philippines 1964–1965; 1975). By 1975, six supermarkets and six department stores (mostly chains) were among the largest 1,000 corporations in the Philippines; so also several book and drug stores, motor vehicle retailers, and appliance outlets (Business Day 1975).

Today retailing in Manila includes organizations that range from the very modern to the very traditional. Expansion in the suburbs, branching, and mass merchandising together with product spe-cialization have been the chief directions in which retailing has moved. The future will tell whether these will prove to be lasting developments, as they have in Japan, or whether they represent an attempt to apply marketing novelties from the United States that the mass of the population cannot economically support. So far these developments have been largely confined to Manila, and the expansion of the "Makati nexus," as some call it, has not dimin-ished the influx of the underemployed into the unorganized service sector, including small-scale trade in Manila (International Labour Office 1974:188).

Ethnic Plurality

While the structure of distribution was subject to some innova-tions, what happened to its ethnic composition during the postwar years? Two events proved important; the Japanese occupation and the decision by the Philippine government, five years later, to press for Filipinization.

The war years saw a steep decline in commerce. Imports ceased, inflation was rampant, and the authorities tried to maximize the movement of goods to the Japanese armed forces at the lowest possible cost. Allowing for this, the occupation did have one positive effect. It forced many Filipinos who had been wage and salary employees to make trade or buy-and-sell their living. This was aided by the pressure the Japanese were exerting against the commercial activities of the Chinese.

The Japanese, in fact, were the first to introduce the long-clamored-for Filipinization program into the country's domestic trade. Its effect is difficult to gauge. A report to the Preparatory Commission for Philippine Independence notes that while before the war 37 percent of the turnover of *sari-sari* stores was in Filipino hands, "it is safe to assume that at least 80 percent of the retail business in essential commodities is [now] in Filipino hands. This [is] due to unemployment and the closing of many [Chinese and Euro-American] firms and the sympathetic attitude of the Administration towards Filipino merchants." Then comes the cryptic remark that "the Filipino should continue to control from between 80 and 55 percent of the total retail trade" (the rest going to the Japanese?) (Preparatory Commission for Philippine Independence 1943:38). However questionable these figures may be, it is true that through government-sponsored retail associations and provincial federations, Filipinos started to play a larger role in commerce. These associations were given preferences in the distribution of essentials (soap, lard, salt, sugar, rice), and their membership was restricted to Filipinos. In addition, trading secondhand goods Americans had left behind kept many Filipinos occupied.

Filipino experience in trade continued to develop immediately after the war. Many ventured into retailing, "having lost their adaptation to steady work under some office or factory manager or foreman. Everywhere in the ruins along Manila's wretched streets, there had sprung up little stores and offices. . . . The places were often very well kept with neat signs, polished show cases, attractive displays. One could sense the pride the new entrepreneurs took in their business" (Hartendorp 1958:275). The same author goes on to say that many of these merchants were doomed to failure because they were too numerous and because they did not have regular supplies or customers (see also Gleek 1977:282–283). Some, though, made it. The pent-up demand for goods and "the hundreds of millions of dollars' worth of surplus Army material disposed of in the Philippines, permitted some practitioners of 'buy-and-sell' to become established merchants and even importers" (Carroll 1965:33). For them the war years and the immediate postwar period offered the crucial incentives and opportunities.

The second factor helping Filipinos enter trade was the postindependence government's increasing concern over the political and economic role of Filipinos in their own country. In its effort to manipulate the economy, the administration not only limited the inflow of finished goods, but also furthered the interests of Filipinos over other ethnic constituents of the country.

To begin with, preference was given to Filipino importers and retailers when import licenses were allocated. This put the established trade houses in a double bind because they were already facing reductions in imported finished products. Later the pressure shifted to the retail level. The government began to assign only to Filipinos the task of retailing essential foods and other imported items at subsidized prices. The National Marketing Corporation (NAMARCO) was established, which in the mid-sixties had 1,000 distributors and 30,000 retailers as members, all Filipinos. A more extreme move was the passage of the Retail Trade Nationalization Law in 1954, designed eventually to eliminate alien (read Chinese) participation in retail trade. Finally, the special privileges Americans enjoyed in the Philippines lapsed with the termination of the Laurel-Langley Agreement in 1974, and Filipino participation in the economy was further stimulated when the BOI allotted 60 percent of corporate holdings to Filipinos.

Because of these incentives and pressures the simple model of a tripartite ethnic division of commerce valid four decades ago represents today only a very rough approximation of actual conditions. Occidental and Japanese interests do continue to be concentrated in large production and distribution firms, Chinese are in wholesale trade and medium-scale production, and Filipinos are encountered in small retailing.[4] But Filipinos now are an integral part of modern retailing as well (many department stores and supermarkets are owned and operated by them), and they, together with the Chinese, play a significant role in large production and distribution firms. It is in between, on the level of importer-distributors, regional and local wholesalers, and wholesaler-retailers, that the Chinese still reign supreme. "Filipino competitive inroads into this distribution strength have been limited to large nationwide organizations that many times end up selling to a local Chinese distributor who is locally strong because of his willingness to provide long-term credit and low prices" (Economic Development Foundation n.d.:51). True, alien Chinese cannot legally trade in certain basic products (rice and corn), but beyond that, government policy on behalf of Filipinos in wholesale trade has been minimal. As I show in Chapters 6 and 8, the most effective pressure against the Chinese position on this trade level has ironically come from those large Manila companies that, with their own sales force, bypass the Chinese wholesalers in the search for provincial markets.

Dagupan

Organization of Distribution

The war years did not leave Dagupan untouched. The Japanese, who kept a garrison in the town, appreciated its central location and, after demoting nearby Lingayen to a municipality, made Dagupan the capital of Pangasinan. For once the highest commercial and administrative functions of the province were united in the same community. Under normal circumstances this conjunction would have provided a healthy stimulus for trade. But times were not normal.

Long before the Japanese entered, Dagupan's position in trade depended on the distribution of consumer products derived from Manila and overseas. When these sources dried up, so did Dagupan's role as the hub of this trade, something even its new title as provincial capital could not prevent. The situation was not helped by a tenuous transportation link with Manila, the considerable pressure put upon the Chinese, many of whom decided to flee the town, and the declining buying power of the population. Large stores on A. T. Bugallon Avenue suffered, and many closed their doors. The inhabitants started to rely on the local trade of peasant produce and on petty buy-and-sell. A few, by handling Japanese-sponsored products, gained entrance into substantial trade, but Dagupan as a whole suffered.

When the Americans returned in 1945 conditions improved. People, including Chinese, poured back into Dagupan, and reconstruction of burned-down districts proceeded. Some American troops lingered for a while, and when moving on they left surplus supplies. What was more important, communication with Manila was resumed, and imports once again entered the Philippines, so that Dagupan's role as a center of distribution was revitalized. Lingayen became again the provincial capital, a loss to Dagupan that was offset in 1949 when it was accorded the status of "city." This enhanced its taxing power and gave Dagupan's administration direct access to the national government.

The subsequent 30 years turned out to be prosperous ones for the city. Its population grew from 36,000 in 1938 to 95,000 in 1975–1976 with an urban (or *población*) population now of 40,000 to 50,000. The city's hinterland currently includes an area of more than 5,000 square kilometers and 1.5 million people (750,000 in the thirties). The fishpond industry has expanded, four colleges attract 25,000 students, and the city has seven hospitals and numerous clinics. The city continues to be the hub of provincial transportation and of entertainment, and although manufacturing—mainly cottage industry—has not grown in importance since the war, it has not declined either. Several fires and urban growth have created in Dagupan a cosmopolitan facade it never before possessed. No longer is the main street lined with ramshackle wooden buildings or sullied by the horse-drawn *calesa* and *caretela*. The latter have been replaced by the tricycle and "teams" (passenger vans), which pollute the air but keep the streets clean. Three-, four-, and five-story concrete buildings now define the borders of several streets—commercial activity has expanded beyond A. T. Bugallon Avenue to Perez Boulevard—with stores on the ground floor and office space above. Even the marketplace has changed. It is now completely packed with permanent stalls, and it is in operation every day of the week. Altogether there are some 2,100 commercial establishments in the city. These are divided into 750 market stalls, 800 neighborhood stores (many in the city's suburbs beyond the *población*), 350 stores along the major business streets, and about 200 full-time hawkers.

Dagupan is exposed to influences that originate from Manila so that innovations in marketing appearing there should diffuse readily into the city. This is true in the case of the vertical channels that connect the two centers, but less so with respect to retail institutions in Dagupan. Supermarkets, malls, department stores may have appeared in Manila; in Dagupan, with the exception of "visions about the future" and loose talk, no one has ventured into such basic novelties. Some establishments are called department stores, which upon inspection prove to be ready-made clothing stores of limited size. Heacock's of Manila did have a branch in the city during the late forties, but it soon closed. The marketplace is called a supermarket, which does not turn it into one. Several superettes have opened their doors during the past few years trying to reproduce on a small scale the self-service policy of genuine supermarkets. Up to 1979 mass merchandising had yet to become part of Dagupan's retailing style.

As the superettes show, however, some moderate innovations have been introduced. Displays behind glass windows and air-conditioned premises exist. Advertising, particularly through radio and slides in local cinemas, has become popular. Several merchants have tried raffles, some indulge in house-to-house promotions, and a few have even adopted, at least on paper, a formalized internal organization between management, sales, and finance. These and similar efforts at modernization are found especially among those who are closely tied to a supplier in Manila—gas station operators, car or appliance dealers, and the like. By and large, though, conservatism dominates retailing in Dagupan. Haggling is combined with a low concern for aggressive marketing, and "firms" are organized familistically, according to the constraints and opportunities provided by the household. The scale of most is small and their numbers are large, relative to the population.

The vertical trade axis between Dagupan and Manila has been less immune to basic changes. In the thirties the typical merchant of imported items in Dagupan obtained them either by placing his orders personally in Manila or by buying them from local sub-wholesalers. Only a few product lines could be ordered through Manila company representatives in Dagupan. Since then suppliers have moved their marketing organization downward, and the need for Dagupeño merchants to order in Manila or through local dealers has declined. The past three decades have witnessed a mounting flood of Manila company salesmen appearing in the city, followed by branch managers and their employees, and by local merchants with exclusive product franchises in their hands. Innovations in vertical distribution that developed nationwide have taken on a concrete form in Dagupan.

Virtually all large firms in Manila today maintain representatives in the city to keep their products visible and under control. Several hundred company salesmen operate in and through the city, each responsible only to one company and over a highly restricted range of products. Specialization has gone so far that some salesmen serve only large dealers, while others promote the same product in small stores. Salesmen of Wrigley, Procter and Gamble, Pepsi-Cola, and many others are encouraged to contact even rural *sari-sari* stores. Over the years the traditional street hawker and peddler have been pushed aside in Dagupan by government harassment and the spread of the neighborhood store.[5] With the entrance of the Manila promotional salesmen, however, a more sophisticated type of this institution has reappeared.

Some Manila companies have found Dagupan a convenient spot for a regional warehouse. Pepsi-Cola, Metro Drugs, Cheng Ban Yek and Company, SEA Commercial Company, and some others have warehouses in the city with attached salesmen and trucks, from which they direct their marketing activities in Pangasinan and beyond. The fact that none of the general-line trade houses in Manila keeps an office in Dagupan anymore says a lot about their diminished position in distribution.

The fifties and sixties also witnessed retail branching and franchising. Nearly a dozen dealers represent Petrophil, Shell, Mobil Oil, Caltex, and Getty in Dagupan with gas stations of a size and layout standard not only in Manila but also in the United States. In appliances Westinghouse-Philacor, Radiowealth, DMG-Admiral, and the like, have ensured their presence through exclusive franchises; so also VW, Chrysler, Ford, Datsun, and GM. Similar close ties between retailers in the provincial city and principals in Manila occasionally exist in glass, hardware, tires, motorcycles, and drugs.

In this connection banks and other financial institutions should be mentioned, even if they are a class unto themselves. During the American period only one bank existed in the city, a branch of the

Philippine National Bank. The situation did not change until that bank was joined by two more in the mid-fifties. Today there are 20 commercial, savings, and government banks and five finance companies represented in the city, which in virtually all cases are branches of Manila institutions. Both in commerce and in finance Manila-based firms have reached out since the war and, it appears, gained control over much of the trade within Dagupan.

This trend also extends into Dagupan's hinterland. Goods that formerly passed into Pangasinan via Dagupeño wholesalers are now often transmitted by company salesmen stationed in the city. Dagupan continues to serve as the breaking point in provisioning its hinterland, but in many lines local merchants have ceased to be the sole intermediaries. A few Manila companies (mainly gasoline companies) have moved into retailing in surrounding communities of Dagupan, thereby dispensing entirely with the entrepôt function of the city. Dagupeños, in turn, have not been sitting entirely on their hands. I mentioned rolling stores used by local traders in the thirties to cover the town's market area. If anything, this practice has grown in popularity, and some local entrepreneurs have created trucking facilities and a specialized sales force that rival those sent out by Manila companies. Several Dagupeños have gone a step further and established retail branches in Pangasinan and adjacent provinces. In other words, the city today relates to its outlying communities in a manner similar to that in which Manila relates to Dagupan, and on a lower trade level the city is the functional equivalent of Manila, at least insofar as distribution is concerned.

The Ethnic Factor

Dagupan had 900 Chinese residents in 1939. Together with a small number of Japanese, Filipinos, and Euro-Americans, they formed the core of those merchants controlling the flow of goods into Dagupan. Petty trade was in Filipino hands. On the national level the ethnic composition of trade was tripartite; in Dagupan it was dual. What changes have the past 40 years brought about?

Of Dagupan's 95,000 inhabitants, slightly more than 2,000 are non-Filipinos, still the largest number of such individuals in Pangasinan. Virtually all of them are Chinese or (first generation) mesti-

zos. Japanese have not reappeared, nor are the few remaining
Euro-Americans active in trade, and both groups continue to have
a hand in Dagupan's affairs only through Manila-based companies, not through their personal presence. A couple of Indian
families operate gift shops. That is all. For all practical purposes
Chinese are the only non-Filipino ethnic minority in the city important in trade. They support a strong Chamber of Commerce that is
busy protecting their economic and political interests, a large
cemetery, and a primary and secondary school.

The following figures show the pivotal position ethnic Chinese
continue to occupy in Dagupan commerce. Of the 2,100 trading
establishments in Dagupan only 160 or 8 percent are controlled by
ethnic Chinese. But they hold their own in turnover: in 1974 they
realized ₱88 million, compared to ₱86 million for Filipino
establishments.[6] If traders of agricultural produce and those handling lumber and cement are excluded, the respective figures are
lower with a slight edge in favor of Filipinos: ₱80 million versus ₱71
million realized by Chinese. Matters do not change much if the
ubiquitous *sari-sari* store is discounted. Then 133 Chinese merchants have ₱50 million in sales and 525 Filipinos, ₱66 million. No
matter how the pie is cut, it is clear that Filipino traders consistently outnumber Chinese, operate smaller enterprises, and have
aggregate sales that differ only slightly from those reached by
Chinese.[7] In simple terms, Chinese control 8 percent of all commercial units and about half of the trade volume in Dagupan.

It is not easy to decide whether this is an improvement for
Filipinos from conditions 40 or 50 years ago. Hard figures are not
available for the early period. The clearest evidence of an improvement comes from the fact that before the war trade between
Manila and Dagupan was in the hands of Chinese wholesalers, and
today Filipinos participate at least to some degree in virtually all
product lines. This trend began with the upheavals of the war and
the resulting opportunities for Filipinos in commerce. In the early
fifties market stalls were restricted to Filipino vendors, and then
the nationwide programs for retail nationalization began.
Throughout these years Chinese moved up and away from small
and medium-scale commerce, and Filipinos filled the gap. Filipinos in Dagupan now virtually monopolize marketing of produce,
and they more than any other ethnic group benefited from the

proliferation of the neighborhood store that took place in the sixties and seventies. Filipinos also control part of the interregional trade of appliances, gas, cement products, drugs, and school supplies, and their role in the grocery and textile trade is less negligible than it once was.

Civic and trade associations established by Filipinos also attest to their greater participation in commerce: two Rotary clubs, a Junior Chamber of Commerce, a Philippine Chamber of Commerce, Masons, a Market Vendors Association, and several more. To be sure, an important motive in organizing them was to emulate the American devotion to such associations and to legitimize the at times quite ostentatious socializing indulged in by their members. Their existence, however, also implies the presence of a relatively large community of sophisticated Filipino merchants, one that has not been averse to using these associations on occasion as a counterweight to the well-organized and powerful Chinese Chamber of Commerce.

When discussing the ethnic composition of trade on the national level I made the point that the Chinese position in commerce is strongest on the intermediary wholesale level. In Dagupan the largest wholesaler-retailers are Chinese. However, the appearance of several substantial local Filipino merchants and the penetration of Manila companies into Dagupan have diminished their once all-powerful position. Filipinos are more apparent in the Manila-Dagupan trade axis than ever before, and the simple duality between Chinese merchants and Filipino vendors that approximated conditions 40 years ago is now a thing of the past.

COMPARED TO DEVELOPMENTS during the American period, changes in the organization of trade channels during the 30 years of Philippine independence have been profound. Not that all old forms have been replaced. New ones, however, have been added and some old ones transformed. Developments that were only hinted at in the twenties and thirties have now come to fruition. Formal, vertical integration is an established part of the Philippine trade scene, and aggressive promotions are widely accepted even among some of the more conservative members of the commercial community. Innovations in retailing have moved beyond Manila, and the participation of Filipinos has expanded to such a degree that it is becoming difficult to identify exclusive ethnic sectors in commerce. In the following chapters the mixture of different distribution channels existing today in the Philippines is disentangled by introducing a typology of market channels and trading strategies. Each type is described by means of various examples. The existing pattern, however, is not static. There are always some traders who try to change established modes of distribution, and new environmental circumstances appear constantly that affect existing channels.

Chapter 4

THE CONSERVATIVE STRATEGY

Introduction

HOW AN INSTITUTION is organized is partly determined by the goals and strategies its members follow. Put differently, "the structure and practice of an organization commonly adapt themselves to the strategy of the organization, not the other way around" (Vernon 1977:30).

Explaining the shape of social systems on the basis of the goal-directed behavior of their members has gained some ground in the social sciences (see, for example, Barth 1966; J. W. Bennett 1976; Heath 1976; Ortiz 1979; Schneider 1974). This perspective emphasizes how exchange and the optimization of one's own position vis-à-vis others leads to institution building, not how exchange is constrained by institutions. Many of those who take this perspective have been interested in the economic sphere of social life, for it is there that "decision patterns," "social exchange," "transactions," "optimization," "utility," "economizing," and so on are most applicable. The firm, after all, is the epitome of an institution devoted to matching appropriate means rationally to given ends. Turning to our subject, distributive channels are composed of firms that share the overall goal of capital accumulation. The marketing strategy they adopt to reach that goal, therefore, shapes not only the organization of the individual firms, but also that of the channel as a whole.

The channel organization between Manila and Dagupan is

based on two sales strategies. In one of them suppliers on the Manila end try to have an active say in the distribution of their products as far down as possible. This I call the "active strategy." The channel associated with it tends to be vertically integrated. The second strategy consists of upper channel members selling their merchandise without trying to control its downward movement by formal means. The degree of channel manipulation is far more restrained in this case than under an active strategy so that I call it the "conservative strategy." It is associated with channels that tend to be vertically fragmented.

As with all bipolar classifications, some caveats come immediately to mind. First, why is downward control emphasized in the active mode? After all, upward channel integration instigated from the retail end is not a rare phenomenon. Second, why adopt such all or nothing differentiation? What about combinations? Isn't the typical situation one in which some members will opt for one, others for the opposite strategy, or in which the same trader will mix strategies according to what products he handles and what circumstances exist? Is it proper, moreover, to assume that traders within any one channel share a goal? It may be that at certain stages of their business life some are willing to take a short-term loss in order to gain a profit over the long run; others will stress profits even if it means decreasing sales; and still others may regard their ultimate goal to be security and survival, not growth via maximization. Third, is it correct to assume that there is a one-to-one relation between strategy and channel organization? Is it not possible, for instance, that actively inclined traders manipulate the downward movement of products in such a way that it does not affect the organization of the channel overtly?

The first objection is easily disposed of by the character of the ethnographic situation at hand. The successful efforts at active marketing in the Manila-provincial trade axis have reached down from the capital into its hinterland, not the other way around. Because the active-conservative classification is intended to illuminate this channel, it seems proper that the supply end be emphasized in this study. This should not obscure the fact that in other circumstances the outlet or retail end may very well be the determining force.

Concerning the second objection, that the division is too simple, all categories of social phenomenon are generalizations and as such they fail to fit every possible empirical permutation. It cannot be denied that in concrete instances systems of distribution will have members who differ in the strategy they follow. This is most likely to be the case if they are located on different trade levels. Whereas an importer or producer in Manila may choose a passive strategy and sell through wholesalers, subwholesalers in Dagupan may prefer an active one by sending itinerant salesmen into neighboring communities. At this point I can only state that channels between Manila and Dagupan tend to fall into either the active or passive mode and to classify them accordingly proves of analytical value. This brings me to the matter of goals. Do those involved in distribution share a goal or not? It would be myopic not to admit that there are different goals held by traders, such as security rather than growth. But the sine qua non of merchants as operators of trading firms, even if these firms are based on the household, is the pursuit of profits and sales. The analysis need only assume that traders pursue this goal to some degree, not that they do so to the exclusion of other considerations.

The presumed overlap between strategy and structure is the third objection. As I use the notion of strategy, it is not only a mental conception held by traders of how to attain a goal, but the concrete method of doing so. The mental image of an active or conservative strategy requires actual behavioral manifestations. Here two complications arise that cannot be eliminated, although reliable and valid enthnographic information helps. These are the issues of relative success and the relations between overt and covert strategy. The active marketing strategy traders follow may prove unsuccessful, and the channel organization may therefore be affected differently from what one might expect. This repeats the old difficulty of whom to call an entrepreneur: those who are growth oriented or those who are successful in their growth orientation? It is also possible that channel members engage in covert penetration which is not brought to light by merely looking at how distribution is organized. Secret trade agreements, private cartels, informal partnerships, or favors based on friendship and kin are examples, all arrangements that are difficult to ferret out since channels remain on the surface fragmented. I discuss these under conservative marketing below.

The simple classification suggested here is by no means original. Students of marketing have been aware of it for a long time. They have discussed it in the American and other national contexts (Palamountain 1955; Yoshino 1971), and placed the typology in a general conceptual and evolutionary framework (Gultinan 1974; Revzan 1967). Most emphasize channel organization, not strategy, in their classification. What I call the conservative mode is known to others as the "loose coalition type" of channel which lacks an identifiable central power or channel leader (Gist 1974:322). Some call it "price coordinated channels" in which channel levels are linked through market forces (Etgar 1975), or "fragmented markets," a term often used to denote a retail structure characterized by many small, independent store traders (Bucklin 1972a:51); by extension, it also connotes multiple, independent channel levels. All these concepts refer to traditional channels exemplified by small and independent producers, wholesalers, and retailers.

The active mode goes under the name of "unified coordinated type of distribution" (Gist 1974:322), "vertical marketing systems" (Kotler 1980:416), or simply "integrated channels" (McCammon and Bates 1967). Although integration can also occur horizontally when a firm absorbs others on its own channel level, my interest is confined to vertical integration in which enterprises extend their control over channel levels other than their own. This process can take different forms. In recent history these forms appeared first in the United States. Integration through contractual agreement is one of them. This includes "voluntary groups" formed by retailers, often under the sponsorship of a wholesaler, or franchise programs that entail bilateral agreements between a supplier and affiliated outlets. Integration can also be based on branching or on chains in which "successive stages of production and distribution are combined under a single ownership" (ibid.:288).

Why, if terms already exist describing active and conservative distribution, do I insist on new ones? The new terms are not designed to replace the established ones. In fact, I have used "integrated," "controlled," and "active" interchangeably in previous pages; so also "conservative" and "fragmented." But this does not make these terms synonymous. By introducing "active" and "conservative," attention is drawn away from the structure of the channel to the strategy of its members (in the present case mainly of the suppliers). In a world in which changes in markets are directed by conscious design, I believe it important to use a classification and terms that recognize this fact.

What concrete channel organizations are included under the conservative and active modes? I already gave some examples of channel integration, but they were derived from the American experience and some of them, like voluntary groups, never evolved in the Philippines. Within the active strategy three types receive attention in this study. Many companies seek integration through an itinerant sales force. This "sales penetration" enables them to reach down to lower wholesale levels or to bypass them and contact retailers directly. The system preserves the autonomy of the downstream traders while allowing the suppliers to do more than sit and wait for others to contact them. The channel receives tighter integration under "contractual penetration." In the Philippines this means exclusive retail franchises. Suppliers help determine what products lower-level traders handle and under what company name they can trade without interfering in matters of proprietorship. The most intense form of downward integration is "corporate" or "ownership penetration." Cases of this are exemplified by Manila firms establishing branches in provincial communities. Here, two or more channel levels come to be joined under one ownership.

The conservative mode is less easily differentiated. After all, can a trader be passive in more than one way? Strictly speaking, no. But if one allows for covert activities within the conservative orientation, as I suggested above, a rough discrimination can be made. On the one hand there is the "passive strategy." In this case suppliers make no attempt to bind outlets to them except through pricing, product availability, and normal and standardized credit policies. This comes close to a purely market-determined fragmented channel in which consumers search out suppliers, retailers look for the best places among wholesale suppliers, and so on up. The second type of conservative strategy, one far more prevalent between Manila and Dagupan, I call "semipassive." It denotes a situation in which the channel appears fragmented, but the traders are actually bound together through informal social ties, often based on kinship or ethnic identity. Under this form of conservative marketing, merchants positioned along a channel extend each other favors which are personalized, covert, and not contractually spelled out.[1]

Passive Strategy

It seems strange that the least common channels of all between Manila and Dagupan are those in which the members sell according to a passive strategy. After all, anyone who displays wares and waits for customers to come by without offering special deals engages in passive marketing. Such behavior is common enough. But entire channels (from suppliers in Manila to provincial outlets) and major product lines are hardly ever organized in this fashion. The passive strategy is encountered in all distributive channels, but it dominates only a few. This makes it difficult to write about. Remember, passive distribution implies the absence of formal *or* informal means to gain control over channel levels below one's own. Much of the trade connection between Manila and Dagupan may appear fragmented and therefore passive. However, more often than not this is because active marketing is informal and covert, not because it is absent.

Not only is the passive strategy rare as a principle of channel organization, it also appears in unexpected quarters. Mr. Aquino is a young merchant of drugs and cosmetics in Dagupan who is unusual in two ways. He is one of the few males in an otherwise female-controlled trade, and he does not usually order his supplies from fieldmen whom drug companies have stationed in Dagupan. He picked up experience while being a salesman for Richardson-Merrell (Phil.), Inc., which taught him to tap sources directly in Manila.

Drug companies often mount lavish promotions involving temporary price reductions of 10 to 20 percent to push special products. Many of these are new, and the idea is to make them attractive to doctors, clinics, and pharmacies. Some Chinese wholesalers in Divisoria buy as many of these promoted goods as possible and resell them at a lower price than that obtainable from the companies once the promotions have been terminated.[2] Aquino has made these promoted goods his specialty. He obtains some of these products through company fieldmen in Dagupan, but mostly he searches for bargains among Chinese in Divisoria. If successful, he transports the goods up to Dagupan and offers them at a price below those offered by standard suppliers.

Others dabble occasionally in this trade, but no one else I know of in Dagupan makes it his chief source of income. The reason is that products receiving promotion are frequently changed, and the amount a merchant can buy of any one item is limited. It is a highly restricted trade which attracts bargain hunters rather than faithful customers. The result is a passive supply organization between Manila and Dagupan. None of the Chinese wholesalers searches for drug outlets in Dagupan. They simply sell to those who come by with the needed cash—cash sales are standard. Aquino has been in this business for six years. He buys according to what prices and products are available, and he canvasses widely. So far the channel has not even been covertly integrated: no semipassive strategy has appeared. This case has its ironic side. Here a passive marketing strategy is maintained on the Manila end by some wholesalers who take advantage of promotions developed by large companies seeking to penetrate the provinces actively. Under the cloak of others' aggressive distribution, a passive strategy is able to flourish.

Aquino is unusual in the drug field where virtually all products find their way into Dagupan via Manila salesmen or wholesale branches. Passive marketing is more common in other commodities. There are the ever popular PX goods. Despite the efforts to stem the flow out of Clark Air Force Base near Angeles (Pampanga), PX products have remained available in Dagupan. Filipino store operators in Angeles have access to base employees to whom the profitable aspect of this activity offsets the risks involved in violating legal injunctions against it. Most of the PX items entering Dagupan are handled by local Filipino gift-shop owners who drive to Angeles to canvass suppliers.

PX trade has flourished now for over 30 years, yet long-lasting exclusive trade links have hardly emerged. Cash has remained the norm even on the wholesale level, and suppliers have refrained from looking actively for outlets in Dagupan. The volume of this trade is too small to provide more than marginal support for merchants in Dagupan. Those who participate handle PX goods as a sideline. Moreover, the product composition that Angeles traders offer frequently changes, which forces customers to canvass widely when they buy. These factors lessen the pressure to adopt integrative strategies downward and also help account for the quite rapid movement of individuals into and out of this business. PX goods are a high prestige, high cost, and high markup commodity with a limited but steady demand and a restricted supply. There is therefore no reason why suppliers should use liberal credit, consignments, or salesmen to lure Dagupeños into permanent trade relations. They come even without such attractions.

Suppliers are also passive in those products that Manila companies, at least for the time being, do not choose to distribute in the provinces. San Miguel Corporation maintains one of the densest and most sophisticated sales networks for soft drinks and beer in the Philippines, but not all of its products pass through it. Choco Vim, a chocolate drink that the company introduced some time ago, is distributed by a fleet of company trucks in Greater Manila. So far demand has not sufficed to justify a similar sales effort in the provinces. Instead, provincial merchants are welcome to see to the distribution themselves. No licenses or exclusive rights are granted. The only incentive the company offers is free delivery for anyone who buys more than 500 cases. Dr. Galvan of Dagupan saw an opportunity in this. A man of many talents—dentistry, sugar repacking, drugs—he started to buy truckloads of Choco Vim and sell them in Dagupan in the early seventies. San Miguel had introduced the brand in nationwide advertisements, beyond which it made no organizational efforts to press the product into Dagupan. In the absence of alternative brands, Galvan had no choice but to buy from San Miguel. The arrangement, however, was strictly business; sales were in cash, and anyone else who wanted to do the same thing as Galvan was free to do so.

The first two examples (Aquino and PX goods) show channels of long duration in which the brands of products handled change rapidly. The last one (Choco Vim) illustrates a channel structure that usually turns out to be transitory in nature even though the product has a long life span. Manila companies that introduce a new consumer line and are uncertain of its sales potential often decide to transfer the initial marketing risks to provincial wholesalers. This could be done by giving them exclusive sales rights or territorial franchises. A cheaper way, and one that tries to encourage local competition, is to sell to whomever comes by and to monitor how these customers fare in their sales efforts. Once demand seems promising, the Manila companies are likely to take over and to regularize distribution through licensing or other active devices. In other words, channels that entail passive marketing behavior in many instances prove to be only a stage, usually the first one, in the overall quite active marketing strategy of Manila suppliers.

Passive supply systems are temporary for another reason: time. When relations between trade levels of an existing integrated channel are rearranged or a new set of products becomes available from sources not previously tapped, the channel structure is for a time disrupted. The supply strategy becomes passive and vertical relations fragmented. Once the new arrangement between channel levels turns out to be permanent or the new products become constantly available from the same source, some type of integration is likely to reappear. With time, what was a passive channel slides back into a semipassive or an active system. The experience of Dagupan's dry goods vendors illustrates this sequence.

Textile vending in Dagupan's marketplace has been a Filipino preserve since World War II. Today there are more than 100 such vendors. Traditionally they bought from Chinese dry goods merchants along A. T. Bugallon Avenue who obtained the product from sources in Divisoria. The channel was informally integrated, and the semipassive strategy prevailed. Suppliers in Manila and Dagupan assured themselves permanent customers through liberal credit and consignment sales based on personal trust.

Conditions changed drastically in 1966. A rumor spread that the marketplace would soon fall victim to arson. Experience of previous fires and the conviction that at least some merchants hope for such catastrophes so that they can renounce their debts, make Dagupeños highly receptive to the subject. This particular rumor persisted, and those of the Chinese traders who had long-term arrangements with customers in the market feared to be caught with outstanding accounts they could not recoup in the event of a fire. Credit is more important in textiles than in virtually any other product so that suppliers in this line have especially much to lose. Late in 1966 they stopped liberal credit and consignment sales, a move that caused many Filipino vendors to turn to Divisoria sources. Monthly or bimonthly the vendors started to travel to Manila, canvassed the market there, placed orders, and had the material shipped north. As a result, the channel lost its informal integrated nature. Market vendors in Dagupan searched for suppliers according to price and product offered and received very little encouragement from the Chinese in Divisoria, whose main concern lay in continuing good relations with their large Chinese customers in the northern city. A passive market organization emerged.

By 1976, however, the situation had changed once again. Divisoria merchants in Yangko and Sampaguita markets were beginning to be more accommodating after Filipino vendors from Dagupan were able to establish a relationship of trust with them. What in 1966 started out as a system of canvass shopping and fluid trade contacts by the seventies had jelled somewhat: Dagupeños had their preferred suppliers who gave "special consideration" to those they considered good customers. Filipino textile vendors of Dagupan once again became participants in a semipassive channel.[3]

Compared to more integrated channel structures, the passive system is rare or at least difficult to isolate in its pure form. This is as true in the wholesale trade between Dagupan and its hinterland as it is in that between Manila and Dagupan. In fact, the above examples should make it clear that impermanence is its chief characteristic. Manila suppliers temporarily choose this strategy to test demand in a region, or new channel arrangements start as passive systems and the longer they exist the more they move toward the active pattern and integration. Those few Manileños and Dagupeños who consistently participate in passive channels switch from commodity to commodity in their perpetual search for special deals and the best buy. Either the channel is permanent but not the product, or the product is permanent but not the channel.

Semipassive Strategy

It is significant that several Filipino dialects contain the word *suki*. There is no equivalent term in English. Similar to *pratik* in Haitian Creole (Mintz 1961) and *kom-ts'ing* in Cantonese (Silin 1972:340), it means "special and permanent customers" and "a long-term trade relationship." *Suki* also connotes trust, reciprocal favors, mutual benefits, and personalism that go beyond the strictly commercial. Traders can refer to each other as *suki* merely for having repeatedly done business with one another. True *suki*s, however, give each other favored terms and patronage not extended to non-*suki*s.

The existence and wide usage of this term of course reflect a certain cultural reality. This is the often-commented-upon propensity for relations in the Philippines to be personalized. In the social sphere this manifests itself through patron-client relations, *utang na loob*, (debt of gratitude), *compadrazgo, pakikisama* (concessions), and intermediation (Kaut 1961; Lynch 1963). It affects political and productive relations (Hollnsteiner 1965; Landé 1965), nor, of course, is trade spared (J. N. Anderson 1969). Market vendors have their close personal or *suki* customers, and neighborhood residents buy from *suki sari-sari* store operators. Market vendors in Dagupan tap *suki* merchants along A. T. Bugallon Avenue and *suki* company salesmen sent out by Manila firms. Store operators sell to *suki* retailers of the city and beyond and depend on *suki* suppliers in Manila. *Suki* is pervasive and important, and is part of the Manila-Dagupan trade axis along its entire length. By means of it, channel members seek to control distribution within the framework of conservative marketing.

Filipinos do not try to establish *suki* relations because of an innate need to be friendly. Despite its social overtones, it remains fundamentally economic in character, and participants calculate that by establishing *suki* they will gain more than they will lose (ibid.:653–654). It increases security in an insecure economic environment. Buyers seek reliable suppliers who give credit, preferred selection of new or scarce goods, and reasonable prices without the need to haggle incessantly. Suppliers search for regular outlets who won't constantly drive a hard bargain and who can be trusted in matters of credit. *Suki*, in short, is an informal way to stabilize commercial relations.

Most Manila suppliers are aware that product availability and competitive prices alone will not enable them to break into the provincial market if demand for their goods is not keen and if aggressive competitors are present. The most conservative and subtle response to these difficulties is to extend special favors to potentially useful customers, and to do so informally without the use of written contracts or other open methods. Open methods improve enforcement of contracts but at the expense of personal trust and flexible terms. Once several Manila suppliers of a product line adopt this strategy and Dagupeños accept it—in no way is this a foregone conclusion since *suki* also entails costs—the channel they represent is well on its way to becoming integrated on the basis of a semipassive strategy. The result is a fragmented distributive structure of far more permanence than one based on the passive mode. Personal trust and favors provide a glue so that the overtly fragmented channel becomes one that is actually quite integrated.

Over the years the Chinese, more than other ethnic groups in the Philippines, have developed the semipassive marketing strategy to a high art. *Suki* is a Filipino concept, yet Chinese practice a certain variety of it to their own advantage in what is simply known as the "Chinese way" of doing business (Ward 1972:384). Their position in the Philippines encourages this. On the one hand, their minority status creates a defensive ethnic identity that leads them to seek trustworthy sources and outlets mainly among themselves; on the other hand, they are sufficiently numerous to have monopolized the wholesale distribution of entire product lines. Groceries and hardware were once Chinese controlled. Today Filipinos play an important part in both of these lines, and large enterprises—many of them non-Chinese—have actively penetrated the provinces. Textiles remain a Chinese domain and continue to be distributed via a channel that comes close to the semipassive ideal. Therefore, to uncover the character of informally integrated channels one can do no better than to examine the textile trade.

Textiles

Import controls and substantial tariffs on cotton yarn and fabrics, introduced in the fifties, reduced textile imports into the Philippines and fostered a local textile industry that now produces low-quality material at high cost. Before World War II two mills were in operation in the country; in 1974, 55 existed with 45,000 workers (International Labour Office 1974:384). These changes had a surprisingly small effect upon the organization of local textile distribution. It remains fragmented, conservative, and Chinese dominated.

A few Indians and Filipinos (often Spanish mestizos) are dry goods wholesaler-retailers in the main textile markets of Manila (in and around Divisoria), and more than half of the mills are in ethnic Filipino hands. There is no question, however, that Chinese control distribution from the mills to the provincial subwholesale level. Their presence is especially noticeable among distributors who buy directly from the mills. This only changes below the subwholesale level in the provinces where textile vendors, peddlers, and tailors are Filipinos.

Mills produce on order from customers or according to their own design. Because each purchase has to be large (50,000–100,000 yards), much capital is needed to buy directly from mills. Those capable of doing so are known as distributors. Their bare-looking offices are located on Soler, Juan Luna, Tabera, and other streets in Manila's Tondo and Binondo districts (all near the Divisoria market), and their warehouses are scattered throughout the city so as to make government inspection difficult. Each specializes in particular fabrics (denim, khaki, chambray) and sells by the bale to wholesalers found in the many private markets of Divisoria. It is only at this stage that provincial wholesalers and wholesaler-retailers normally enter the picture. They buy from the Divisoria wholesalers and have the goods shipped to their place of business.[4] The channel is vertically fragmented. Each level is independent from the other, and if the movement of individual merchants is traced, buyers are seen to search and contact suppliers, not the other way around. Dagupeño wholesaler-retailers visit Manila monthly or bimonthly; they do not sit in Dagupan waiting for sales representatives from Divisoria.

The channel is also horizontally fragmented. In Dagupan alone there are 110 dry goods stall vendors, and nationally there are 7,417 textile retailers (between one-half and one-third of them in Manila) (Republic of the Philippines 1975). In addition there are some 25,000 tailors and dressmakers in the Philippines (103 in Dagupan). Strictly speaking these are part of production or processing, not trade, but I include them here to give an idea of the atomized condition of retail organization. After all, many consumers buy their clothing materials from tailors. The national census lists 471 enterprises as wholesalers and wholesaler-retailers in textiles. Half of them are in Manila, 12 in Dagupan. About 10 major Manila distributors set the pace of the textile trade nationally. Even if the channel is fragmented on the retail end, at the top it is concentrated in a few hands.[5] How do the members of the channel relate to one another vertically?

The large textile distributors in Manila are legally independent businesses, but most enjoy special arrangements with mills from which they obtain the bulk of their inventory. One form such linkage takes is the "peculiar characteristic of local textile industry [of] having the same investors in both the manufacturing and distributing establishments" (Studies on Philippine Industries 1974b:36). In many cases this identity dates back to the surge into textile manufacturing that took place in the Philippines during the fifties. "The incentives granted the industry in the 1950s, coupled with restrictions on imported textiles, induced many wholesaling establishments to embark on the manufacture of textiles while still retaining investments in wholesaling concerns" (ibid.). Marketing and production were kept apart to take advantage of lower tax assessments, to smooth the way for financing, and to keep the fact secret (especially important for Chinese) that the same individual or family was involved in production and distribution. Shared surnames are common. Angs in textile distribution serve Universal Textile Mills, Inc., owned by individuals of the same surname. Tai Lu Commercial Company (distributor) on Soler enjoys a special relationship with Eastern Textile Mills, Inc.; both are owned by Dys. Yujuicos and Family control Evertex Sales Corporation and General Textiles, Inc., the first being the former distributor of the latter.

Arrangements between mills and distributors are not always based on kin or investment ties. Distributors are also the suppliers of capital for the textile mills simply through their repeat purchases. Banks are the chief source of funds for production expansion, whereas the day-to-day operation of mills is made possible by distributors who place orders and pay in advance for fabrics of their choice. "In some cases, distributors have agreements with a producer to purchase the total output of the mill. This is due to the fact that some mills do not have sufficient financial or manpower resources to handle the distribution of their products. Furthermore, the millers are badly in need of working capital which can very well be provided by the distributors with pre-paid orders" (ibid.). This pattern of semipermanent trade contacts based on familial or ethnic trust and financing is repeated between the lower channel levels, except that there product credit is extended downward and prepayment of goods is rare. Distributors serve as the pivot. In their effort to obtain goods and sell, distributors play the dual role of providing capital for the mills and financing the lower-level wholesalers. Credit is their chief tool of downward channel manipulation, which smaller wholesaler-retailers repeat on their own selling side.

Credit plays a prominent role in all phases of Philippine commerce. In dry goods, however, it takes on unusual proportions. Provincial grocery merchants have to contend with 30 days from the Manila suppliers, druggists do not fare much better, and those in appliances and hardware get 60, maybe 90 days, and usually a ceiling on the amount is set. Compared to this, the textile trade is a haven of liberality *if* the credit rating of the provincial merchant is good. On the wholesale level, between Divisoria suppliers and Dagupan outlets, credit has no stated limit (it is "sky high"), and the repayment period is flexible ("several months," "six months," "until the coming New Year"). Unpaid accounts of ₱500,000 are not out of the ordinary.

It is difficult to generalize about the trade terms in textiles, since they are kept secret and because on-the-spot negotiations vary from case to case. Extreme liberty and flexibility are characteristic of the system; so too is the means by which it is maintained. Informal credit ratings among Chinese and personal contact between those managing the businesses prevail. As long as the ratings of Dagupeño merchants are good and purchases indicate healthy sales, credit is forthcoming. One personal check that "fired" (bounced) or even the bad reputation of some fellow traders can ruin a dealer's reputation. This is why textile merchants in Baguio City often buy in Dagupan. The credit reputation of that community is very low in Manila because of the improper conduct of some Baguio merchants.

To gain sufficient trust and thereby attract first-class credit treatment is an arduous task for individuals, even if Chinese. This is illustrated by Charlie Ang, the proprietor of Ang To Dry Goods in Dagupan. In 1971 his business nearly went bankrupt when he faced two crises: expenditures for his imminent marriage and the default of his brother-in-law in Manila (a textile wholesaler) on ₱600,000 he had piled up in debts. On both counts Ang had to spend considerable sums, and when his predicament came to be known most of his *suki* suppliers in Manila thought that he would go under. To make things worse, Ang had innocently paid for purchases with some of his brother-in-law's postdated checks, which then bounced. So his *sukis* tried to collect his past accounts and restricted or altogether terminated new ones.

It became now a matter of saving face for Ang. After repaying his Divisoria sources in full, he stopped buying from all but one of them. The real test began. For four years Ang struggled to find new and reliable *sukis*. Were it not for the one old *suki* who remained loyal and continued to provide liberal credit, he might not have made the transition. By 1976 he had survived the worst and had access to new suppliers who were opening up their credit doors. He had suffered in the interim because he faced a passive supply side in Manila, while his competitors had access to suppliers who operated according to the semipassive strategy. In an environment in which informal integration is the key, the loss of "special considerations" (or credit *sukis*) can mean commercial death. The Japanese had to learn this the hard way in the thirties when they faced the Chinese boycott in the textile trade.

Despite the importance of credit in dry goods distribution, not all distributors and wholesalers offer it. Some sell only on a cash basis, and most refuse credit sales or impose tight terms on high demand items. Under normal circumstances Dagupeños of good standing will pay for part of their previous purchases on the next trip to Manila. Unless he faces a dire emergency, no one lets his account pile up over more than, say, six months without making some payments. The semipassive channel is quite resilient in such emergencies. In the case of fire or other emergencies not caused by gross mismanagement, required repayments of outstanding debts are usually reduced to a fraction (at times down to 10 percent) of the original value. Alternatively, "when a distributor or retailer 'suffers' a 'loss' due to fire or insolvency, it is customary for the 'big boys' to re-finance [him]. The textile mills or their distributors extend further credit, to be able to collect on past debts—going against the primary principle of banks of not putting good money after bad" (*MH* February 1963). Of course the motive here is not benevolence, but the desire to hang on to a potentially useful customer and, more important, not to lose everything. As in Java (Geertz 1963:37–38), creditors in Manila find it difficult to balance judiciously the need to extend financing with the risk of doing so. The only difficulty for the immediate victim of the emergency is to reestablish his credit reputation with his suppliers, a tedious undertaking, as I have shown. No wonder Chinese facing a serious downturn in business fortunes spring back with greater ease than others not so well placed.

Credit has costs for those who receive it and some wholesaler-retailers in Dagupan who can afford to go without it. Purchases on account involve price increases of 1 to 2 percent, which mount up for large orders. Some Divisoria suppliers also insist on postdated checks, at least to have some documentary evidence on hand. Finally, purchases on credit give an understood right to sellers to ship more of particular items than is actually ordered. These are not gifts. The textiles involved are difficult to sell, and the provincial dealer handles them like consignment sales: only after disposing of them does he pay the supplier. The dealer can return the excess goods if he is willing to incur the loss of his supplier's goodwill. Excess delivery is simply another weapon suppliers use to push sales in the provinces.

Liberal credit, personal trust, ethnic and kin identity, and lack of fixed terms create a channel in which a paranoid secrecy is observed. Marketing according to semipassive principles breeds it. Which outlets are one's favorites and, even more important, on whom one depends for supplies are considered sacrosanct and confidential not only from outsiders (that is, Filipinos), but also from fellow Chinese merchants. In the words of one distributor, "to reveal one's sales and sources only invite others to bid into the relationship."

Chinese are united only against non-Chinese, not among themselves. For example, Charlie Ang, the operator of Ang To Dry Goods in Dagupan, was accused by Kim Pian, a textile dealer across the street from Ang, of selling pants (Ang retains a tailor) at the extremely low margin of 50 centavos, which undercut the position of others. After hearing this, Ang made the mistake of charging into Kim Pian's store clutching Manila receipts in his hand. They showed that he could buy fabrics at a lower than normal price, but they also showed the names of Ang's *suki* suppliers. The next time he was in Divisoria Kim Pian started to contact these suppliers. He was unable to receive credit from them, but he could still hurt Ang by getting the same kind of cloth that the Ang To store is noted for. Ang was furious and stopped buying from two of his *sukis* until they broke their relation with Kim Pian.

Stories like these are legion in Dagupan as well as Manila and reflect a state of affairs in which a trader's position is reinforced at least in his own community if he monopolizes some trusted and confidential trade contacts. Only where terms are more uniform and contracts standardized is the need for confidentiality less pressing. The same is true when an ethnic minority has less to lose should outsiders decide to cut in.

Secrecy of the type discussed here should be considered a kind of informal channel manipulation, a semipassive strategy like flexible credit and other tactics (cf. Geertz 1978). Textile dealers pursue secrecy consciously (to the recurrent distress of the investigator) in order to maximize sales at minimal long-term cost, or, what amounts to the same thing, at minimal use of their own capital. It also increases the chances for traders to manipulate the channel downward (or upward) without fear of interference.

Another characteristic of textile merchants can be interpreted in a similar way. Virtually all firms, from the distributors down to the provincial wholesaler-retailers, are also families or households. Centralization of authority within them is extreme, and the internal division of labor, insofar as it exists at all, is very informal. Centralized familism is the result.[6] All purchases and sales of any significance pass through the hands of the proprietor-operator during at least one stage. When absolutely necessary (as when the Dagupan operator is off buying in Manila), authority is delegated to a close kin or to long-time employees of Chinese descent.

All textile merchants in Dagupan hire Filipino assistants, but these remain strictly auxiliary. They help carry bales, keep the store in order, unwrap and cut, and serve customers. Even simple tasks like changing money have to pass through one of the responsible individuals. This is deemed necessary for internal security and to enable the proprietors to negotiate the terms of trade effectively. The need for trust in the face of credit agreements that are guaranteed by no or only minimal documentation forces owner-operators to be personally involved in the selling and buying process. Dagupeño dry goods merchants feel that far better deals can be clinched if they go to Manila and negotiate themselves than if they send a representative or wait for one from the Divisoria suppliers.

It is not unusual to find familism pervading business organizations in developing societies. One interpretation of this states that premodern traditions and customs of these societies do not die easily. Obligations toward kin precede considerations about effective business management. It has been argued that in the case of textile mills in the Philippines, the management groups running them represent transitional Filipino values—they "try to reconcile demands of the traditional familial system with requirements of the business" (Stiefel 1963:109). The incorporated form of ownership maintained by virtually all mills, for example, is a superficial device adopted merely for tax purposes and to secure dollar allocations. Ownership and managment are restricted to family members, yet most would-be investors hesitate to invest equity without personal representation in the mills. Because the mills are large and considerable skill is required in running them, this tradition of nepotism has led to less than effective management.

Among textile traders, however, the same organizational propensity is exactly what is needed from a rational entrepreneurial point of view. The use of the family in commerce makes sense. What appears as an encrusted tradition handed down from the past is in this case actually the conscious use of an organization well suited to a high-risk situation where secrecy is important—not to mention the saving in labor costs that results from using family members.

Familistically organized firms and the semipassive character of trade in textiles reinforce one another. The need to participate in confidential trade negotiations and the need for internal control foster centralized familism among textile firms; the acceptance of kinship as a mode of organizing businesses enhances confidential negotiations and protects trade secrets. This is especially true among Chinese with their emphasis on the patriline and a more selective sense of kinship obligations than is found among Filipinos (Amyot 1973; Omohundro 1974). The point has been made that the family serves as a viable framework for medium-sized enterprises in developing settings (Benedict 1968). Chinese and Filipinos provide good examples of the skillful manipulation of familial relations for business ends, and those in the textile trade are among the most skillful.

Many of the semipassive strategies I have reviewed (secrecy, flexible terms, personalized trust, excess deliveries, familism) are not unique to textile distribution, nor are they unique to the Chinese. American and Filipino merchants occasionally play the same game of personalizing trade contracts and holding on to flexible terms under a cloak of informality and secrecy. Among Chinese, irrespective of product line or trade level, this strategy is nothing else but the Chinese way of doing business I have mentioned before. It, in turn, differs little from protective devices used in trade by ethnic minorities the world over (Bonacich 1973). Between Dagupan and Manila it is played by Chinese in the grocery trade, hardware, and even such modern lines as electrical appliances. Given this, what is so special about the textile trade? First, the terms tend to be more flexible than elsewhere, trade relations more guarded, contacts more personal, and firms more familistically organized. Second, so far textile suppliers have failed to use widely other, organizationally more active and formal means to penetrate the provincial market. The first point has to stand as is until I turn to other marketing methods and products; the second deserves some comment here.

Attempts at an Active Strategy

The position of wholesalers is so strong in the Philippine textile trade that it is easy to overlook the fact that mills at times have succeeded in bypassing them. They have done so in the export trade where foreign importers now send their orders directly to the mills. Mills also sell to large garment manufacturers without using intermediaries.

Forward integration has been less pronounced in the domestic market. Some mills limit active channel penetration to operating their own wholesale stores in Divisoria. Others are more radical and have decided to enter into retailing themselves. Some large distributors have done the same. In 1972 a report on the amount of money textile mills and distributors pumped into advertising—it found the total woefully inadequate—could already point out that Evertex Sales Corporation (distributor for General Textiles) managed six retail outlets, that Island Textiles had one, and that U-Tex had one through its U-Tex Distributors Corporation in Makati. It also noted that P. Floro and Sons had two retail outlets in Escolta, and Litton Mills, Inc. a display in Rustan Department Store, also in Makati (Ronquillo 1972:78).

Since then some distributors and mills have strengthened their position considerably. Evertex Sales is now independent from Gentex and associated in milling with Evertex Industries, Inc. It operates 11 branch retail stores in Manila. In the provinces the company has done something almost unheard of in dry goods distribution. It has established franchise outlets in Davao, Cagayan do Oro, Iloilo, Bacolod, Angeles, and Ilagan (Isabella). Evertex still waits for applicants from Dagupan. How successful this venture into contractual penetration will be no one can tell, but the fact that inexperienced individuals, such as attorneys, are accepted as dealers does not bode well. Evertex was encouraged to move into extensive retailing by the fact that it handles garments alongside textiles. Clothes have a greater brand appeal than cloth and therefore can be more easily retailed through exclusive stores. A similar example is the House of Ramie. It used to be the distributor of Ramie Textiles until it failed to keep up with the sales requirements of the mill. It sells textiles together with embroidery and native craft, items that have helped its retail efforts. By 1975 it had nine retail branches in Greater Manila and several in the provinces.

Turning to mills, Litton Mills now has three retail stores in Greater Manila (in Pasay, Mandaluyong, and Makati) and plans additional outlets in Cebu, Baguio, and Pampanga province. In the opinion of the chairman, George Litton, however, "retailing is just a sideline or just a means to engage in some promotion for most mills," including his. The mass market represented by Divisoria wholesalers remains important to all producers. The vice president of Eastern Textile Mills, Inc. has put it in a nutshell:

"Going directly to the retailers would cost the mills millions."
Given the nature of the product and channel, such outlays are not
worth the effort. "Since the textile producers manufacture largely
on the basis of job orders from the large-scale distributors, the
former depend to a great extent on distributors for market information regarding styles, color scheme, design, weaving patterns, fiber blends, and others. Also because of this, many textile
mills do not have professional marketing organizations" (Studies
on Philippine Industry 1974b:36). It is not surprising, therefore, to
learn that promotional and advertising costs for mills amount to
only 0.5 to 1.5 percent of total sales and that the ratio of selling
expenses to net sales only ranges between 2 and 4.9 percent (*EM*
October 14, 1968).

For fear of alienating their favorite distributors, most mills will
enter into retailing only when they face an emergency. When
Columbia Textile Mills, Inc. brazenly bypassed its distributors and
started to retail in Cubao market (east of downtown Manila) in late
1975, Divisoria merchants did not like it. But Columbia saw the
move as its only viable alternative. The year had turned out de-
pressed for the dry goods business so that the mill was ill prepared
when a large overseas order was canceled because of poor product
quality. The distributors did not want to take the order off Columbia's hands. It seemed therefore to be a good idea to organize a
bargain sale in one of Manila's largest middle-class shopping areas.
This was a very exceptional affair, and by late 1976 Columbia was
mending its fences with its distributors.

In an effort to adopt an active marketing strategy, some distributors and occasionally even mills organize sales penetration. They
employ itinerant salesmen to take orders in the provinces and
appoint local dealers who are given territories and quotas. This is
most frequently done in the Visayas and Mindanao because dry
goods merchants there find it difficult or inconvenient to travel to
Manila. The only problem with this service is that salesmen cannot
make major decisions regarding terms without having to report
back to management. The alternative would be to depend on an
intermediary channel level, thus lengthening an already long
channel.

Salesmen and dealers are used more sparingly in the north. Only
during periods of sagging demand is there a tendency for the

normally marketing-shy Manila textile firms to adopt this strategy. Thus in the early sixties some salesmen from Manila were searching for orders and dealers in Dagupan. This diminished in the mid- and late sixties with the improved market, and only in the first half of the seventies, when inflation hit the economy and credit tightened, did the salesmen reappear. The terms they offer are tighter than can be obtained personally in Divisoria, and they have difficulty breaking the ice, especially with the local Chinese merchants who are used to far better prices and credit treatment.

So far no retail establishment of a Manila mill or distributor has successfully operated in Dagupan. Perhaps the well-entrenched position of the local Chinese store traders and Filipino vendors in dry goods is responsible for this. One of the most blatant attempts to defy their power happened when Allied Textiles in late 1975 opened its doors on the west side of the town's plaza, prudently removed from the Chinese concentration on A. T. Bugallon. This event was heralded as the long-hoped-for direct link between Dagupan's consumers and a large textile mill in Manila.

Allied was advertised as a retail branch of Gentex. Actually it turned out to be a branch of a store in Cabanatuan that was owned by the wife of Gentex's president. The Dagupan store was managed by the owner's brother, and the two helpers were his brothers-in-law. Instead of buying from the mill, the Dagupan outlet obtained its goods from Cabanatuan and sent its remittances back there. The store in Cabanatuan had had to battle a court case against a local vendors association that feared cutthroat prices. Allied expected a similar reception in Dagupan. It need not have worried. The fact that it had no direct access to Gentex, the fact that it indiscriminately mixed together A-, B-, and C-quality merchandise, the fact that it sold only on cash and that it failed to lift itself into wholesaling, eliminated any serious challenge it might have posed to the local traders. Neither was its location propitious, and in late 1977, two years after having opened with such fanfare, Allied quietly closed its doors.

Other attempts at active market penetration into Dagupan have been less blatant. In addition to its branches, the House of Ramie maintains salesmen and dealers in the provinces. Its salesman responsible for Pangasinan, La Union, Baguio, and Ilocos Sur decided in the late sixties to open a store in Dagupan that would sell Ramie products and be managed by his wife. Of course, such a move hurt Ramie's main dealer in Dagupan, a Filipino wholesaler-retailer (Salonga). The company compromised and appointed both of them as subdealers and required each to buy 1,000 yards a month with a 20 percent discount and 30-day credit terms. A short time after, the proprietor of Salonga stopped selling Ramie products, charging that Mr. Caolite (the Ramie salesman) was underpricing him because he received favored treatment from the House of Ramie. Whether this was true or not, the Salonga proprietor had every right to be suspicious because Caolite remained an employee of the company. Two years later, in 1973, the salesman also gave up the dealership because overall sales were down, and now both stores handle Ramie products only as a sideline.

The examples of Allied and Ramie represent attempts at active integration into Dagupan that did not involve the Chinese community. Even with its assistance, success is not assured. Instead of buying from the House of Ramie, Chinese prefer to obtain their ramie in Divisoria where prices are lower. There Ramie Textile, Inc. (or Ramietex, a mill partly owned by San Miguel Corporation) has its principal distributor, a Filipino whom the Chinese do not like because he sells only on cash. This would not be so bad if demand for the product were low. But the output is of good quality, and the mill is willing to lower its production to keep prices and demand high.

Except for heavy mass advertising, the mill has followed a quite conservative marketing strategy in northern Luzon. Robert Ngo of Dagupan therefore was surprised when one day in 1975 he was approached in his textile store by an Agency for International Development official, known only as Melvil, who claimed that Ramietex was planning to appoint an exclusive distributor for northern Luzon. The appointee would be a Mr. Rowe who is famous in the Philippines for his TV shows. Rowe had not the foggiest idea of the textile trade, but he had money and was convinced by some of his associates to enter the line. Before signing the distributorship, Rowe was test selling some ramie in a retail outlet in Baguio. He and Melvil planned to locate the distributorship in that store and hoped to expand it into a fancy and large wholesale-retail outlet that would also cater to tourists. Rowe represented the capital and Melvil the entrepreneurial encouragement. What they needed was someone well placed in the Chinese textile network to give advice and open up contacts.

At this point Melvil remembered Ngo whom he had come to know well when he was stationed in Pangasinan. He asked Ngo what it would take to set up a distributorship in Northern Luzon and whether he would care to join them. Ngo was horrified to hear that they planned an extensive retail operation, because that would scare away local wholesalers who would fear being undercut. First, confine yourself to wholesaling, he advised, and gain experience and the confidence of customers; only then, maybe after two or three years, enter into retailing if you must. He also opined that at least ₱1 million in capital would be needed to initiate the distributorship properly. Ngo agreed to join them with the idea that he would be responsible for sales. He planned to sell "aboveboard" north of Manila through Baguio and Dagupan, but secretly also in Manila by supplying his brother-in-law and his best *suki* supplier. Ngo's plan was to put pressure on the Manila distributor of Ramietex by selling the goods at the same price and allowing for a few days' credit. Ngo believed that even with such short credit, the Chinese would prefer him to the Filipino distributor who gave no credit, and "they will keep their mouths shut because they are Chinese."

If everything had gone as planned the curious situation would have arisen in which Divisoria wholesalers would buy Ramie fabrics produced in Manila via a source located some 200 kilometers to the north. Whether the goods were to be shipped physically north before entering the Manila market had yet to be worked out. In this case more than downward integration was at stake. An attempt was made to make Dagupan a conduit through which would pass much of the ramie actually destined for Manila. Perhaps fortunately for the consumer (though retail prices need not have been pushed up), but certainly unfortunately for the participants, the experiment never got off the ground. The Manila end fizzled out before anything substantial was begun. The three had not even drafted an agreement among themselves. Spring 1976 was the last Ngo ever heard of Melvil and Rowe, and so far no new attempts by Ramietex to establish a distributorship in northern Luzon have materialized.[7]

Up to this point I have described only unsuccessful attempts at integration between Manila and Dagupan. The fragmented textile channel does show some exceptions to this bleak record, but they are few and even they retain much of the semipassive flavor. One exception of this kind involves the material used for boy scout uniforms.

Virtually every year the Boy Scouts Council of the Philippines decides on a new color or pattern to be used for the uniforms. To guarantee a standard product, one mill is given the responsibility for producing the material. Here the trouble begins. Mills need cash advances to produce such a large order, but the Philippine Council lacks sufficient funds. Hence a bid goes out that offers the exclusive distributorship of boy scout uniform fabrics for the entire nation. Established distributors in Divisoria shy away from government bidding with the result that usually an outsider acts as distributor.

In 1975–1976 Shoe Mart, Inc. in Manila, a Chinese-controlled store chain, was the lucky bidder. The Sy family manages it, and not surprisingly a Sy was the head of the Boy Scouts of the Philippines. Shoe Mart then placed orders with Central Mills and pumped ₱10 million into the affair. Though Chinese, Shoe Mart was less "benevolent" than traditional distributors and demanded cash when orders were placed. It had a monopoly, after all. It delivered two to three weeks after the order, and the amount was shipped out in irregular installments.

Theoretically each provincial Boy Scouts Council placed the orders with Shoe Mart. But they faced the same capital shortage as their counterpart in Manila and thus turned to those with resources, usually Chinese. There was not even any bidding. Instead, each council or (what amounts to the same thing) each council executive chose a distributor. This was legal enough, but the kickbacks that accompanied the arrangement were not.

In Dagupan Robert Ngo has been the exclusive distributor for three years. His "appointment" happened by chance. Even before Amor became the council executive of the Western Pangasinan Council, he was a good customer of Ngo's. One day he asked Ngo whether he would be interested in acting as distributor with the understanding that for each yard he bought from Shoe Mart, 20 centavos would go to the council executive as *lagay* or under-the-table payment. Ngo agreed. To order from Shoe Mart he had to show a certificate of distribution. Downstream he sold only to licensed tailors. One of these was assigned to each municipality, and they had to pay five centavos per yard to the council for the privilege (and probably more as *lagay*). The system works well for Ngo because he can claim that the wholesale and retail prices are set by the supplier; actually they are his own. In 1976 he served 50,000 scouts through 20 tailors, handled 100,000 yards, and made about ₱2 on each yard after purchasing and *lagay* costs were deducted. The business has become his bread and butter during the sluggish monsoon season.

The success of this effort at downward integration can be attributed to the monopoly of those who are interested in it and their political clout which enables them to decide which applicants are to be given the plum of distribution. Success in this example also depends to a considerable degree on special personal and confidential agreements so typical of the semipassive strategy. In general, active marketing has so far failed to prove viable in textile distribution, and this case represents one of the few exceptions. Unless powerful extraneous forces for whom formal channel integration is profitable are present, the existing channel based on the semipassive strategy appears to be a strong conservative force against change.

Dagupan and Its Hinterland

Pangasinan is wide open for Dagupan dry goods wholesaler-retailers. Except for local fellow traders and the distant challenge of Manila, they face little competition in the province. Other than Dagupan, only Alaminos, Tayug, and Rosales have textile dealers, and in each case only one or two. The semipassive strategy also typifies this lower trade level, with Filipino vendors and tailors now the beneficiaries of the (considerably less)[8] flexible terms. One group of customers greatly appreciated by Dagupan's merchants is about two dozen peddlers from Batangas province, south of Manila. They buy a lot, pay promptly, and carry the trade into Dagupan's hinterland at no direct cost to local merchants.

Batangeños represent an old tradition in central Luzon. At least since the turn of this century writers have commented on the regional specialization of trade and cottage industry existing in the lowland Philippines (Miller 1911): hats from Calasiao, Ilocano blankets, Mangaldan *bolo* knives, Binmaley pots. Over the years individuals from Batangas have gained a reputation for coming to Pangasinan during the dry season where they perambulate from barrio to barrio, selling dry goods to consumers on short-term credit. Their tactics are sophisticated indeed, and Dagupeño traders could not wish for more effective "sales representatives." They belie the notion that aggressive marketing is strictly a modern phenomenon.[9] Some specialize in cheap materials, others in expensive fabrics; they divide themselves by territory and usually go in pairs. When entering a barrio they first contact the barrio captain to offer him the initial choice. They might have bought enough material for three pairs of pants in Dagupan for ₱24, and in the barrios they sell material for two for ₱50 and give the buyer the remaining material "free."

Men who carry under their arm a large package of fabric wrapped in plastic are immediately identified as Batangeños. Their reputation smooths the way for them. What they carry around they typically represent to unsuspecting customers as stolen or smuggled goods of exceptional quality, although the goods were actually bought in Dagupan. Their success is sustained by such myths, and Dagupeños find it an entertaining sight when the customer of a Batengeño encounters him busily buying his supplies in a dry goods store in Dagupan.

The hesitant attempts by Manila enterprises at downward integration hardly ever go beyond Dagupan. This is left to others. Aside from Batangeños whose main concern are consumers, a few Dagupan merchants have done more than just sit and wait for customers. Two of them personally operate rolling stores in central and eastern Pangasinan and southern La Union. In their travels they seek out market vendors and tailors. Three more send someone around to collect accounts and to take orders on standard products like zippers, lining, and T-shirts. Occasionally they try to sell fabrics by showing samples. But here the same limitation applies that vexes Divisoria merchants when they send out salesmen. Unless the proprietor or a close confidant of his goes, it is difficult to negotiate terms on the spot. There is therefore a more pronounced tendency for wholesale customers to come to Dagupan than for Dagupeños to reach out.

Dry goods merchants are among the most conservative traders the city has to offer. Yet, even they are willing to experiment if that will keep them abreast of local competitors. Their small numbers and intimate awareness of each other's moves guarantee that they relate to one another by copying each other's tactics. When Kim Pian of Dagupan decided to send letters to potential customers to offer his services, Charlie Ang of Ang To felt he had to do the same. When the proprietor of Payas Dry Goods decided to enter western Pangasinan with delivery service, Kim Pian followed, and when Aljas of Aljas Textiles put out feelers in Alaminos about doing the same, Payas intensified his efforts. As long as some merchants see it as to their advantage to market according to principles that are more active than implied under the semipassive strategy, others will be tempted to do so too. The dynamics involved here, as I show in Chapters 5 and 6, are very similar to the ones that led Manila companies over the past decades to penetrate Dagupan and Pangasinan actively.

THE TRADE CHANNELS considered in this chapter have one thing in common. Manila suppliers are reluctant to adopt openly an aggressive sales strategy. Vertical connections between traders either occur on the basis of prices and product availability alone (the passive mode), or are acted out on the basis of personalized and informal favors which frequently are embedded in close ethnic and kin identities (the semipassive mode). If I were dealing with prewar conditions, much of the trade channel between Dagupan and Manila would thereby have been described. Today, however, those merchants sitting in Manila's Binondo, Tondo, and Santa Cruz expecting customers to contact them are joined by many more who project their efforts into the provinces via their own sales organization. The fact that even in textiles attempts at downward integration are made is symptomatic of the popularity this strategy has come to enjoy in the Philippines. In many products the conservative strategy has either been replaced or complemented by a more formal and active type of distribution. For the majority of suppliers this means sales penetration.

Chapter 5

SALES PENETRATION

SALES PENETRATION is the most popular type of active marketing strategy in the Philippines today. Sending out itinerant salesmen to take orders enables Manila firms to establish direct personal contact with a wide range of provincial customers among whom sales can be pushed aggressively. Sales penetration gives the supplier greater control over distribution than conservative marketing and entails lower costs than is implied by ownership or contractual penetration.

Several hundred Manila companies employ a mobile sales force in the provinces, and more than 160 of them have "traveling merchants" registered in Dagupan alone.[1] Many keep more than one representative in the area so that a total of about 250 company salesmen tie Manila to Dagupan by means of this marketing strategy.[2]

Sales penetration is far from monolithic in character. It takes on different forms depending on the resources of the supplier, the type of provincial outlets served, the character of products, and related factors. The most distinctive variation is the degree to which salesmen accompany their products. The rolling store is the simplest type. Salesmen begin their route in Manila, sell the stock from the truck to provincial customers, and then return to the head office for more merchandise. Somewhat more elaborate are arrangements in which salesmen book orders in the provinces, and take them to Manila; delivery of the goods is made some time later by a trucking firm. More elaborate still are provincial branch warehouses of Manila firms. Attached to these are fieldmen who use rolling stores or act as booking agents. A great number of other variations exist: Manila producers may retain distributors or enter into sales penetration themselves; the market can be nationwide or cover only one region; only large wholesalers may be contacted or the target may be the small-scale retail level. Differences also exist in how the field force is organized and controlled: salesmen may be permanently stationed in the provinces, or they may visit provincial customers from their Manila headquarters; some suppliers allow their sales force considerable freedom in setting sales terms, others do not.

These and other differences are best examined if sales penetration is discussed according to particular product lines. Hardware, pharmaceuticals, and groceries are the principal commodities that are moved into Dagupan through this marketing strategy. Of the three, the grocery line is the largest and the most wide ranging. Virtually all variations of sales penetration are found in it. This is to be expected given the extraordinary breadth of this line, which includes everything from matches, rubber bands, and cigarettes to canned goods, soft drinks, repacked sugar, flour, and lard. Ninety-eight of the 164 firms keeping sales representatives in Dagupan handle groceries. Hardware, in contrast, is represented by eight, and drugs by 20 companies. The following discussion of sales penetration therefore revolves mostly around institutions in the grocery trade though I look at hardware as well. I deal with the drug trade separately at the end of this chapter because of several features unique to it.

Grocery and Hardware

To understand the distributive strategy used by Manila grocery and hardware suppliers, it is necessary to identify the provincial outlets each faces. To start with groceries, trader multiplicity and retail fragmentation are even more extreme in this product than in textiles. Seventy-five percent of all retail establishments in the Philippines, or 247,000 outlets (240,000 of these are *sari-sari* stores), handle groceries. To these must be added 41,000 *carinderias* (eateries), and restaurants (Republic of the Philippines 1975).

The upper end of the grocery channel in Dagupan is capped by Chinese wholesaler-retailers.[3] There are nine of these, which I am calling "first-order merchants." Their stores are located along A. T. Bugallon Avenue, and most of their sales come from grocery and neighborhood stores in Dagupan's hinterland. Several of them have rolling stores. Below them is an intermediary level not found in textiles. It consists of 35 "second-order merchants" who participate in local, intra-Dagupan wholesaling and retailing. Their stores are scattered in the marketplace and *población*, and half of them are operated by Filipinos. On the bottom are small "third-order retailers," of whom Dagupan has 950, virtually all of them Filipinos. These operate the famous *sari-sari* stores which are to be found primarily in residential and rural Dagupan. Their individual size may be small, but together they are of great importance to the channel. Forty-five percent of all trade units in Dagupan are *sari-sari* stores, and in 1974, 39 percent of the total grocery sales passed through them (Dannhaeuser 1980). The city has some 200 eateries, *carinderias*, and restaurants, and also 22 bakeries, all of which are important to soft drink and beer distributors and to those in the flour and sugar trade.

Facing such extreme retail fragmentation, the Manila supplier can keep his marketing costs low by relying on Divisoria wholesalers. This was the usual practice until the fifties. With the exception of suppliers like Getz and Brothers (Klim milk) or PCC (sardines, canned milk) who had their own provincial sales force, the grocery channel before World War II was as vertically fragmented as the textile channel is today: importers passed merchandise on to Divisoria distributors or wholesalers; these resold to provincial wholesalers; these, finally, supplied the subwholesale and retail level.

After the war the position of the Divisoria distributors deteriorated considerably. Chinese grocery distributors never did build up a position of dominance over the sprouting local manufacturers of processed foods comparable to their position in textiles, with the result that producers found it less difficult to extend their own marketing organizations into the provinces. Moreover, the fact that brand loyalty can be easily created in groceries and the fact that American interests played an important role in this sector— food processing has traditionally been an American preserve in the

Philippines—meant that grocery suppliers were subjected to considerable pressure to integrate downward. Today many of them bypass Divisoria entirely.

The provincial end reflects these changes. Dagupan's first-order grocers continue to visit Divisoria wholesalers in Manila, such as Sy Tan and Company, Eng Hiap Sun Candy, and King Sim Trading, who wait in their offices with tempting terms for good provincial customers. But these customers patronize them only for selected items (Alaska and Frisian milk, Hakkado salmon) and special buys (imported apples during the Christmas season). The highly specialized company fieldmen, hired by giants like Pure Foods Corporation, Filipro, Inc., San Miguel Corporation, and many more, revolutionized the trade for provincial grocers of all sizes, and most of them now depend on this service for supplies.

The trend toward sales penetration has been less distinct in hardware despite the fact that Manila suppliers face a less fragmented market than in groceries and the fact that a larger portion of the trade is absorbed by institutional end users (construction firms, contractors). There are 1,500 hardware stores in the Philippines. The trade structure in the provinces is simple. In Dagupan the product is handled by close to 30 store merchants along the major business streets. These act as dealers of Manila companies and engage in both wholesaling and retailing. Five of them are the equivalent of first-order grocers; the rest are of the second-order variety. No small-scale trade has evolved into which Filipinos could find an entrance, nor did the government's Filipinization program drive Chinese into wholesaling. The provincial hardware market is too small to carry a separate wholesale level. The result has been that the retail trade in hardware has not opened up to Filipino participation to the degree it has in other products.

Divisoria wholesalers continue to be important in the distribution of hardware. Changes of course have taken place. Marcelo Enterprises, Marvex Commercial and Manufacturing Corporation, Union Carbide, Philippines, Inc., Philippine Blooming Mills Company, Inc., and other firms have entered into production since the war and now have their own provincial sales force. There are also the large limited-line trade houses of hardware and construction supplies (such as Amon Trading Corporation, LCC Corporation) and the general-line trade houses with one of their divisions devoted to this product (Connell Brothers, Marsman and Company). All of them participate in active provincial marketing.

Overall, however, the Chinese import houses and wholesale suppliers around Divisoria still dominate much of the hardware field. Their position has been helped by the slow development of local production of hardware and the hesitant participation of American capital in the trade. Among the more important Divisoria sources for Dagupan are Cham Samco and Sons, Inc., Yutivo Corporation, Go Soc and Sons and Sy Gui Huat, Inc., and Hap Seng Hardware. Until a few years ago, none of these suppliers had a formal field force to contact provincial customers. Some of them developed one on a limited scale only within the last decade, much later than companies like Union Carbide and Amon Trading, and their sales penetration was less extensive than that in groceries. For them the semipassive strategy remains of considerable importance.

The Problem of Delegation

The first question Manila suppliers face is whether they should organize their own provincial sales or leave the effort to others. In the grocery trade these others are general-line trade houses and more specialized distributors. Divisoria wholesalers are of little importance. An idea of the variety of existing arrangements is provided by the canned milk industry.

Some overseas suppliers were happy with general-line trade houses until import controls were imposed in the fifties. Darigold Milk Company employed the services of Marsman and Company, Inc. to channel its milk products into the provinces. Established in 1929 as a mining company, Marsman by the mid-fifties was selling business machines, construction equipment, foods, beverages, drugs, and agricultural chemicals. It was (and is) a trading company par excellence with departments even in insurance and travel, and it became locally known as the "*sari-sari* store of Manila." But after import controls pushed Darigold into local production, Marsman shared the fate of many other distributors and lost one more lucrative account.

Other suppliers of canned milk continued to depend on the general-line trade house despite the upheavals of the fifties. Liberty Milk (produced by General Milk Company) is distributed by Connell Brothers. Up to the mid-seventies this company also represented Carnation Milk, Silver Swan Soy Sauce, Gillette, Krieger candies, Kraft, Libby's, and Kellogg's in the Philippines. Its other division traded in hardware (Dutch Boy Paints) and machinery (Matsushita).

Connell Brothers is another classical general-line trade house. Unlike Marsman and many others, however, it has been successful in retaining important accounts over the last two decades. One reason is that like distributors in textiles, it has considerable investments in some of the manufacturers it represents. It holds 49 percent of National Lead Company (Phil.), Inc. and the same fraction of Silver Swan Manufacturing Company, Inc. Another reason is its aggressive entrance into marketing. Before the war orders from merchants in Luzon had to be placed in the Manila office. Since then it has built up a sales force numbering in the hundreds and warehousing facilities covering all major islands. Marsman and others could not offer equal services.

This worked well until the mid-seventies. Then Connell Brothers had to submit to the Filipinization rule that required 60 percent of the capital of local corporations to come from Filipino investors. The creators of modern Makati, the Ayala family, bought the 60 percent share, and it was not long after that Connell Brothers witnessed the mysterious exodus of some of its major accounts. Kraft left, Libby's left, and Carnation Milk. So far, though, it has held on to Liberty Milk.

Others in the milk business prefer more specialized agents to be their distributor. Milkmaid, Alpine, Bearbrand, and Magnolia (San Miguel) are marketed by Filipro, Inc. (formerly Anglo Swiss Company, an American concern). Similar to Connell Brothers and Marsman, Filipro is a trade house with a long history, but the merchandise it represents is less varied. The only other important principal it represents is Nescafé. In other words, it handles imported and locally manufactured products that are closely allied.

In all of the cases so far described the distributor's fieldmen are asked to handle the products of different principals at the same time. Salesmen of Connell Brothers promote Liberty Milk together with soy sauce, corn flakes, and other items, each licensed by different manufacturers. Filipro fieldmen sell Magnolia Milk together with coffee and other milk brands. This is one of the reasons large producers try to avoid trade houses; they fear that their own product will not receive sufficient attention. As I mentioned in Chapter 3, one way to alleviate this concern among manufacturers is to have the distributor assign salesmen exclusively to their product. This is what the agreement between Marikina Dairy Industries, Inc. (producer of Dutch Baby Milk and under Australian ownership) and Foremost Traders Corporation (which handles the accounts of many principals) stipulates.

The contract between them does not leave much to the distributor's discretion. The agreement is quite specific about what type of sales organization Foremost has to construct. It is expected to appoint dealers (or subdistributors) in Manila, Baguio, Legaspi, Zamboanga (Mindanao), Bacolod, Cebu, Iloilo, Davao, and several other places. In 1971 it had 11 in Manila, seven in the rest of Luzon, three in the Visayas, and four in Mindanao. Foremost has to supply each of these with a panel truck. The result is an island-wide distribution network that is shallow; sales penetration by the distributor reaches no further down the channel than large provincial wholesaler-retailers. Credit and collection are the responsibility of Foremost, and it markets the product at a price set by Marikina Industries. In return, Foremost receives a commission of 10 percent of gross sales, and Marikina Industries sees to mass advertising. There is more to the agreement than this, but it ought to be clear the degree to which the principal has seen to it that its products receive adequate attention from the distributor.

Even explicit agreements like these cannot gloss over the fact that the relationship between the manufacturer (or importer) and the distributor is unstable. They need each other, but all too often there comes a time when either the product is not salable and the distributor wants to drop it, or the distributor cannot keep up with the demands of the product and the principal wants to terminate the agreement. In the hardware trade, for example, Go Soc and Sons and Sy Gui Huat in Binondo was for 10 years a distributor for Philippine Standard, producer of bathroom fixtures. It agreed to maintain sales of ₱400,000 a month, which required keeping a burdensome inventory valued at ₱800,000. Because of keen competition, its profit was very low, and eventually Go Soc decided to drop the agreement. Another instance is Republic Glass Corporation (sheet glass manufacturer) which relies on several distributors for its national sales. One of its practices has alienated some of them. Whenever Republic faces excess inventories it offers "opportunity deals" to its distributors. These deals are sales at a liberal discount which none of the distributors can refuse for fear of being undercut by the others. The result is chronic excess inventory holdings by most of Republic's distributors, forcing some of them to quit.

More common are cases in which the principal drops the distributor. I already mentioned Darigold terminating its agreement with Marsman, or Kraft and others leaving Connell Brothers. Another example occurred when Bacnotan Consolidated Industries, Inc. (cement production) in the early seventies canceled its exclusive agreement for cement distribution with LCC and moved into warehouse branching itself. The occasion for this switch was a glutted market and concern that LCC did not press Bacnotan's sales sufficiently. A more elaborate instance is that of Pure Foods Corporation. It illustrates the tension that often exists between three actors: the overseas principal, the licensed producer in the Philippines who also tries to promote his own products, and the local distributor.

Pure Foods was founded in 1956 by several Manila Chinese grocers who decided to establish a meat-packing plant for the production of cold cuts. In the late fifties the company obtained the license to manufacture Vienna sausage, and shortly thereafter it began to produce pork and beans and tomato sauce under the Hunt label. In 1961 it began to do the same with French's mustard. Ever since, cold cuts and canned meats have been the company's mainstay, and the turnover of the concern grew from ₱3.5 million in 1963 to ₱78 million in 1974.

To distribute cold cuts and fresh meats Pure Foods from the beginning had its own sales force contact groceries, supermarkets, and institutions with freezing facilities. In canned goods the story was different. In 1959–1960 Atkins Kroll and Company, Inc. handled the nationwide distribution of Hunt products for Pure Foods, and at first the market penetration was quite impressive. In 1960–1961 the first difficulties arose. Atkins Kroll sold only 2,000 cases a month, far below the quota, but it assured Pure Foods that new efforts would be made to increase sales. As in the case of

Marikina Industries and Foremost, Pure Foods financed the advertisements. At this time Pure Foods introduced its own brand of canned meats and marketed the product through Premium Brand, Inc. But sales did not take off despite the fact that Pure Foods pumped 8 percent of sales revenues into promotion. So in 1961–1962 the agreement with Premium was canceled, and Pure Foods took over the distribution of its own brand product. Atkins Kroll in the meantime continued to fall short of its quota, and pressure mounted within Pure Foods to drop its services. After protracted negotiations with Hunt Foods and Industries back in the United States, an agreement was worked out whereby Atkins retained exclusive access to GMA (Greater Manila area), while Pure Foods received the right to sell Hunt products in the provinces by means of its own sales force. Normally this arrangement is reversed: the manufacturer first enters into sales penetration of the GMA and leaves the provincial market to distributors.

Another source of strain between principal and distributor occurs when a principal uses distributors to market a product in a new territory and then, after the product has become popular, takes over the marketing itself. This happens less frequently than one might think, however. Aside from having to take on the burden of credit risks and sales costs, such a move into distribution is painful, especially for manufacturers who have yet to become marketing oriented. Such a move would mean a reorganization of their business. When Pure Foods canceled the agreement with Premium Brands, it finally decided to hire a marketing director and to establish a marketing department. At that time it had only two vans supplying the Luzon area. The new marketing director drew up a plan indicating the number of vehicles needed, the number of salesmen required, their compensation, and related matters. Production decisions began to be affected more and more by marketing needs. The marketing director pushed for the creation of an extensive dealership network first in Luzon, then in the center and the south of the Philippines.

In 1963 the general manager resigned, and the new one appointed another marketing director. This one introduced quotas for salesmen and organized sales contests between them—in other words, the company began to adopt gimmicks of American marketing management. He also hired some mestizo-Chinese sales-men in recognition of the fact that most of the merchants the company supplies are Chinese. By the late sixties about 90 percent of grocery retail outlets (not counting *sari-sari* stores) in the Philip-pines were carrying Pure Foods products, and the larger of these outlets were served directly by the company without the use of middlemen. From being a licensed manufacturer dependent on one or two distributors, Pure Foods had evolved into a producer of its own products and one that has its own mature sales organiza-tion. The transformation from production to marketing orienta-tion can be made, but it takes a long time, much expenditure, and a willingness to devote a substantial part of a firm's organization to distribution.

The Loose Dealership System

After deciding to enter into provincial sales penetration using their own resources, Manila companies face the question of how far they should reach down the channel levels and what portion of ap-propriate outlets they should contact, in other words, how deep and how extensive their coverage should be. Some grocery sup-pliers contact only large wholesaler-retailers found in one or two commercial centers of each province. They act as if the only worthwhile customers in Pangasinan were the first-order grocery merchants in Dagupan and a few other municipalities. The task of subwholesaling and retailing is then left up to these dealers.

Alhambra Industries, Inc., the largest producer of traditional cigarettes in the Philippines, dates back to the nineteenth century. It seems natural that the company prefers a conservative type of sales penetration. In Manila, though, this conservatism is hardly noticeable. The marketing strategy there is deep and extensive, and the company promotes its products even among small *sari-sari* stores. Alhambra does not do this because it is infatuated with marketing—management considers the main role of the company to be production, not distribution—but because of competition stemming from modern cigarettes.

In the provinces demand for traditional cigarettes remains high, and Alhambra limits direct sales there to large wholesaler-retailers. These buy in bulk and place advance orders, thereby carrying the burden of stocking and subwholesaling for Alhambra. The company's sales force in Manila is divided into "propagandists" who contact small retailers and salesmen who deal with larger customers. In the provinces fieldmen are not ranked in this way because only one type of customer is served.

An even simpler and less costly method of sales penetration is that employed by the medium-sized Chinese firm Siga Vegetable Lard Repacking (White Rose brand). Until his recent death, the proprietor, who doubled as salesman, visited Dagupan once a month. He used the rolling store method, selling goods from his truck and collecting on previous purchases. He proved even more reticent about spreading his sales than Alhambra. His calls in Dagupan were confined to three first-order merchants. In fact, as his products gained in popularity he did the opposite of what marketing-inspired entrepreneurs would have advised. He restricted his sales more and more to those who could afford to buy in bulk. This annoyed many traders in Dagupan, and some smaller merchants begged his daughter (who attended Chinese school in the city) to intervene on their behalf. Their efforts were to no avail—the proprietor wanted to minimize the number of customers, so that he could personally take care of northern Luzon. And he wanted to contact the customers personally because he liked to shift aspects of the semipassive strategy from Manila into Dagupan and other provincial centers. He preferred to operate on the basis of flexible terms, and as the proprietor of the concern, he was in the best position to do so.

Alhambra and Siga represent Manila suppliers who minimize the cost of sales penetration by shifting much of the sales costs onto the provincial wholesale level. I call this type of sales penetration the "loose dealership" system.[4] Suppliers select dealers on the basis of buying, paying, and warehousing capacities; these dealers in return receive favored treatment in matters of credit and pricing. Each company has three to five of these in Dagupan and one or two in other major towns in Pangasinan (Alaminos, Tayug, San Carlos, Lingayen, Carmen, Rosales). Instead of organizing advertising and promotional campaigns to increase sales, they manipulate the terms offered to their dealers—often they do so confidentially and under cover. Here features of the semipassive strategy are very much alive.

Moderately sized and Chinese-controlled companies are most prone to resort to the loose dealership system. The fact that two or three trucks and an equal number of salesmen are sufficient to cover central and northern Luzon makes this type of sales penetration sensible for firms with limited resources. Also the ethnic angle enters, since those whose support is essential for the success of this system—the provincial dealers—in most cases are Chinese. Not only do flexible prices, credit terms, and the Chinese way help to obtain their allegiance, it also helps if the Manila supplier, or at least his sales representative, happens to be Chinese. This explains Pure Foods' scramble to hire salesmen with a Chinese background. Ethnic identity, paramount in textiles, appears also in groceries at this point; but here it only underlies one of several types of distribution systems, whereas in textiles it suffuses the only one that exists.

Turning for a moment to hardware, there the loose dealership system is the typical mode of sales penetration. This is to be expected given the position of Chinese in the trade and also the nature of the market structure in the provinces. Once a hardware supplier decides to enter into distribution, aside from institutional customers, there are only large- and medium-sized hardware stores to contact. No lower-level retail customers are served because none exists. This means that the Manila hardware supplier needs only a small and simple field force for effective sales penetration. Cham Samco of Divisoria, for example, which regards itself as a "contented cow" in the business and avoids open aggressive marketing, has had fieldmen since the thirties. Up to recently these were family members organized in an informal manner. Now Cham Samco has 10 hired fieldmen, each responsible for a territory and a fixed set of provincial dealers. Go Soc and Sons and Sy Gui Huat copied Cham Samco in 1972 when it launched its own sales force, now consisting of 10 booking agents. Yutivo Corporation has a slightly more complicated system because much of its sales goes to institutional accounts (for example, San Miguel Corporation). It has 10 salesmen headed by a sales manager, two assistant sales managers, and two supervisors. About half of them specialize in taking orders from institutions, the rest in selling to wholesaler-retailers.

Deep Sales Penetration

Manila's involvement in provincial distribution would be shallow indeed if the loose dealership system were the only form that sales penetration took. The only way in which this system differs from the former one, with its reliance on Divisoria wholesalers, is that the trade negotiations have shifted to the provinces. The provincial actors have remained the same. First-order grocer Jimmy Lim (City Grocery) in Dagupan used to get Royal Oil products from wholesalers in Divisoria; now the company salesman takes orders from him in Dagupan. Then, as now, Lim controlled much of the distribution of that product in and around the city.

Many Manila companies in the grocery line are not content with the loose dealership system and seek to extend their sales to the small subwholesale and retail levels. They find at least some of Dagupan's 950 *sari-sari* stores worth contacting individually. Such a move has certain implications for the Manila supplier. A larger number of fieldmen must be mobilized than under the loose dealership system, they are likely to be classified according to what outlets they serve, the territory each is responsible for is probably smaller, and a greater need for warehousing facilities will be felt. In other words, the cost of distribution will experience a steep rise.[5] To keep control over such an elaborate sales organization the head office must impose standardized terms. Deep sales penetration also calls for a product with mass appeal, amenable to sales gimmicks, special promotions, and heavy advertising aimed at small retailers and consumers. Under these circumstances American-inspired aggressive marketing comes alive, and mass merchandising of consumer products receives considerable development.

A step toward deep sales penetration was taken by the Philippine Packing Corporation (PPC, formerly California Packing Corporation), a subsidiary of Del Monte (California). Until the late fifties PPC assigned two distributors to market canned pineapples in Luzon. When its main competitor, Dole (Phil.), Inc. (subsidiary of Castle and Cooke), moved into the Philippines, PPC decided to change sales policies. First, it increased the number of distributors in Luzon to five. Second, Del Monte intensified its advertising, and PPC stepped into distribution on its own account. In 1964 it employed one salesman for northern and central Luzon, and in the late sixties it had five. The salesmen book orders, set up displays, and promote among small outlets not contacted by PPC's distributors.

La Perla Industries, Inc., exemplifies a further step toward deep sales penetration. It is one of three large Chinese cigarette producers which until the early fifties formed one family concern (the others are La Suerte Cigar and Cigarette Factory and Associated Anglo-American Tobacco Corporation). All of them produce and distribute American brands under license. To begin with, La Perla's provincial distribution was quite shallow, but in the late fifties it was forced to change from a dealership system because of pressure from competing companies and demands from overseas principals.

Early in 1960 the company took on (for a period) the representation of Liggett and Myers, and one of the stipulations of the agreement was that La Perla increase its marketing effort. The company had already improved control over provincial sales by creating the position of field supervisor. Now it formed "saturation sales teams" consisting of five aggressive salesmen who were shifted from area to area in an effort to promote the cigarettes among subwholesalers and retailers. The regular salesmen of La Perla continued to contact dealers. The company divided the Philippines into five regions, which were subdivided into provinces and areas (such as West Pangasinan), and assigned a salesman to each area. Out of the saturation teams eventually grew the company's permanent promotional salesmen, at least one of whom is now assigned to each of the area salesmen.

During the past two decades Philippine Packing and La Perla faced demands leading them to expand their sales force and establish direct sales contacts with a wide range of customers. Other companies subject to similar pressures have developed even more elaborate systems. S. C. Johnson and Son, Inc. divides the Philippines into 15 territories, each subdivided into five regions. Every region is headed by a supervisor who is responsible for three senior salesmen, and to each of these two junior salesmen are assigned.

Altogether the company has 225 fieldmen. California Manufacturing Company, Inc. (Lady's Choice) has 336 fieldmen. Each of its 21 area managers has four supervisors, and each of these is responsible for four salesmen who are divided into booking salesmen (selling to dealers) and peddling salesmen (selling to retailers).

Elaborate sales organizations also exist in hardware, although they are rare. Two kinds of companies have them: large hardware and construction–supply trade houses and firms that handle products that crosscut the hardware and grocery field. Amon Trading Corporation belongs to the first kind. It markets Sherwin-Williams paints, Republic cement, and many other items, and it likes to cover all potential customers (hardware stores, lumber yards, construction companies). Nationally the company has 120 salesmen and supervisors. These specialize either in institutional accounts ("retail") or dealer accounts ("wholesale"). This division is overlain by territorial specialization: a Retail Sales Department is responsible for Manila and a Wholesale Department for Manila and the rest of Luzon; several warehouse branches with retail and wholesale fieldmen take care of the Visayas and Mindanao.

Union Carbide (Phil.), Inc. is an example of a firm producing an item that finds buyers among a broad range of customers. After starting to manufacture Eveready Batteries in 1956, the company began to market and promote the product itself. Flashlight and radio batteries can be sold to grocery and *sari-sari* stores and to gift shops, as well as to hardware stores. To cover this market, Union Carbide chose to construct a field organization that now includes eight area managers, about 40 account salesmen (contacting large customers), and 42 van salesmen, all of them capped by a complement of supervisors. Amon Trading and Union Carbide, however, are exceptions in hardware. The loose dealership system of sales penetration reigns supreme, especially among Divisoria suppliers.

Most companies that pursue deep sales penetration find it convenient to divide their fieldmen according to the outlets they serve and to add a supervisory level. What the categories are called differs from case to case, but the functional division tends to be the same. The lowest-level salesmen are known as "promotional," "assistant," "route," "truck," "van," "peddler," "direct," "bond," or "junior" salesmen. Their job is to push the product in small and highly dispersed outlets. They break supplies into small units and sell from a van or truck, sell on cash, offer promotions and sales advice, and see to display. They take over if a new product is to be introduced. The promotional salesmen are the final capillaries of those Manila companies that can afford them, and in nearly all cases they form the bottom rung of a career that can propel a person up to sales manager or beyond. It goes without saying that the promotional salesman is superfluous in most hardware products. If a distinction is made, it is between those salesmen selling to hardware stores and those serving institutional end users.

For large accounts the counterpart of the promotional salesmen are the "booking," "district," "foot," "account," or "senior" salesmen. They serve dealers and handle only large lots, they can give credit and discounts, and they collect and usually book while delivery is made by others. Senior salesmen are the lowest echelon of field personnel allowed some autonomy in setting terms by the Manila companies.

Either promotional salesmen have to report to senior salesmen or both are administered directly by a supervisor. In the typical case the supervisor—this term is widely used—does not participate in sales. His job is to accompany and otherwise check on his subordinates, report shortages and local developments further up, and make the initial decisions about hiring and firing of fieldmen. The following list of functions of the Union Carbide supervisor emphasizes his role as "leader of men."

a. Guide the salesmen in selection and training of assistant (promotional) salesmen;
b. Develop leadership qualities in salesmen;
c. Organize the men under him into tight teams to achieve sales goals;
d. Develop and train men;
e. Develop himself into an executive by developing others to replace him (*MH* November-December 1968).

Only occasionally do managers contact provincial customers personally. When they do, it is in an attempt to promote a new product by showing personal commitment to the well-being of the customer or by appealing to his loyalty to the company.

Warehousing and Jobbing

So far I have discussed two variations encountered in sales penetration: first, whether suppliers engage in provincial distribution themselves or leave it to others; second, whether sales penetration is extended only to large wholesaler-retailers (the loose dealership system) or whether a deeper range of sales contacts is sought. Another variation I want to turn to now concerns the warehousing policy of Manila enterprises.

Companies following a loose dealership system of distribution seldom maintain provincial warehouses or bodegas. The need for those facilities intensifies as sales penetration becomes deeper and geographically more extensive. It hardly makes sense to expect promotional salesmen in remote places to travel to Manila whenever their supplies run out. The most obvious way to shift merchandise into the field is to establish bodegas under the ownership of the Manila company. Here ownership penetration is combined with sales penetration, and salesmen fan out from the provincial warehouse instead of from Manila.

Warehousing is most prevalent in the south where overland access to Manila is not available. Cebu, Davao, Bacolod, and Iloilo traditionally are the preferred spots. Luzon, especially the north-central portion of it, is less favorable to warehousing. Access is easier, and there exists less potential for combining distribution with assembly. For the vast majority of Manila grocery and hardware companies, warehouse branches in Dagupan and similar provincial centers to the north simply make no economic sense.

Exceptions, both temporary and lasting, of course exist. Getz and Brothers had a warehouse in Dagupan, which it gave up after the war. Connell Brothers plans to open one in Calasiao to the immediate south of Dagupan, and its fate is unknown. In 1960 Rufina Patis Factory (seasoning) opened a large one in Dagupan to cover all of Luzon north of Pampanga province, but today deliveries to customers come from Manila, and the warehouse is closed because of declining sales.

Some maintain a bodega in Dagupan because of special connections within the city. Cheng Ban Yek and Company, Inc. (cooking oil and soaps) has warehouse branches in Davao, Cebu, Iloilo, Legaspi, and since the forties, in Dagupan. The choice of Dagupan was helped by the fact that a close kin relation exists between the head of the company and the proprietor of a large local trucking firm. Other Manila suppliers keep a warehouse in the Dagupan region because they are committed to a very deep and extensive distribution policy. Union Carbide has 14 bodegas, three of them in Luzon (1 in Dagupan). Colgate-Palmolive (Phil.), Inc. has one in Iloilo, Cebu, Cagayan de Oro, Legaspi, Ilagan, Laoag (Ilocos Norte), Tuguegarao (Cagayan), and San Fernando (La Union; this one as an alternative to Dagupan). Amon Trading has warehouse branches in Cebu and Davao, a subbranch in Iloilo, and depots in Cabanatuan, Dagupan, Angeles, Naga (southern Luzon), and Cagayan de Oro. When it still had the distributorship of Bacnotan Consolidated Industries in 1971, LCC Corporation had 19 branch warehouses, most of them in Luzon (including one in Dagupan). Beer and soft drink companies, however, have constructed the most extensive network of all. In addition to having a large number of bodegas, they have invested in an extensive system of processing plants in the provinces, including north-central Luzon. I present their case in a moment.

What if warehousing is considered too costly, yet Manila suppliers want to control the trade of their product down to the provincial retail level? An acceptable compromise is jobbing. Jobbing is a dealership system of distribution with a twist. Senior salesmen sell to their dealers or jobbers at a discount price. Whenever promotional salesmen run out of stock for their own customers, they buy from these dealers at company price (normally 2 percent higher than the dealer discount price) and resell the stock to *sari-sari* stores and similar outlets without markup. Dealers serve as warehouses in this arrangement. They take title to the goods and sell as much as they can. The twist lies in the understanding that promotional salesmen of the Manila company will help dispose of the goods. Before the 30-day payment and discount period is over they are expected to repurchase part or all of the lot for their promotional purposes. The dealer receives his remuneration in the form of the price difference between buying from the senior and selling to the promotional salesman. Both the supplier and provincial dealers gain. While common in groceries, jobbing is rare in hardware (Union Carbide is one of the few exceptions) because a small-scale retail level is absent.

Companies committed to this system—usually they have no warehouses, but pursue deep sales penetration nevertheless—try to maintain several jobbers in a community in order to guarantee that products are available for promotions. All of Dagupan's first-order grocery merchants and some of the second-order ones serve as jobbers to several Manila firms, the ability to buy and to pay being sufficient to qualify.

Jobbing is perhaps more open to abuse than other types of active marketing. Abuse occurs, for example, when senior salesmen ask dealers for a profit split in return for favorable treatment (such as positive credit ratings). The salesman sells goods to the jobber at a discount, and the promotional salesman rebuys the lot at less than the company price. If the official price difference is 2 percent, the senior salesman may ask the dealer to be satisfied with 1 percent and then pocket the rest, while on paper the dealer receives the full margin. For the Manila supplier danger also exists in the fact that since his buying salesmen are in all cases expected to pay in cash for merchandise they rebuy, they have to carry large amounts of cash. Some receive as much as ₱30,000, enough to tempt anyone to take off, never to be heard of again. It is standard practice now to have these salesmen bonded.

Another problem inherent in the jobbing system lies in the potential conflicts between the supplier and the dealer (jobber). The longer a dealer serves as bodega for a shipment of goods, the better for the supplier because storage costs do not mount over time for him. This is not true for the dealer. Unless the inflation rate is very high, it is in his interest to have the promotional salesman rebuy the merchandise as soon as possible. Should the salesman visit less frequently than expected, the dealer feels neglected. Suppliers, in turn, are easily convinced that their jobbers rely excessively on the services provided by the buying salesmen, without giving adequate attention to their own sales effort.

Sales penetration through jobbing is therefore hardly an ideal arrangement. Warehouse branching is safer, even if costlier. It gives the head office maximum control over its products, which is not the case if it passes them to jobbers. This is so because warehouse facilities allow the suppliers to bypass provincial wholesalers, whereas jobbing requires their services.

Coke and Pepsi

Companies handling cigarettes, soft drinks, chewing gum, house-hold soaps, batteries, and similar mass consumer items are more aggressive than others in provincial sales penetration and ware-housing. Among them beer and soft drink companies have out-shone the rest. Their efforts have achieved the logical conclusion of active marketing by means of deep sales penetration. San Miguel Corporation, the largest company in the Philippines, is the best example of deep penetration and, therefore, deserves some detailed attention.

San Miguel has dominated the domestic beer market since the nineteenth century. It moved into soft drinks in 1922 when it bought the Royal Soft Drinks plant in Manila. After it obtained the distributorship of Coca Cola in 1927, it began to construct a marketing network the likes of which the Philippines had never seen before. By the onset of World War II, it had bottling plants in Manila and Cebu City, 20 warehouses in the islands, and a routing system in which all easily accessible retail outlets were reached through sales trucks used as rolling stores. In remote areas local distributors took over. After the war San Miguel signed a new contract with Coca Cola which gave it exclusive rights to sell and distribute Coke in the Philippines. Up to that time this was the largest single concession Coca Cola had granted anyone in the world. San Miguel now made every effort to establish a tight and wholly owned nationwide sales network. A good reason for this was the threat coming from others. Pepsi-Cola had begun operat-ing in the Philippines in 1945 with a new plant in Quezon City, and in 1952 Seven-Up joined the fray. And there were numerous local brands (Uro, Ideal, Avenue) that sprang up selling at half the price of the international brands.

In 1947 San Miguel had 23 warehouses, 191 route trucks (139 in Manila, 20 in Luzon, and 32 in the south), and 27,000 dealers. Although this was for all of its products, the major component remained beer and soft drinks.[6] In GMA it had 5,000 dealers for Coke alone; these were serviced on a weekly basis by a fleet of 44 trucks. The company had bottling plants not just in Manila and Cebu, but in Guiam (Samar), Polo (Leyte), and San Juan (La

Union), as well. A decade later San Miguel had succeeded in its quest for nationwide distribution. By then it had 100,000 dealers nationally, more than 1,000 route trucks, and about 100 warehouses for all its products. It also operated 13 bottling plants. By this time the market was becoming saturated, and during the following decade the pace of expansion slowed. In 1975 San Miguel had 16 bottling plants and some 150,000 dealers.

San Miguel's enormous effort to build a total network reflects a long-term marketing strategy going back several decades. In 1954 it justified placing bottling plants in remote areas by noting that "in addition to providing for maximum production efficiency, provincial plants are instrumental in substantially reducing distribution costs and the benefits of these investments will be gradually realized as new highways are opened" (San Miguel 1954:21). It appears that they have been. Distribution by means of company trucks now reaches virtually all urban and rural *sari-sari* stores accessible by road. San Miguel has seen to it that no one stands between it and the final retailer, whatever the distance from Manila. The case of Pangasinan shows just how intensive distribution by this firm is.

Up to 1966 San Miguel directed the marketing of soft drinks in central and eastern Pangasinan from a bottling plant in San Juan (later Catalina), La Union. After 1947 a warehouse in Alaminos took care of western Pangasinan, and another large one was opened in 1959 in Urdaneta (central Pangasinan). Up to then Dagupan was important to the company only as a local point of consumption. This changed in 1966.

Seven-Up Bottling Company had constructed a bottling plant in Calasiao in 1956. Because of a "temporary" setback in its competition with San Miguel and Pepsi, it closed its operation in northern Luzon. Following a strategy developed long before of acquiring those it drove into the ground, San Miguel bought the plant. At that time the plant had seven route trucks; today it has 20 and nine more are on order. The Alaminos warehouse has three trucks, and the one in Urdaneta is now used only for beer. Each of the trucks has a driver, a helper, and a salesman. These are headed by six district sales supervisors who are led by the regional sales manager of the plant. The only area where retailers are not contacted by salesmen of either plant or warehouse is in the extreme eastern section of the province. This region is taken care of by several local merchants who buy entire truckloads at a time (like Galvan with Choco Vim in Dagupan). In Dagupan and the rest of central Pangasinan, a subwholesale level for beer and soft drinks was eliminated a long time ago. The only time that first-order merchants still handle the item is when a windfall is in sight, as when an increase in price is pending. Even then they can buy only limited amounts because supply is tight and the product is allocated according to the amount previously purchased.

Each of the company salesmen and his companions contact about 300 customers on a weekly route, or (with six days to the week) 50 customers daily. In the large towns, high turnover outlets are "hit" twice a week, which amounts to 150 customers per route. All in all, through 20 fieldmen and 40 assistants San Miguel contacts between 4,000 and 6,000 retailers in Pangasinan every week. This is not bad considering that in 1972, 12,000 wholesale and retail establishments (including restaurants and hotels) existed in Pangasinan (Yambot 1975). Marketing is so thorough that some salesmen are assigned to individual streets; one salesman, for example, serves only stores and restaurants along A. T. Bugallon Avenue.

One might think that San Miguel monopolized soft drink distribution in Pangasinan as a result of such complete coverage, or at least that it held a monopoly in cola drinks. But no, Pepsi's coverage is equivalent. In fact, Pepsi was the first to choose Dagupan as a center for soft drink distribution by opening a warehouse there in 1950, and it has had an edge on San Miguel in the city ever since.

Like Coke, Pepsi was first distributed in the Philippines by a licensed company; however, in 1957 a subsidiary of Pepsi took over—Pepsi-Cola Bottling Company of the Philippines, Inc. It first sold to retailers in Manila and then moved into Cebu; in other areas the firm had regional distributors. Pepsi's operations spread rapidly. In 1952 a plant opened in Bacolod, in 1954 one in Tarlac (central Luzon), in 1955 one in Iloilo, and so on. In the mid-fifties the company had 48 warehouses and 380 trucks, which was less than San Miguel had, but it must be remembered that Pepsi dealt only in soft drinks. In the early seventies Pepsi had 11 bottling plants throughout the Philippines. During the last two decades growth has been more important to the company than profits, and no outsider knows how much it cost the mother company in the United States to keep abreast of San Miguel.

Pepsi supplies much of Pangasinan from a bottling plant located in Rosario (La Union). This plant takes care of the eastern section of the province, it stocks the warehouse in Dagupan, and it supplies a depot in Dasol that serves the province's remote western region. The Dagupan warehouse sells to retailers in central Pangasinan from Alaminos to Santa Barbara south of Dagupan. It covers this area with 10 trucks, four of which are devoted to Dagupan alone. One serves A. T. Bugallon Avenue, one the marketplace, one the southern edge of the *población*, and one the eastern section. In this core zone customers are contacted up to *three* times a week.

Although they do not participate in retailing, San Miguel and Pepsi have managed to construct a system of distribution that allows them to deal with every type of outlet virtually everywhere. Road conditions and the receptivity of customers are the limiting factors, not hesitant sales tactics. Production for them is entirely subservient to marketing. Another characteristic they share is a simple sales organization. Customers are categorized according to the size of their orders. Thus Pepsi distinguishes between those who order 100 cases a week and more, those who buy 11–99, and those asking for 10 or less. But the salesmen who contact them are considered of the same type; no distinction is made between senior and promotional salesmen. The stress is on serving the needs of retailers, and production facilities or warehouses are so near to the customers that such a distinction is considered unnecessary.

This remarkable channel has helped "pop" to become the drink for everyone and for all occasions in the Philippines. Whatever the occasion—whether a *merienda* (snack break), a reception, or a "blowout"—if it calls for imbibing in public, soft drinks will be part of it, at least as long as females are present. It also means that wherever communities are found, irrespective of whether they are urban or rural, the imagery of soft drink advertisements is present. This does not confine itself to large billboards towering over skylines, or ads in the mass media. Much more fundamentally, it shapes the appearance of the small-scale urban and rural scenery. It is the rare *carinderia* and *sari-sari* store operator who does not display proudly his or her business name above the store between two Pepsi, Coke, or other company signs. This commercial symbolism suffuses much of the countryside because there are so many of these stores and eateries. It also reflects a mutual dependence between small retailers and the large soft drink companies.

On the one hand, neighborhood stores, eateries, and similar institutions are the main customers for San Miguel and Pepsi. On the other hand, access to the soft drink salesman is imperative for these small operators for three reasons. First, a large portion of their sales is in soft drinks so that Manila enterprises, by creating the popularity of the product and making it locally available, help these minioutlets survive. Second, access to the company salesmen by neighborhood store operators lowers their dependence on local Chinese intermediaries. Third, company salesmen bring promotions to the stores. However meretricious most promotions may seem to us, to the operators of small *carinderias* and *sari-sari* stores, special sales and incentives loom as a very important means to success in the market.

Flexible Terms versus Centralized Control

In Chapter 4, I made the point that trade terms are more restricted in groceries than textiles. Credit extended to Dagupan textile merchants by Divisoria suppliers can run over months and accumulate to dizzy heights. In groceries the norm lies between 15 and 30 days, there is a ₱50,000–100,000 limit on the outstanding amount, and strictly enforced COD policies are not uncommon. The difference goes deeper. With several exceptions I present in "PMC, PRC, and IOF" (this chapter), the tight terms available in groceries are uniformly applied to all customers. No customer receives favored treatment not also potentially and publicly available to others, nor are trade agreements renegotiated at every transaction. Under active marketing standard enforcement of terms has replaced the particularism of the semipassive strategy, and it is now common for Manila suppliers to write out terms in Chinese, Tagalog, and English. Why is this so? Is there anything peculiar about groceries that fosters such a practice?

One factor comes immediately to mind, and that is the tremendous impact American capital and marketing philosophy have had on the grocery trade—it is much greater than in the textile and even the hardware trade. Many in the Philippines believe that Americans have a penchant for keeping matters open, above board, and contractual. There may be a kernel of truth in this opinion, especially if one compares the methods of arranging channels by most American companies with the far more informal strategy preferred by the Chinese. For the present purpose, however, it is sufficient to note a more immediate factor. The way in which groceries are distributed forces suppliers to restrict and, above all, standardize trade terms. The main culprit is deep sales penetration.

If a Manila merchant decides to distribute in the provinces, he has, among other things, two problems to consider: first, controlling those who collect orders and deliver for him; and second, negotiating the terms of trade in such a way that the traders in the community he tries to serve are not made envious of one another. When the Manila supplier follows a conservative marketing strategy and waits for provincial customers to come to him, he can personally oversee the negotiations and thereby minimize the problem of control. What is more, the supplier need not worry about the envy of other merchants operating in the community his customer comes from because special favors the supplier extends to his customer are not known to them. Thus Charlie Ang of Ang To Dry Goods does not know the deals his fellow textile merchants of Dagupan have been able to negotiate in Manila.

Control is also of little moment for those Manila merchants, like the proprietor of Siga Vegetable Lard, who venture into the field on their own. The deals made are entirely their own personal responsibility. But even this simple type of sales penetration can create difficulties with envy. Giving preferred treatment to some merchants in a trade community at the expense of others equally capable of buying can sour the prospects of a supplier in that community. This La Fuerza, Inc. had to find out the hard way. Some time back, this producer of rum appointed a distributor in Iloilo. For a period the setup worked well, and according to a company official, "they did not need to worry about distribution." But soon sales were dropping off rapidly, and an investigation found that other merchants were avoiding the product and turning to other brands in order not to "see the distributor make money on them."

As sales penetration expands and deepens, the problems of control and envy grow for the Manila supplier. What kind of distribution system would S. C. Johnson have if it permitted each of its 200 plus fieldmen to negotiate confidential and special deals with provincial customers? What would the consequences be if the 84 supervisors of California Manufacturing Corporation were at liberty to offer terms as they saw fit? Chaos for the supplier and dissatisfaction among most customers would result. The widespread use of extensive sales organizations in groceries explains the restricted and standardized terms typical in this trade sector. A similar point can be made with hardware. There the loose dealership system of distribution and the Chinese presence on all trade levels lead one to expect less rigid and uniform credit and price arrangements. Indeed, that is the case. In hardware, terms tend to fall between the extremes of what is practiced in textile and grocery distribution.

The probems of control and envy (or goodwill) dovetail. In order to keep an elaborate sales organization manageable, Manila firms restrict the autonomy salesmen are allowed in the field, and that, in turn, keeps them free of the problem of envy. A policy intended to reduce envy demands equivalent treatment of equivalent customers, which, in turn, restricts the range of terms salesmen can offer. In a nutshell, the problems of control and envy lead to the same thing: standardized terms.

To impose uniform and well-defined trade terms has various additional implications. For one, it affects the business organization of those who follow the policy. For another, suppliers will try to find some kind of substitute for personalized deals. While discussing the textile trade, I made the point that a mutually supportive relation exists between flexible trade negotiations and family firms personally supervised by one individual. In groceries the relation between organization and the trade process leads to a different outcome: uniform terms make it possible for the owner-operator to be removed from the buy-and-sell negotiation, and the fact that he is absent requires uniform terms. The result of this circular relation is evident on the Manila end. Large suppliers in

Manila may still be in the hands of individual families, but provincial sales are conducted by personnel way down the ladder of authority who are not supposed to offer personal favors in matters of credit and pricing. In the provinces standardization of trade agreements has had less of an impact on sales organization. There the centralized family firm operated by one person through whom all transactions pass is still typical.

Another implication of standardized terms is that suppliers try to replace personal treatment of individual customers with something equivalent. Without being able to give confidential specials to individuals on personal grounds, Manila companies attempt to approximate this through the use of promotions. Certain territories and types of customers are chosen as temporary targets for special sales. This permits the supplier to offer some flexible terms without overlooking the problems of envy and control.

Soft drink companies, creators of the most elaborate system of sales penetration so far devised in the Philippines, are masters of promotions. They started with the road shows in the fifties and the boxer Rocky Mariano publicly feeding his baby daughter Coke; they continue today with the massively advertised prizes for anyone lucky enough to collect crowns with the correct combination of letters in the bottle caps, a promotion begun in 1976. The main prize of this particular contest is a fully stocked *sari-sari* store valued at ₱5,000—the winner is expected, of course, to carry only the appropriate brand of soft drinks. What better way is there to capture a customer? Other promotions involve an exchange between a handsome sign for the store and the promise by the customer to handle only the giver's soft drink brand. Pepsi even offers small plywood shelters that can be folded for transportation and are used as shells for *sari-sari* stores. The relationship here is almost as paternalistic as the one between market vendors and Chinese suppliers in Baguio City reported by Davis, in which the suppliers tell the customers every week what they should order (Davis 1973:205). It also approaches a franchise system by encouraging the customer to become product exclusive in exchange for certain favors.

Of course, soft drinks are not the only goods pushed through promotions. Virtually every supplier of mass consumer items who taps provincial retailers and faces competition uses them, whether he is in grocery, hardware, drugs, or any other field. Promotions mean attractive low prices on new products for retailers, "take two and get one free" incentives, free samples to be test marketed, help with displays, prizes for especially conscientious and successful dealers. Even the employed field force is not immune: individuals receive a special commission for overfulfilling a quota, or junkets to Manila after top sales. Manila companies find that if their competitors organize promotions they have to do the same or not survive. In this manner, a self-feeding, self-perpetuating system of promotions supports competing companies' sales penetration into the provinces, and local color is replaced by imported form. Only when a monopoly is enjoyed, as in the case of the Philippine Match Company, Ltd., are promotions dispensed with in mass marketing.

Once Manila suppliers decide to apply tight terms uniformly among customers, envy between traders may be minimized, but the problem of controlling the salesmen becomes all the more formidable. Who or what is going to guarantee that none of them bends the rules so as to fill his own order book? Manila companies try everything: requiring daily and weekly written reports by the salesmen to the center; entrusting the selling and collecting responsibilities to different individuals; rotating fieldmen between territories to avoid formation of close allegiances; hiring only married individuals with children; organizing fieldmen's conferences in Manila attended by management to boost morale; offering extensive sales training. Attempts along these lines go as far as Union Carbide's policy of instilling into employees a feeling of loyalty and attachment to the company by emulating the permanent employer-employee relationship typical in Japanese firms; others do the opposite and rely on the threat of dismissal to keep their salesmen cheap and in line. The last procedure fits in with a hiring and firing policy widely used by Manila companies. A large portion of the labor force is employed on a temporary basis and let go if expenses grow or savings are to be made. Promotional and other junior sales personnel are often among the first to feel that treatment. Aside from lowering costs, this practice makes it easy to eliminate actually or potentially harmful individuals, even if it does not encourage the development of loyalty and skill. Finally, control is sought through personal contacts by sending supervisors into

the field. Of course, that still does not guarantee proper conduct since ultimately the supervisors themselves want supervision.

PMC, PRC, and IOF

I have made the point that increasing the depth of sales penetration, other factors being equal, encourages standardized terms and decreases the autonomy of fieldmen. This association is only rough, and other factors are not always equal. At times companies using similar organizations in their sales penetration are at opposite poles with regard to the uniformity of their terms and the centralization of their control. Comparing them brings several interesting details to light. The trade in detergents provides a ready example.

Before 1958 clothes in the Philippines were washed with bar soap manufactured by about 70 (mostly Chinese) enterprises scattered over the archipelago. They shared the market with several large Euro-American-controlled companies, among them Procter and Gamble Philippine Manufacturing Corporation (PMC) and Philippine Refining Company (PRC, a subsidiary of Lever Brothers) (Montanez 1971). This began to change in 1958 when PMC introduced Tide, the first powdered detergent ever marketed in the Philippines. In 1962 PRC countered with its Breeze, and soon after that the market was transformed. The manufacturers of bar soap were pressed against the wall as the oil-based powdered detergent gained popularity, and slowly the distribution of laundry soap slid into the hands of PMC and PRC. In 1972 only 27 soap and cleanser producers remained in business. The Chinese dominance was broken by means of a product requiring large capital investments to produce and the skillful use of mass advertising. Of equal importance was the aggressive sales strategy followed by PMC and PRC: they outbid the traditional manufacturers who limited their marketing efforts to local first-order merchants.

PMC and PRC are good examples of firms that had already incorporated a "proper" marketing orientation into their organization two decades ago. That is, they assigned the responsibility over distribution to a few people in high positions. PMC did so by having its department heads (sales, advertising, research and development, and so on) report to the vice president and general manager. PRC has its division heads (sales, marketing, product) report to a marketing director, who, together with the directors of manufacturing and finance, reports to the managing director. Similarities between the firms continue on lower levels. Up to the late sixties both relied on provincial warehousing; since then they have switched to jobbing, PMC in 1967 and PRC in 1971–1972. Both employ a large field force with promotional and senior salesmen. Both like to keep their fieldmen permanently in one territory, and each company has one booking and two van (promotional) salesmen assigned to Dagupan and its environs. A more perfect case of competition between two contenders leading to parallel sales organizations can hardly be found.

Despite these similarities, merchants in Dagupan classify PMC and PRC as companies working according to opposite principles because they differ in how much autonomy in setting terms they allow their salesmen. The senior salesman of PMC and his assistant are known to be strictly bound to company policy, which over the past several years has meant 2 percent discount with payment expected in five working days after delivery, and 30-day credit without discount. Not even damaged products can be returned for a refund. Salesmen have no authority to bend these rules. Formally this can only happen when management from the Manila office decides to check on sales in the field and allows some personal favors. For example, one day the Luzon district manager stopped by for a chat with Jose Dy, a second-order grocer in Dagupan. At this time (1971) the company maintained price brackets and sold one case of Tide for ₱31.50 each to dealers, two or more for ₱28.50. After a lengthy conversation, the manager confidentially agreed to the lower price for Dy regardless of how much he bought. This little episode did not make PMC appear flexible to Dy. On the contrary, the experience reinforced the fact that control over sales is tightly in the hands of high-level personnel from the head office.

Centralized control extends into the upper hierarchy of PMC. Usually three to five times a year the firm launches a promotional campaign which the advertising department organizes. Within this department each brand is handled by a brand manager whose duty it is to conceive and formulate new campaigns. Before it is adopted, the plan must move through all other departments (sales, manufacture, finance, and so on) for an OK. This is not enough! Procter and Gamble insists that all major proposals of its subsidiary, including promotions, be referred back to the main office in the States. Only if the Cincinnati office gives its blessing will the proposal be tested by research and development.

Matters are handled differently by PRC. It prefers to organize promotions on a more continuous, slightly less massive scale than PMC. It has campaigns under way throughout the year, each confined to particular regions and aimed at a limited range of outlets. The brand manager is the key person designing them also in this case, but he does so in cooperation with the promotion manager and the manager of research and development. The project is then handed to the marketing director who has the final say. The project is not passed on to the U.S. head office (Lever Brothers) for final approval. PRC develops and implements its marketing strategy independently of its mother company.

This tolerance toward lower-level autonomy is replicated in the provinces. Whereas PMC requires the personal authority of a district manager before bracket discounts can be extended to small purchases, PRC salesmen have the authority to extend such favors. It seems like a little thing, but this right lends the PRC salesmen an aura of independence and flexibility in Dagupan that those attached to PMC cannot match.

Similar marketing organizations between companies, therefore, do not guarantee that marketing policies are centralized to the same degree. In the case under discussion, two companies identified with the same nation (the United States), dealing in the same product line, and with nearly identical sales organizations, encourage sales activities by their fieldmen according to different notions about autonomy: by minimizing it in one case (PMC) and, with prudence, allowing it in the other (PRC).

I insert "with prudence" because the degree of freedom PRC allows its fieldmen is quite restricted. Except for the leeway in bracket pricing, they cannot interfere with discounts, credit rates, prices, and other matters. A company that combines an even greater degree of local autonomy with deep sales penetration is the International Oil Factory (IOF, a subsidiary of Cheng Ban Yek and Company). This Chinese firm is celebrated in the field of cooking oil. Its Baguio Oil continues to be the best-known brand in the Dagupan region. In 1967 IOF took advantage of its existing distribution network and launched its own detergent brand, Marvex. This move appeared to be an attempt to recoup the position the Chinese had enjoyed in soaps before the 1960s. By the late seventies this proved illusory, and Marvex continues to lag far behind Tide and Breeze. More important for us, however, is the method of marketing used by IOF.

If PMC is the archetypical "American way" company in groceries, IOF represents the Chinese option of personalism and flexibility. Like the other two, IOF has a deep distribution network in Pangasinan, but this network differs from theirs by retaining a warehouse system of distribution. The Dagupan warehouse serves north-central Luzon by means of five salesmen. Small outlets are contacted only in Pangasinan and Dagupan: beyond this distribution is limited to dealers. A senior and one promotional salesman are responsible for Pangasinan, and one salesman is assigned to Dagupan. Given the deep distribution in Pagasinan, one would expect centralized control over marketing to be strong. But this is true only with respect to the promotional salesman. He cannot negotiate terms. It is different for the other two salesmen. The one assigned to Dagupan, Fred Lo, is not subject to field supervision, and the warehouse manager, who is his immediate superior, does not interfere with his modus operandi. In contrast to what PMC or PRC would demand, IOF does not ask Lo to report periodically to Manila in person, he has no quota to meet before receiving a commission, and he can have sidelines as long as they do not interfere with his sales. These are enviable conditions for fieldmen of many companies.

Lo has become a fixture in Dagupan. He has been in sole command of booking and promotions for IOF during the past 20 years, and, as a Cantonese, he has established a remarkable degree of goodwill among the largely Hokkien and Filipino grocers.[7] The main point in his favor is that he has discretionary power over whom to sell to and how to regulate trade contacts. Manila's control is gentle, a fact that Dagupan's traders try to bargain into their favor. The official company terms are 2 percent discount if payment is received within 30 days. But whether a customer loses the 2 percent discount after the 30 days have elapsed is for Lo to decide. He can even tinker with the discount and credit line. Dy, the second-order merchant in Dagupan I mentioned above, is occasionally able to obtain from Lo a discount of 3 percent on purchases of ₱5,000 or more. After delivery he signs the invoice and pays perhaps two months later. Even then Dy usually convinces Lo to accept postdated checks for two days if he expects many checks to reach his account. The company sends the check to Manila for clearance, and Dy gains another couple of days. This trader, therefore, receives an effective credit line of close to 70 days at 3 percent discount when the company officially demands 30 days and 2 percent. In this case conditions are not far removed from those in textiles. Of course, by allowing a 3 percent discount Lo cuts into his own commission. Autonomy is permitted in one direction only; Lo cannot increase prices or limit credit beyond the levels publicized by the company. This way a sense of fairness is maintained among Dagupan's merchants and envy avoided.

Discussing suppliers who permit local autonomy to their sales force leads us back to the ethnic angle. After all, IOF is a Chinese enterprise, which in itself makes it more likely to follow such a strategy than PMC or PRC. But ethnicity is not all. Some companies, irrespective of the ethnic composition of management, have discovered that it is to their advantage to maintain what seems to be a contradictory policy: in order to increase *actual* control (in the sense of honesty and reliability) over their fieldmen, they reduce *formal* controls. Union Carbide has done this so far (it seems) with success. I have already mentioned that this firm has tried to instill into its sales force a feeling of personal commitment to their colleagues and the company. Within this overall goal, it initiated the following reforms: (a) salesmen are authorized to hire and dismiss their juniors; (b) detailed instructions on selling have been terminated, and the development of management talents is encouraged; (c) decisions on extending credit to dealers is left up to the salesmen. These steps have increased the feeling of responsibility among fieldmen. They also are reported to have eliminated favoritism between fieldmen and higher-level personnel, reduced the antagonism of fieldmen about controls, and lowered the expense of supervising them (*MH* November-December 1968).

When facing competitors who permit local trade autonomy among their fieldmen, what do companies like PMC and their local sales representatives do to keep ahead, or at least abreast of them?

To enforce standardized terms has the advantage of easing administrative complications and presenting an image of absolute fairness. But the cost of control is high, and customers usually prefer those suppliers who offer a modest amount of personal goodwill and favors. I have already pointed out several means used by firms to overcome these limitations: mass promotions among consumers, advertisements, incentives for salesmen, and deep and extensive sales penetration. Frequently this combination works. All too often, however, the nagging problem remains for the salesmen in the field that "I cannot offer flexible terms and stretch rules, while my competitor can. How can I keep from losing potential orders?"

One response is to "grin and bear it," as most promotional salesman do in the hope that specials offered by their company will eventually even things out. Others are driven to reinterpret the rules and to be innovative on their own accord. This does not involve outright violations of rules—if this were done consistently the salesmen would hardly survive in their positions. More subtle means are available, such as not warning those who have been inadequate in their patronage when future price hikes are imminent, or offering special promotions to good buyers first and when the less favored are contacted later noting with regret that the stock for the promotion has been exhausted. Some fieldmen show an extraordinary ability to create a flexible position for themselves through these and similar means.

Alex Muñoz has been the PMC senior salesman of central and western Pangasinan, including Dagupan, for 10 years, and he has had the unenviable job of fending off the senior man of PRC and Lo of International Oil. So far he has managed well despite his handicap of being tied to strict and standardized company terms. He considers himself as belonging to a "certain breed of men" widely believed in the Philippines to be typical of salesmen and which comes close to a picaresque character: lonely, independent, and aggressive; outgoing when with others; not really trusted by others, but needed by most; irregular and irreverent; a hard worker and a hard player; ready to use imagination for one's own good and that of others. The last point is illustrated by the following series of events.

In late January 1976 Muñoz had faced a costly misunderstanding with his company and customers from which he recovered by using some imagination and taking advantage of the timely government decision to raise the price of oil once again. In December 1975 Muñoz received a telegram from the head office which seemed to say that he could sell as much Calmay soap as he wished at a 5 percent discount, instead of the usual 2 percent. During that month alone he took orders on these terms for 2,000 cases with the blessing of his supervisor. Then the revelation came. The telegram he had acted on contained a clerical error (or Muñoz "misread" it), and the promotion had been intended for another region. The company did allow 400 cases to be absorbed into Muñoz's territory under the 5 percent discount, which he distributed to those whom he feared would not take kindly to the error. On his next cycle Muñoz apologized to the rest of the customers who had placed orders and blamed himself; some canceled their orders. "Over-commitment by the salesman," said Muñoz, "especially under PMC, can cost him his head because the company will not back him up."

In mid-January of 1976 the "good news" came that the government-pegged oil price would be raised. Now he could recoup his loss. Local grocers know that detergents are oil based, so it would be easy, Muñoz thought, to argue that a price hike of this product was imminent, leaving the exact when and how much properly nebulous. Muñoz asked for guidance from Manila, and in its characteristic way PMC refused to commit itself to such a deal. Thus Muñoz turned creative and decided to schedule a special trip on a Saturday to tell customers that new orders at the old price would be subject to company approval, but that orders placed with him immediately would most likely be accepted. To clinch the matter and add an aura of authenticity, he asked the author to accompany him. I learned only later that I was presented as a representative from the Manila office who came to hand carry the orders down to Manila for company approval. He contacted dealers in Alaminos, Lingayen, and Dagupan, and by playing on the fear of missing out on the windfall profit, by drawing up suggestive orders for dealers, and by letting an "American representative of the company" stand by, convinced most. On this day he booked orders for 1,000 cases, far in excess of his daily quota. This time the representatives of PRC and IOF, despite their greater authority to set terms, lost out. Companies can restrict the autonomy of field personnel, but they cannot eliminate their imagination.

Provincial Sales Agents Acting as Wholesalers

Many of the organizations responsible for provincial sales penetration are veritable bureaucracies: specialization is formal and rational, line and staff duties are separated, personnel receives training, and goals and responsibilities are spelled out. The exceptions are proprietor-operated rolling stores and companies that depend on the loose dealership system. I have not yet mentioned another exception. Some companies have constructed a channel structure reminiscent of the old *cabecilla* system of the nineteenth century. This is especially common in the cigarette trade where Chinese are nearly as dominant as in textiles. Cigarette suppliers either employ this method to the exclusion of others (La Suerte Cigar and Cigarette Factory) or use it together with a standard field force (La Perla Industries, Inc.).

La Suerte represents the popular Marlboro brand, and over the years it has outcompeted its former sister companies, La Perla and Anglo-American, to become one of the two largest cigarette manufacturers and distributors in the Philippines. Because of its size and because it is licensed by an American company, one would expect the company to channel its products through an elaborate marketing network. Instead, distribution is simple, and company control over the provincial retail level is indirect and covert.

Pangasinan and environs are covered for La Suerte by five so-called wholesalers. This title suggests that they are not hired employees or even commissioned sales agents, but independent merchants who act as cigarette wholesalers. Actually their connection with the company is more intimate. Secrecy, so typical in the semipassive strategy, is repeated here under sales penetration. Paul Chiao of Dagupan obtained the distributorship for the city, central Pangasinan, and La Union from the company two years ago. The Manila firm agreed to defray the expenses for two vans, four salesmen, and two *cargadores*. Chiao receives the cigarettes on consignment, and at the end of each selling week he forwards his receipts, retaining a commission. He never gains actual title to the goods. Yet La Suerte tries its utmost to make it appear as if Chiao and the other distributors own the merchandise they handle. Distributors of La Suerte, therefore, are treated locally like any other independent merchant, despite their de facto status as consigned sales agents of a Manila company. This means Chiao has to pay a city tax of 1 percent on sales. With a turnover of several million pesos annually, the amount involved is considerable.

Facing this prospect, Chiao and similar distributors in Dagupan try to reach an accommodation with the city, or to shift the local tax burden to the Manila supplier. If nothing else works, they intend to move their businesses to a municipality having lower or no sales taxes. It is for this reason that the local distributors for United Cigar and Cigarette Company and U.S. Tobacco Corporation operate out of Rosales and Mangaldan to the south and east of Dagupan. Some distributors are located in areas so remote that their activities in Dagupan appear like that of any other company salesman who is subject to a fixed yearly license fee, and city officials and customers alike may not even be aware of their true identity. Chiao feels himself too exposed in his present location, and Dagupan is likely to lose his business soon.

The system of distribution is awkward, though very lucrative, for the local representatives. For Manila companies it has definite advantages. It enables them to roll local taxes onto the shoulders of their sales agents and to blame them for any irregularities that may occur because, after all, they are "independent." A fracas between the Bureau of Internal Revenue (BIR) and La Suerte in the fall of 1975 illustrates this. In September of that year the BIR charged La Suerte with having underpaid the taxes due on its August sales by some ₱13 million. The company argued itself out of the difficulty by pointing out that its products were sold through wholesalers to retailers at a fixed price of ₱2.75 a pack. If the retailers followed the marketing agreement, the cigarettes would retail at ₱3. But the BIR was assessing the sales on the basis of actual retail prices, not those set by La Suerte. In the words of one of its officers, "it is not our fault if retailers turn greedy and increase our mark-up of 25 centavos. We have no way to control the action of these retailers much as we want them to follow our own pricing" (*EM* September 22, 1975).

What La Suerte actually had done was to accept the suggestion of sales agents (its "wholesalers") and offer a discount to large customers. It did this by increasing the price for those who bought by the carton and not by the case. Naturally, small retailers increased their price instead of agreeing to a lower margin. This event terminated the discount and nearly exposed the true relation between the "wholesalers" and La Suerte.

La Suerte has considerable, though hidden, control over the provincial distributors. It sets the maximum price they can charge and demands that no credit be extended to retailers and that sales be restricted to the assigned territory. Sales agents, in turn, are free to charge lower prices if they are willing to accept a lower commission. They receive hardly any supervision in the field, they are not subject to minimal sales quotas, and how they organize their business is up to them. Distributors are also permitted to engage in other business activities—in fact they are encouraged to do so because it legitimizes their appearance as independent cigarette merchants.

The fine balance between provincial freedom and Manila control, between overt autonomy and actual agent status this case exemplifies is effective. Sales go well for La Suerte and its distributors, and competition with more formal sales organizations poses no threat. There are two reasons for this success. The first is the old theme of trust generated by ethnic and kin identities across channel levels. Virtually all of these semiindependent distributors are of Chinese extraction, and the following account of Chiao's selection shows the typical procedure involved. When the previous representative in central Pangasinan proved unsatisfactory, La Suerte sought a replacement it could trust. Chiao's wife is related to the owners of Cheng Ban Yek and Company. A subsidiary of this company (International Oil Factory) has a warehouse in Dagupan, the stocks of which are delivered from Manila by the flourishing trucking firm owned by Chiao. The owners of Cheng Ban Yek and Company, in turn, have links with La Suerte, so that Chiao was a natural choice. Such ethnic and kin identity is indispensable for a partly informal and covert form of sales penetration like this to survive.

The second reason for the success is, ironically, mass advertising and the identification of the Marlboro brand with the "rugged American life." Why do Manila firms so often impose their own sales organization on the subwholesale level? It is only occasionally owing to their love for administrative clarity. More often it is to maximize turnover and meet the challenge of deep sales penetration of others. Thus most cigarette manufacturers depend on both semiindependent distributors and their own promotional sales force in the provinces, or they forgo the local distributors altogether in favor of employed fieldmen (Columbia Tobacco Company, Inc.).

La Suerte's ability to refrain from using a fully controlled and formal sales force is attributable to the extraordinary demand for the major cigarette brand it carries. This demand also enables the company to ask for terms that are among the most restrictive in the grocery trade. Up to late 1975 the market was such that La Suerte had to limit sales to customers to assure fair allocation between them, and in 1976 sales continued to be brisk in spite of rising prices. La Suerte is the only company that can insist on COD terms; all the others in the cigarette trade operate on a 15- or 30-day credit basis.

The tremendous demand Philip Morris has generated through American-inspired advertising makes it possible for La Suerte to rely on a sales organization steeped in the Chinese idiom. The ready demand has simplified marketing. The company needs no extra promotional component in the sales force, nor imaginative sales talk. Once the Marlboro truck parks in front of a marketplace, customers, most of them small retailers, gather around it to buy. The Chiaos (the proprietor or his sons) enter only the stores of large customers to collect orders. Here their behavior contrasts sharply with that of, say, Alex Muñoz of PMC. He has to be Mr. Friendly and Funny. He has to cajole and to twist the truth to make sales among Chinese and Filipinos alike. When the Chiaos, on the other hand, pick up orders it is simply a matter of asking "how much this time?" and no more. There is no sales pitch, no haggling. Terms are fixed and demand is high so that professional groveling is not needed. If demand were not so high, the Chiaos and similar distributors would have to change their sales tactics drastically or, what is more likely, they would contact only large dealers and leave the small fry to be served by the company's promotional salesmen.

The Chiaos and others like them are retained by cigarette companies not so much to push sales as to guarantee the safe execution of the marketing process. For this purpose an organization approaching the *cabecilla*-agent system is well suited. Today's arrangement, however, is not an exact replica of the *cabecilla* system of a century ago. In its heyday the provincial agent was totally dependent upon his "head" in Manila; and not only did he sell for him, he also bought. The link exemplified by La Suerte and its provincial distributors is nearly as confidential, but less all-embracing (see also Omohundro 1978:125–129). For an agreement that is almost as all-embracing but less confidential, one has to turn to contractual and ownership penetration. However, first I want to say a few words about sales penetration in pharmaceuticals.

Pharmaceuticals

Because sales penetration appears in such a great variety of forms in the grocery trade, it may seem redundant to discuss this marketing strategy in the context of other products as well. Thus, I was able to handle the hardware trade in a rather perfunctory manner. But drugs deserve a more extended treatment for two reasons. First, they constitute a major and well-defined commercial sector and to overlook them would skew any picture designed to show how provincial distribution centers, like Dagupan, are tied to their source of commodities. Second, and more important, sales penetration in drugs takes on a character that differs more than in mere nuance from that in grocery and hardware.

The Philippines is one of the most advanced countries among Southeast Asian nations in the assembly and distribution of pharmaceuticals. Several companies maintain a nationwide marketing network that allows delivery of special orders within one to two days in all easily accessible regions, and some, like Winthrop Stearns, Inc., use their Philippine subsidiary as the regional headquarters for Southeast Asia. Production (or rather laboratory assembly) has experienced a phenomenal growth since the fifties, and many well known overseas companies have opened facilities. Also, local enterprises (such as United Laboratories, Inc.), most of which have technological ties with overseas concerns, have entered the field. And there are several large national distributors (Metro Drug Corporation, Philusa Drug Distributors, Inc.). In 1972, 81 manufacturers of pharmaceuticals (27 with 100 or more employees) existed in the Philippines. These, together with 80 wholesaler-importers, supply 4,400 hospitals, clinics, and rural health and puericultural centers, 5,700 drugstores, and 17,000 physicians (Republic of the Philippines 1975; Studies on Philippine Industries 1974a:10, 22). The retail level is less fragmented than in groceries, but the necessity of serving a large professional group makes distribution a difficult affair.

History

Before World War II a pharmaceutical industry hardly existed in the Philippines. Botica Boie Watsonal Castoria and some house remedies of Arambulo Products represented virtually the only ventures in the production of Western-type medicine. The indent channel was the most important means by which pharmaceuticals were made locally available, and general-line trade houses, some of which (like Marsman) have continued their activities in drugs to this day, also played an important role in this product. Specialization and active marketing were early introduced by a company that goes back to the Spanish period. Botica Boie was established by Germans in 1867 and turned American in 1917. It imported, indented, distributed under license, dabbled in production, wholesaled, and retailed, and in the twenties it opened the most prominent American-style drugstore in the Philippines.[8] At the same time it began to have wholesale-retail branches in Cebu, Legaspi, and Iloilo.

Drug retailing did not take off in the Philippines until 1902, when the Philippine Public Health Service established a network of dispensaries and health stations over the islands and when colleges of medicine and pharmacy (most notably the University of Santo Tomas) opened their doors. Professionalism spread fast, and as drugs became available, "illegitimate" competition began to be a matter of concern: "Many ordinary merchants sold simple remedies and patent medicines until the Philippine Legislature passed a law in 1915 prohibiting any one but a registered pharmacist from selling drugs, compounds and patent medicine within a radius of 10 km. of an established drug store" (Botica Boie Drug Company n.d.:19). Laws have become more restrictive since then, but the fact that antibiotics can be obtained in *sari-sari* stores today attests to their effectiveness.[9]

Despite competition from nonprofessionals, officially sanctioned pharmacies flourished during the interwar years, and for once a trade was closely identified with Filipino entrepreneurs. In the early days Filipinos were the only ones seeking degrees in pharmacy from the University of Santo Tomas, and this gave them a head start in the trade. Americans operated the few large wholesale and retail outlets and Filipinos the many small and medium-sized stores; the Chinese concerned themselves with Chinese drugs. Divisoria never got a firm hold on the trade. Until today Filipinos (mostly females) have defended their strong position in drug retailing.

Immediately after the war, leading drugstores were able to import by renewing prewar connections with American sources. Demand was high and provincial merchants came to Manila to buy. As more drug merchants entered the import trade, competition increased, and some saw it as to their advantage to begin a policy of active provincial penetration. Botica Boie, for example, expanded its branches with outlets now in Cebu, Iloilo, Bacolod, and Davao, and depots in Zamboanga and Dagupan. At the same time, exchange controls forced overseas and local firms into production. Muller and Phipps Manufacturing Corporation was one of the first (1950), followed by Merck Sharp and Dohme (Phil.), Inc., Abbott Laboratories (Phil.), E. R. Squibb and Sons Philippines Corporation, United Laboratories, Inc., Parke Davis and Company, Inc., and many others.

National distributors like Botica Boie marketed their products at a uniform and fixed price throughout the Philippines. There were also regional wholesalers who limited their activities to individual regions (Iloilo, Cebu, central Luzon) where they were able to offer drugs at lower prices than distributors operating on a national scale. Up to the late fifties manufacturers used as many outlets as possible, including these regional wholesalers. Under these circumstances national distributors had a difficult time maintaining themselves, and some, like Botica Boie, virtually ceased to exist. In 1959 one of them (Metro Drug Corporation) saw a way out. It signed an exclusive licensing agreement with a major manufacturer, convinced that if it were the sole distributor of a brand, no one would underbid its price. What had already been standard practice in grocery and hardware for quite some time became common in the drug trade only now. A few suppliers dispensed with Metro's services, charging it with favoritism, but eventually they came back to conclude similar agreements.

By the mid-sixties national distributors controlled much of the drug sales to the provinces. Only in remote areas have regional wholesalers retained an advantage, and so far only a few manufacturers manage sales penetration themselves. The typical national distributor uses warehouse branches to cover the provinces. The largest of these, Metro Drug Corporation, has 22 warehouse branches. Smaller distributors and some manufacturers have provincial depots instead of warehouses, keeping invoicing and credit control in the Manila office. In addition to ethical and over-the-counter (or proprietary) drugs, the larger companies offer veterinarians' supplies and cosmetics, each of which is handled by a different department and sales force. In effect they are limited-line trade houses.

It is more difficult for drug manufacturers to enter into sales penetration than for grocery producers. This is not because these manufacturers are less conscious of the market; if anything their close affiliation with overseas interests makes them more market oriented. The reason lies elsewhere. To distribute pharmaceuticals requires a high degree of expertise. It is costly, therefore, to create a marketing organization out of nothing. Moreover, the strong position of the national distributors damps the incentive for manufacturers to contact retailers themselves.

Organization of Distribution

The close to 40 traveling salesmen of Manila drug companies active in Dagupan are well placed. They have seven hospitals and 10 clinics to serve and 110 doctors and 23 drugstores to contact, not to mention customers in the rest of Pangasinan and beyond. Except for Aquino (see "Passive Strategy," Chapter 4) and two Chinese pharmacists who personally buy in Binondo, drug merchants in Dagupan order through Manila company salesmen. The trade structure in Dagupan is simple. Three large wholesaler-retailers form the equivalent of first-order merchants found in groceries and hardware. They are dealers for many Manila suppliers, and much of their sales effort is directed at retailers in Pangasinan and Ilocos whom they serve through rolling stores. The remaining drugstores in Dagupan are mainly in the retail business.

Active marketing into Pangasinan goes back to before the war when Botica Boie, Botica de Santa Cruz, and others in Manila started to send their trucks to north-central Luzon. Companies supplying Dagupan today are different, but the trend toward sales penetration has continued. Other developments have been of more recent vintage: professionalization of the detail men;[10] breakdown of the equilibrium existing in the local trade structure after a Manila retail franchise entered the city; and the spread of branch warehouses of Manila companies in Dagupan. I consider the first two developments later; the last I turn to now.

The late sixties witnessed a concerted push into Dagupan by a handful of Manila drug firms. First two distributors, then two manufacturers established branch offices there. In 1967 Pharma Industries, Inc. (a subsidiary of F. E. Zuellig, Inc.) and Metro Drug Corporation opened depots in the city, in 1969 Johnson and Johnson (Phil.), Inc. entered with a depot, and in 1973 Warner-Chilcott Laboratories (Phil.), Inc. did the same. The competitive drive into provincial marketing was in full swing, and channel integration was the result.

Pharma and Metro distribute drugs and related products under license.[11] Their depots in Dagupan have matured into full-fledged branch warehouses which provide complete credit and billing services. They are elaborate affairs, and of a size unusual for such outlets in Dagupan. The Metro warehouse employs 22 individuals. This includes the branch manager, cashier, bookkeeper, statistician-pharmacist, ledger clerk, two bodega men, two assistants, and one inventory man. Together with 12 employed salesmen, they realize annual sales of more than ₱10 million. Six detail men, who are paid by the companies Metro represents, are also attached to the branch.

Since the mid-sixties Pharma has expanded its provincial network "because of the pressure arising out of its chief rival, Metro Drugs" (as put by a local detail man), and when a few years ago the company joined forces with Muller and Phipps Manufacturing Corporation and took over its drug line, Pharma started to be particularly aggressive. The company now has 16 branches in the Philippines compared to Metro's 22. Fifteen detail men of the Dagupan branch scour hospitals and talk to doctors in Abra, Ilocos Norte and Sur, La Union, Tarlac, and Pangasinan provinces. Routine orders and all collections are handled by seven salesmen. The branch has 25 employees, is divided into administration, sales (responsible for salesmen), and promotion (takes care of detail men), and plans are to add 10 more men to boost the sales force.

Both branches have grown into substantial investments for the Manila firms. Among such facilities in Dagupan, only the Pepsi-Cola warehouse overshadows them in personnel. The warehouse of Cheng Ban Yek, the gas storage depots in Dagupan, and branches of cement distributors boast larger physical plants, but their permanent administrative and sales personnel is smaller.

Why are the drug warehouses so large? Aside from Metro's and Pharma's competitive zeal, which has driven them to expand, several factors, some unique to the drug trade, are important: (a) these branches are responsible for a territory covering much of northern Luzon, and the medical community in Dagupan itself is unusually large; (b) drug distributors have to serve doctors and hospitals that can be ignored by most other Manila suppliers; however, for their over-the-counter items they have to keep in touch with a broad range of store outlets; (c) it is far more difficult for drug suppliers to rely on jobbing than it is for suppliers in grocery or hardware because of the technical know-how needed to handle the commodity; (d) delivery speed is crucial in drugs; (e) these distributors also merchandise products other than drugs.

The last point explains why Johnson and Johnson and Warner-Chilcott have offices in Dagupan. They are among the very few drug manufacturers in the Philippines who organize sales penetration through their own provincial branch depots. In fact, their presence in Dagupan would be surprising were it not for the fact that in addition to pharmaceuticals, they distribute other mass consumer items: Halls candies in the case of Warner-Chilcott and baby powder in that of Johnson and Johnson.

In the typical setup, overseas or local producers have contracts with distributors to market their products. This includes holding several month's worth of supplies, physically distributing them, booking orders, and collecting. The principals (producers), in turn, retain the responsibility for detailing. Detail men, usually employed by the producer, are attached to the distributor's offices and coordinate their activities with salesmen. They pass samples to doctors and other professionals and explain them; if the professionals place orders, detail men pass them on to salesmen. In essence, detail men are the promotional component in the drug trade. Their function is similar to that of promotional salesmen discussed in "Deep Sales Penetration" (this chapter), but their position is different. Because they receive more training than the ordinary salesmen and because they rub shoulders with lofty professionals, their status is very much above that of the rest of the sales force in drugs, not to mention salesmen in other products. The relation between fieldmen in Dagupan makes this clear.

Itinerant salesmen representing Manila companies in Dagupan have never formed a homogeneous group. Supervisors stay in different, fancier hotels than the ordinary salesmen, resident salesmen with their families in Dagupan stand apart from those who are totally itinerant, and, of course, Chinese and Filipino fieldmen do not mix with one another as freely as they do with their own kind. But it has only been during the past 20 years that another differentiation has appeared, this one according to product line.

Until the early sixties drug fieldmen stationed in Dagupan were very much part of Manila company salesmen in general. They lodged in the same hotel and belonged to the same association (Philippine Fieldmen Association of Northern Luzon), and their sales responsibilities did not differ much from those of others. Then the medical boom had its repercussions in Dagupan also. Training was intensified on the Manila end, the role of the detail man was carved out, and slowly a bifurcation appeared in Dagupan between "professionals" in the drug trade and the rest.

Today, detail men and pharmaceutical salesmen have their own association, and all of them stay in two hotels that cater only to them. These have been opened within the past 10 years by shrewd drugstore operators, who created goodwill for themselves by charging low rates. Detail men are on the top of the heap and, therefore, are most resented. The ultimate indicator of snobbery to other salesmen (including those in drugs) is their use of the M.D. symbol on their cars, which actually stands for medical detail man. The extremely large-scale and deep sales penetration found in groceries, above all in soft drinks and cigarettes, never evolved in drugs. What has happened instead is the creation of an "elite" distribution force, which likes to identify itself more with those it serves than with other company salesmen.

One of the central tenets of aggressive marketing states that it is not enough to have wholesaler-retailers place orders for particular products; it is also necessary to convince consumers that these products are to their benefit. This tenet is shared by Manila drug companies. They face one complication, however, in the form of ethical products. For over-the-counter drugs standard promotions, discounts, and advertisements are appropriate. In the case of ethical products a different form of morality enters, and some of these techniques, most notably advertisements directed to consumers, will not do. Instead of approaching consumers directly, a roundabout procedure is used in which the promotional efforts are aimed at those who advise consumers what to take. The tactic is to get doctors and health institutions committed to particular products through the effort of detail men. Once this happens, doctors prescribe the products to patients who buy them in drugstores. These, then, begin to place regular orders for the items with salesmen.[12]

Here doctors, midwives, and similar professionals are the prime target. They are showered with so many free samples, brochures, and favors that it borders on the unethical. Competitive pressures among suppliers hardly help. Wyeth-Suaco Laboratories, Inc., for instance, recently complained that a competitor outbid it in provisioning the nursery of Makati Medical Center because Wyeth-Suaco was unable to offer air conditioners to the new facility. Restrictive orders from the home office in the United States forbade it to give special favors to institutions and other customers because of the recent scandals that revealed shady business dealings by American companies (such as Lockheed) overseas. The Manila office tried to convince those on the American end that business is done differently in the Philippines than in the United States, but to no avail. The only counterpunches it can offer are to show that its product is of better quality, to lower its price, and to rely on female sales personnel to push the item among midwives, none as effective as offering needed capital equipment in exchange for goodwill!

The need for flexible trade relations is greater in drugs than in groceries because many techniques of mass marketing cannot be used. Unlike in textiles, however, in drugs this does not express itself in the realm of terms. Vertical relations between channel members are not steeped in ethnic and personal trust. Terms are standardized within 30 days, 2–3 percent discount, and brackets on prices are the norm. Some leeway of course exists. Special "house accounts" are allowed exceptional deals. Mead Johnson Philippines, Inc. gives 90 days to the Mercury Drug retail chain because this chain buys more than ₱1 million worth of goods a month from them. The three largest drug merchants in Dagupan receive "unlimited" credit for 15 to 30 days at 3 percent discount from their important sources. Salesmen of Johnson and Johnson are even allowed to offer at their own discretion a 3 percent overdraft to their credit customers. This is unusual. Most suppliers grant autonomy to their salesmen only in the matter of scheduling visits, a privilege that is really an empty gesture because the obligation by salesmen to meet specified quotas effectively restricts their choice.

Flexibility in the drug trade is expressed instead in the form of special gifts offered to those deemed important and receptive. On the cheap end this means free samples, calendars, and brochures; on the inflated end it involves cars to doctors ("to enhance their professional service") and appliances and other goodies to institutions. Up to a point this is similar to the strategy followed by Pepsi and San Miguel which supply refrigerators to commercial outlets in return for patronage. In the drug trade, however, these are confidential gifts, and the expected return is not written down or publicly announced.[13]

Like the targets of promotions in grocery, the recipients of favors and gifts from drug suppliers do not refuse them. Wyeth-Suaco once held a seminar for doctors during which it was proposed that all marketing paraphernalia used by the drug companies should be terminated except for samples and brochures. The provincial doctors in particular disagreed vehemently. They already consider themselves discriminated against compared to their urban colleagues and feel they need all the help they can get from drug companies.

In more general terms, under conditions in which a professional group that is not receptive to simple advertisements and sales talk mediates between suppliers (drug companies) and consumers (patients), "corrupt" methods will flourish, unless strict ethical standards are enforced. In the United States such standards and enforcement are far from perfect; in the Philippines they barely exist.

Until 1976 all pharmacies in Dagupan were independent family proprietorships, and those facilities controlled by Manila firms confined themselves to wholesaling. Then a certainly not unanticipated, but long opposed, event happened. In 1976 Mercury Drug Corporation of Manila opened a retail franchise in the city after it had done so in several other provincial centers. It is no wonder that Dagupan's druggists dreaded the entrance of this franchise since it is tied to the largest chain in the pharmaceutical field, one that is famous for low prices and efficient distribution. For the first time a Manila company was undercutting the position of Dagupan drug retailers. Full channel integration has become part of the pharmaceutical trade—long after it had conquered other product lines.

WHEN ACTIVE MARKETING of industrial consumer goods began to make inroads in the Philippines during the twenties and thirties, it did so mainly in the form of sales penetration. The preponderance of this marketing strategy has continued ever since. Today most consumer products enter the provinces through channels organized in this manner, and most suppliers engaged in active marketing opt for sales penetration. One reason for its popularity is that it allows traders to maintain direct links with lower-level merchants at acceptable costs. It also creates at least a facade of personalized trade, an important fact in a culture that stresses personalism. It is also popular because it enables traders to bridge organizational gaps, which often exist between the upper and lower ends of channels. Large suppliers in Manila find it easy to manage transactions with tiny neighborhood stores in the provinces by means of itinerant salesmen.

Over the years sales penetration has matured into a strategy within which a large number of subtypes exist. Suppliers either confine themselves to a loose dealership system, or they try to reach as many provincial outlets as possible. Many rely on a simple sales organization, others prefer complexity. Local autonomy is stressed by some, others choose centralization. Manila firms may use jobbing to overcome storage problems, or they may have their own warehousing facilities. Put simply, sales penetration varies from shallow to deep. It is deep when it tries to impose control over provincial retailers. At this point sales penetration begins to overlap with other types of active marketing strategies that have become popular in the Philippines during the past three decades. These I examine in the next two chapters.

Chapter 6

COORDINATED PENETRATION:

AN EXAMPLE OF FAILURE

EVERY STRATEGY has positive and negative consequences for those who carry it out. It is primarily, and this is its positive side, a means to an end, a way for actors to reach a goal. Its negative side is the cost accumulated by virtue of pursuing that strategy, and the opportunities forgone because of not choosing another course of action.

Marketing strategies are no exception to this duality. Active marketing by means of sales penetration improves downward control, expands regional coverage, and makes brand loyalty a more certain proposition. But it also requires expenditures to maintain the field force, and it fails to achieve what aggressive firms often see as their ultimate aim: direct management of retail sales. Even the deepest form of sales penetration only serves retailers; it does not participate in retailing. To satisfy this goal, ownership or contractual penetration, or coordinated penetration for short, is available to the supplier.[1]

Under coordinated penetration the supplying firm integrates downward and has a hand in the management of the stores through which its products pass to consumers. Compared to sales penetration, its costs usually are higher because considerable outlays for land, buildings, and personnel are needed. This strategy also intensifies local resistance to commercial penetration by outsiders. After all, retail branches and franchises are very visible compared to company salesmen, and they compete with local retailers.

Ownership penetration offers (at least on paper) a greater degree of control over retailing than contractual penetration. The supplier retains ownership of the product until it leaves the branch, he employs those who retail, and the physical plant of the retail store is owned or rented under his name. Ideally there is nothing that keeps the owner from replicating his sales outlets from province to province in a manner entirely to his liking. The form in which products receive distribution—displays, prices, credit, quotas—and how centralized the business is are up to the owner.

Contractual penetration, in turn, is preferred by many because it allows the supplier to eat his cake and have it too. It lowers the expense of distribution borne by the supplier and enables him to retain much of the direct supervision over retailing he enjoys under ownership penetration. The franchise dealer has the title of the goods he retails, but his sales and buying strategy and even his business organization are restricted by the contract he has signed. Contractual penetration therefore is an ingenious compromise for the supplier, but it also has its negative side. It is always possible for franchise dealers to turn independent after they have accumulated enough experience and capital, and to compete with the original franchisor. Also the willingness to conform to the contractual agreement by either party tends to be fragile because they relate to one another, at least legally, as independent firms.

A widely shared model of channel modernization assumes that in open economies undergoing development there is a trend away from conservative distribution toward active marketing strategies. Within the active mode, moreover, coordinated penetration is said to be the most recent stage in the evolutionary progression (Bucklin 1972a; Gultinan 1974). This model is derived from the Euro-American experience, and the expectation is that trends in distribution evident in these societies will be repeated in countries that are currently undergoing development (D. Anderson 1970; Takeuchi and Bucklin 1977). If this is true, one would expect vertical channel integration to be more prevalent in developing societies today than several decades ago. The Philippines generally corroborate this expectation. Sales penetration has emerged as a strong force since the war, and the deep version of it (as in soft drinks) matured only recently. Trade contacts have been formalized (written terms, contracts, postdated checks), and the internal organization of trade establishments is now often rationally planned. Also contractual and ownership penetration has become common only since the fifties. Retail branches and franchises of Manila companies are today found in virtually all of the more important towns of the Philippines and handle a wide array of goods.

In this and the following chapters I illustrate the structure of ownership and contractual penetration and trace its historical development. My main concern is with household appliances, cars, and gasoline. Earlier it was seen that textiles have defied the trend toward formal channel integration. This chapter presents another exception. It illustrates how vertical integration in the appliance channel dissolved into a more fragmented condition. Chapter 7 shows the opposite. It describes how the distribution of cars and gasoline has followed a trend predicted by models of channel evolution. In fact, trade channels in these products are the acme of nationwide coordinated penetration found in the Philippines. At the end of that chapter I present cases in which suppliers are currently adopting coordinated distribution in products that typically are moved through less integrated means. Perhaps these cases are harbingers of future developments.

Home Appliances

History

Limited local buying power and electrification provided a highly restricted market for home appliances in the Philippines before the war.[2] Only ₱4 million worth of electrical goods (including appliances) were imported in 1932 (*MH* March 1963). Most of these were traded by general-line trade houses with exclusive agency agreements from overseas suppliers.

Distribution of home appliances received a boost in the Philippines when an American in Manila acquired the agency of General Electric early in this century. This agency—"a plum many were reaching for" (*ACCJ* November 1935:16)—was eventually taken over by Pacific Commercial Company, which retained the license even after GE opened its own office in Manila. By the thirties more than 20 electrical supply businesses existed in Manila, and the demand for home appliances began to stir among Filipinos. "At some of these stores, more than 4 customers in 5 are Filipinos; even the demand for electrical refrigerators is chiefly among Filipinos" (ibid.). The market, though, remained largely confined to Manila. Until after the war few salesmen ventured outside Manila, and provincial dealers were very scarce. Americans dominated the scene in both the products traded and the enterprises that handled them. Among the more prominent firms were Singer Sewing Machine Company, Heacock's (radios), GE, Erlanger and Galinger (refrigerators), American Hardware and Plumbing, Pacific Commercial Company, and Manila Gas Company (gas ranges).

Of this list, GE and Singer were unique in being overseas producers that maintained branch offices in Manila. The considerable business GE had built up as a result of the electrification of Manila made such an outlet convenient. Singer is a special case entirely.

The Singer Manufacturing Company opened a Manila branch as early as 1878. The American occupation 20 years later increased its sales, and in 1910 Singer Sewing Machine Company, the trading arm of Singer Manufacturing, took over. The really impressive fact is that by the twenties the company had more than 150 branch stores throughout the islands, and in 1938 it had 368. This network made Singer unique not only in appliances but in all imported consumer lines of the day. Even after the war only a few companies managed to match such a large-scale system of ownership penetration.

Singer is famous for its long-standing tradition of creative marketing procedures (Jack 1957). As elsewhere, its success in the Philippines was based on three components. First was the product: sewing machines can be used by consumers to earn money, and they need no electricity. Second was the channel organization: experience had taught Singer when entering a new market to establish first exclusive agency agreements with local merchants— the company developed franchising 100 years ago. Once sales improved substantially in a region, the company would move into retailing through branching. Third were the retail terms: in the late nineteenth and early twentieth centuries Singer was a pioneer in installment selling, which became standard in the appliance field only much later.

By the thirties each branch outlet in the Philippines was identified by a Singer sign and had a branch manager. These "stores" were (and most of them still are) modest affairs, but their large number and the commissioned agents attached to each resulted in a thorough coverage of the rural population. The outlets sold machines worth nearly ₱200 each on ₱10 down and ₱5 a month installments. COD sales went for a price 20 percent below that of installment sales. The agreement was kept as simple and clear as possible. The contract was short, and only one cosignee was needed; "the claim [was] limited to the machine itself, *no other collateral stands behind the peasant's words*" (*ACCJ* 1938:8). How the system worked is illustrated by the following case. A clerk is earning ₱100 a month.

> He has an aunt . . . who thought she might make herself
> more useful if she had a sewing machine. It was talked over
> [and] accordingly she bought a machine and someone signed
> with her for it. She made some of the payments herself. The
> clerk's mother made some for her and other members of the
> family made some. The aunt now makes the clerk's shirts, he
> is buying the material—also dresses for his children and
> things for his wife. There is of course no charge but if you
> think to send your Auntie rice once in a while, or chicken
> for Sunday dinner, this is what you should do (ibid.).

With this policy of relying on character credit and the ability of the customer to earn the installment payments while using the machine, Singer experienced minimal losses, and the distribution network was (and still is) impervious to the encroachment of even the Chinese. Before the war the Philippine agency was the largest one Singer had overseas, and in the thirties it imported and retailed some 8,000 machines a year. More than 95 percent of them, so the company claimed, went to poor families.

Home appliances, other than Singer products, either reached the consumers at this time through the few retail outlets of import houses located in the major cities, or were sold by importers to independent, often Chinese, wholesalers, who passed them on to subwholesalers and retailers in Manila and the provinces. Except for sewing machines, no brand-exclusive, integrated channel for appliances was in sight.

By the early fifties several factors conspired to turn appliance distribution in a new direction. The principal ones were: (a) expanding demand occasioned by the spread of electrification; (b) an oligopolistic market in which a small number of dominant competitors began to relate to one another by emulating each other's novel marketing strategies; (c) the rising popularity of coordinated marketing strategies in the United States, which U.S. companies began to extend into their overseas operations; (d) the imposition of import controls, which undermined the position of established trade houses.

The combination of these factors meant that downward sales control became the order of the day. This development was facilitated by the fact that no traditional channel specializing in the movement of these products existed. The principal form this took on the upper channel end was for large overseas firms to license limited-line distributors or to enter into joint ventures with them. These distributors (such as Del Rosario Brothers Marketing Corporation, Ysmael Steel Manufacturing Corporation, Refrigeration Industries, Inc.) were made exclusively responsible for marketing and, in many cases, for assembling the appliance brand. Instead of handling a variety of products, each distributor was now expected to devote much, if not most, of his organizational and capital resources to the sale of the principal's products. The degree to which the channel was marketing oriented and brand conscious became the measure of potential success.

Such commitment had several implications for the distributor in Manila. First, it meant that he was able to engage in heavy advertising and sales gimmicks so as to establish brand identity. Second, it implied that the distributor, to ensure local brand availability, would build a closely controlled distributive network down to the retail level throughout the islands. Third, it often meant constructing local assembly facilities to back up the sales effort and comply with governmental expectations. Even with the help of the principal, these requirements meant that the distributor had to have considerable capital resources. The one group in the society with access to ample funds, the Chinese, remained dormant during this

period, refusing to become exclusively attached to any one supplier. Filipinos were found willing to accept exclusive representation with starting capital derived from food processing, from real
estate, and, in the case of joint ventures, from overseas suppliers.

So, with the encouragement of their principals, large license
holders built a fully owned retail network that eventually covered
all major urban centers of virtually all provinces. As the channel
matured, however, each company developed its distributive
organization, not according to the needs of the product and constraints of the consumer market, but according to the strategies
followed by its competitors. This left the door open for more
effective traders to disrupt the channel later on.

The first decade of appliance distribution after the war was
dominated by the competitive minuet danced by two companies,
Del Rosario Brothers Marketing Corporation (DRB) and Ysmael
Steel Manufacturing Corporation. Companies like Radiowealth,
Inc., Refrigeration Industries, Inc. (Frigidaire), and Aircon, Inc.
played a secondary role. The background of the first two companies is similar. DRB began in 1952 as a real estate company for
the Del Rosario family. In 1953 it formed a marketing arm, because one of the brothers had managed to get the exclusive distributorship of the International Harvester (IH) appliance line. This
was not to last. A few months later IH decided to bow out of the
appliance field altogether and sold its assembly plant to DRB. A
short time after that DRB picked up the distributorship for GE
electrical appliances, which it kept for the following two decades.

In 1950 the president of Juan Ysmael Company, also a real
estate company, decided to form Ysmael Steel Manufacturing
Corporation to produce filing cabinets. As a result of a visit to the
United States in 1954 by the president's wife, the company received the right to manufacture and distribute Admiral refrigerators and air conditioners for the entire Philippine market.

Ysmael and DRB, the "arch rivals" as they became locally
known, reacted to one another as if they were the only ones in the
field. Ysmael had an edge in manufacturing; DRB was the innovative one in distribution. Under IH, DRB used an independent
dealership system of distribution, which it changed when it took
over the GE agency. The company had two aims in the fifties: to

extend distribution to consumers into all provincial centers of the country and to control sales down to the retail level. To accomplish this it chose ownership penetration. Management felt that this stratgegy maximized control. In addition it turned out that independent dealers did not have sufficient funds and know-how to take up distribution themselves. DRB built up its branch network, and by 1960 it had 40 retail outlets. Next to Singer's, this was the most ambitious system of centrally owned appliance retail stores in the Philippines.

Because it was a manufacturing firm to begin with, Ysmael Steel's main interest to start with was in production. It left the task of selling to a distributor—Sun Brothers, which had its own national marketing network. This lasted until Ysmael decided to take over distribution itself, or, what amounts to the same thing, until it felt that Sun Brothers could not keep up with demand. Either way, the aggressive expansion of DRB and the pressure from its principal, Admiral, to capture a certain share of the market had much to do with this decision. By 1961 Ysmael had 26 branches and was in the midst of further expansion.

During the late fifties Ysmael Steel and DRB had created a standardized, branch-specific, formal, and nearly totally integrated channel. Radiowealth had also developed an exclusive network of its own with 27 branches, and Singer continued its long-established branch system. In 1962 each of these firms (and a few others) had a branch in Dagupan, and those few local merchants who had handled appliances on the side stopped doing so.

Ownership penetration flourished in appliances. Sales activities by Manila firms reached directly into barrios where commissioned or salaried salesmen from their branches showed catalogs to potential consumers with easy credit. The channel could hardly have become simpler and more direct. Relations between the levels were fixed through single ownership, and the internal organization of the retail outlets was specified by the mother company. Personnel attached to each branch showed an elaborate division of labor: receptionist, secretary-clerk, bookkeeper, technician, credit man, stock boy, salesman, sales manager, branch manager, and perhaps assistant manager. Branches were restricted in the products they could carry, they had an assigned territory (except in Manila) and a quota to meet, and each was bound by centralized pricing and credit policies. Modern business organization had entered the provinces and was there to stay.

In 1963 DRB performed what to observers of the day seemed to be a radical turnabout. It changed its branches into franchise dealerships and thereby moved from a tight form of coordinated penetration to one that is (at least on paper) looser. Several reasons for this change existed. The branch system of distribution proved to be costly for all. Even when sales were good and control effective, the expense of this marketing system became a serious limiting factor. "Distribution cost control was unheard of. A firm that starts to operate in Manila seemed compelled by the *gaya-gaya* [copy] mania to branch out to the key cities" (*MH* October 1968). For some distributors matters were made worse by the fact that, in their competitive zeal, they expanded their retail credit line too rapidly. Not infrequently the sales manager was made responsible for credit sales with predictable devastating results. Ownership penetration did not even guarantee that the head office effectively controlled the sales activities of its branches. It turned out that branch managers could easily pad the payroll with fictitious employees, or pad their business expenses with receipts collected from friends. To eliminate these and other abuses while retaining the same distributive mode would have required a substantial force of auditors, which would have greatly added to overhead expenses. DRB tried to tackle this problem by imposing a ₱20,000 bond requirement on each branch manager, demanding daily reports on collections and weekly reports on sales, and asking its branch and sales managers to report monthly in person to the Manila office. The effect was less than promising.

A final consideration that motivated the change, one that is more specific to DRB, was Ysmael Steel. For several years DRB watched Ysmael copy its system of distribution until it got to the point that communities boasting a DRB appliance branch almost invariably also had one representing Ysmael. In 1962–1963 Ysmael Steel was expanding its branch network, and DRB could not resist the temptation to throw Ysmael off balance by changing its own marketing strategy.

Franchising seemed to provide an admirable compromise between total control over provincial retail outlets by Manila suppliers and total independence of these outlets. This form of retail organization was experiencing extraordinary success in the United States during the fifties and sixties, so that it was only a matter of time before it became a fad in the Philippines. Moreover, for alien-controlled suppliers franchising sidestepped potential conflict with the government's rising demand for Filipinization.

So in a smooth and rapid move DRB changed its branches into franchise dealerships, keeping the same buildings and personnel it had used under ownership penetration. At the same time the firm increased the number of retail outlets to 75. The reaction of Ysmael Steel was immediate. It stopped expanding its branches, closed some, and converted virtually all of its provincial branches into franchises. Ysmael's commitment to the idea that the best way to overtake its chief rival was to copy its strategy was one reason the company reacted in this fashion. Another was that franchising became a method of drawing capable retail managers away from others. DRB and several newcomers in the appliance field were enticing branch managers away from Ysmael by showing them how they could become "independent."[3] Ysmael had to swim with the tide to survive, and so did most others. At the end of 1966 there were four franchise dealerships (Ysmael, DRB, Radiowealth, and Philacor for Westinghouse) and two branches (Singer and Madis for Philco) of Manila appliance companies in Dagupan.

The first 15 years of appliance distribution, therefore, saw the rapid creation of an exclusive channel where none existed before. Vertical integration became as tight as could be. At the end of the period the channel structure had become more loosely coordinated as ownership was replaced by contractual penetration. The degree of this transformation, however, should not be overestimated. Manila franchise companies (like those the world over) liked to boast that they encouraged independent retail merchants to take up the distribution of their products, thereby replacing mere branch employees of the company. The implication was that they allowed an autonomous retail level, required to handle the company products, to develop. Through this almost benevolent action they helped form a local entrepreneurial force. As I show later in this chapter and in Chapter 8, in the long run some of this was true, but when franchising first became a craze in the Philippine appliance trade, it was not.

Under the new contractual system Manila companies did not relinquish as much control over retailers as the move from branching to franchising implied. In contrast to former times, the dealer now received title to the goods he obtained from the supplier, but otherwise his upward dependence remained essentially the same. Several points of the dealership contract used by DRB make this clear:

a. The franchise is exclusive; no partner is permitted to enter in any capacity.
b. The dealer cannot sell any products other than those carried by the company.
c. Each dealer is assigned a territory, and sales made beyond it by the dealer are not credited to him.
d. The company fixes the terms and prices of goods sold to the dealer.
e. The dealer must sell the company products at the retail prices and discounts the company has set.
f. The store location and facilities must conform to company standards.
g. The dealer must provide office space free of charge to the company's finance company representative.
h. The dealer must provide a service shop according to company standards.
i. The dealer is not permitted to open another outlet in his territory without written consent of the company.

Add to this list monthly sales quotas and a bond upon which the size of the dealer's credit line depends, and the actual degree of freedom enjoyed by the fledging retailer for DRB becomes clear (cf. Magbag 1966; Nam 1971:152).

During these early days, therefore, the "independent" dealers were little more than commissioned sales agents. The products handled, the margin to be set, the financing offered, the charge for service, and the business organization of their retail outlet were determined by their principal. True, over time franchise agreements have become less restrictive for dealers, especially concerning the retail and service prices they can charge. In the words of one appliance merchant in Dagupan, very restrictive controls "may be attractive to new dealers with no capital; anyone with a large organization, capital, and a credit line would find them unsatisfactory," something suppliers have taken into account. But franchisees today are still far from being independent merchants, and certainly in the early sixties contractual penetration did not substantially decrease the degree to which Manila firms had control over the retail level. What it did do was lower the cost of marketing for the Manila supplier and increase the incentives for retailers to market aggressively.

The mid-sixties proved to be a watershed in the appliance trade. By now total sales reached ₱200 million a year. American concerns, such as Philco, Westinghouse, Admiral, and GE dominated the field through their local representatives. These, in turn, controlled in an orderly and replicative fashion—mainly by using contractual penetration—distribution to the retail level. Full control and stability seemed indestructible. But this was only the lull before the storm.

A stimulus for drastic change came when import controls on appliances (and other products) were relaxed during the early sixties. A wave of goods from Japan was the result, exacerbating an already existing situation of oversupply. These imports found their way through nonexclusive import and indent channels to general-line retail stores and to a growing number of independent retail centers in Manila. Firms like Ysmael Steel, which had built up their sales network according to their manufacturing capacity and the position of their major competitors, were particularly vulnerable, but even suppliers who had been more prudent in their expansion found it difficult to dispose of products through their exclusive retail outlets. For many it became a question of whether to increase sales or stick to their exclusive trade channels. Something had to give.

During the fifties Chinese activity in appliances, as I have pointed out, was subdued. Very few entered exclusive agency agreements, though they had the capital, because it would mean relinquishing other products and giving up discretion over decisions that are the hallmark of the independent trader.[4] A few did handle appliances, but refused to become allied to any single source. One of the more successful examples of this was Benito Lim of Automatic Electrical Appliances. His business was already flourishing in the fifties. A rather colorful, but basically accurate write-up has this to say about him: "Benito would smell a bargain in an appliance manufacturing firm that was strapped for cash. As inventories would pile up, Benito would time a visit to such firms, and he could literally wave a cashier's check under the very nose of the cash-starved executives of the firm. If you wanted to get hold of the cashier's check, all you had to do was agree to give sizeable inventories to Benito, by-passing your own distributors and dealers, at liberal discounts" (*MH* March 1972:28). At this time Lim did not pose a serious threat to the existing exclusive channel since demand still outpaced supply. He was one of the very few who was successful in this type of trade. But he helped pioneer a buy-and-sell strategy that soon revolutionized appliance distribution.

The situation changed in favor of operations like Automatic during the following decade. Access to capital and credit together with the flexible trade organization that typifies the textile trade also became advantageous in appliances. Established producers, facing the rising flood of goods and a market that refused to expand to a corresponding degree, found it increasingly difficult to sell only through their own channels. In an effort to overcome this constraint, some improved their credit terms, repair services, and pricing. Others juggled their system of distribution. GE, for example, started to produce different brands for different exclusive outlets. Norge was sold through Heritage Marketing, Universal brand was sold directly to dealers, and Hotpoint was handled by Homemakers Appliances. DRB continued to carry the GE brand itself.

Another adjustment was to restructure the relationship with the franchisees. In 1968 Ysmael, and two years later DRB, established "corporate dealerships" under which 51 percent of the retail business was owned by the head company (or its finance company) and the rest by the dealer. This led to more effective dealer financing by the company. The arrangement was also designed to allow dealers considerable leeway in determining their own terms. Corporate dealers under Ysmael Steel enjoyed good credit—for every peso of capital put up by the dealer, Ysmael gave ₱3 worth of inventory on credit. The dealer could set his own prices and had the right to finance consumers himself, instead of being bound to the company's finance company. And he could charge at will for repair services.

None of these adjustments, however, could dispel the increasing problem of product disposal. To deal with this effectively suppliers began, at first secretly, to restructure their mode of distribution more fundamentally. They began to bypass their own exclusive distribution channels, which they had built up with so much cost, and sold directly to independent wholesaler-retailers. What was only an occasional practice in the fifties began in the late sixties to be the norm. Appliance wholesaler-retailers similar to Benito Lim started to proliferate in Manila. Automatic was joined by Western Marketing, Cosmopolitan, Anson Emporium Corporation, Abenson, Inc., and several more. All of them handled allied lines, all of them pushed the concept of "appliance supermarketing," and all of them were in Chinese hands.

Sales to these outlets, of course, violated the producers' up-to-then sacrosanct integrated system of marketing. Particularly damaging to the established channel was (and is) the ability of the Chinese to obtain more favorable terms because they purchase larger quantities than the exclusive dealers. Abenson, for instance, a company established by the sons of Benito Lim, typically buys a quarter of the total stock of an assembler at a time, occasionally even the entire monthly output so that it forces dealers to buy from it. The company also underwrites manufacturers who lack capital, not unlike distributors who place orders with textile mills. Only the ethnic and kin link is missing. At times Abenson pays three months in advance under an agreement that it will receive a large portion of the output at a considerable discount. If the producer's price is 30 percent above costs, then it is only 10 to 15 percent above costs for Abenson. Even with bulk buying alone and without advance payments, Abenson can get from the assembler a price 4 to 6 percent lower than the "exclusive" dealers can. To return to the case of Benito Lim whose business started to take off in the sixties, "he was there through it all, disrupting the orderly distribution system that the marketing executives would have preferred, selling below official or suggested retail prices, even supplying dealers of other distributors at prices that the distributor himself could not extend to his own dealers!" (ibid.). The business strategy of the Chinese wholesaler-retailers was jobbing in the broad sense: tapping multiple sources and outlets, maximizing turnover speed, and as much as possible, using the capital of others without *ever* proving a credit risk. These were family concerns in which the owner-operators or active partners controlled the business throughout. Most of their sales were on cash, and by self-financing the credit they gave, instead of relying on finance companies, they maximized their receivables. To retain tight control over operations, most kept their branches and otherwise affiliated businesses under the management of family members and confined them to metropolitan Manila. Until recently they made no serious attempt to establish an exclusive retail network in the provinces. There has been little pressure for them to do so. As independent appliance traders began to multiply in the provinces, many of them were forced to buy from Chinese wholesaler-retailers in Manila for want of alternative sources.

During 1968 the inevitable happened in Dagupan. First one and then a second local Chinese decided to enter the trade after suppliers who did not insist on channel integration became available in Manila. Neither of them was an established merchant. The family of one operates a first-order grocery store in Dagupan; that of the other had been in the soap-manufacturing business. The sons were breaking away from these traditions, and they received capital from their families to do so. They differed in this from the Filipino franchise dealers who had typically risen to their present position while working for one or several of the major distributors.

The two newcomers also varied from the other retailers by handling a wide range of appliance brands, by retaining their autonomy from Manila sources, and by organizing their firms in a manner that minimized formal internal division of labor and stressed, instead, the authority of the owner-operator in virtually all matters. They took advantage of close personal ties to Chinese appliance dealers in Manila, and the ample resources of their families made it possible for them to self-finance their installment sales. Now it became only a matter of time before a Filipino opened an independent and full-line appliance business in Dagupan. This happened in 1969 with the establishment of Ricafort Trading.

The time had come for trade terms offered by Manila sources to be renegotiated from transaction to transaction. Prices, products, credit, and discounts received by provincial appliance retailers began to depend on the retailers' skill in selecting suppliers and their bargaining power, not on a contract they had signed some time before. Also the number of retail outlets increased phenomenally in the Philippines from 183 in 1961 to 1,800 in 1972 (Republic of the Philippines 1964–1965; 1975). As the opportunity to obtain goods from different sources expanded, independent appliance establishments proliferated. Filipinos, many of them former branch managers and franchise holders, run most of them. However, Chinese are responsible for much of the turnover. An estimated 25 to 50 percent of the appliance wholesale trade is handled by them, a percentage that may be higher on the retail level in Manila.

Given these changes, only a few of the producers (Singer, Radiowealth) decided to retain their exclusive channel system after 1970. The more typical accommodation was for franchise contracts to be maintained with retailers without including the stipulation that franchisees be brand exclusive. Now dealers could also buy products from sources other than their franchisors. This course was followed mainly by those distributors who had lost exclusive access to their former overseas principal. In compensation for this loss some of them started to market their own brand (for example, after losing the GE account, DRB began to market its own SEARS brand).[5] Several producers and distributors, finally, discarded coordinated penetration altogether and began to sell to anyone who could buy in sufficient amounts.

In Dagupan these national developments took the following form. In 1969–1970 the fear grew among exclusive dealers in the city that they were not only effectively competed against by well-financed local independents (that is, by Ricafort and the two Chinese), but that their own mother companies were undermining their position by selling covertly to independent merchants in Manila and elsewhere. The demand grew that these sales either cease or that dealers be allowed to broaden their inventories. To oppose the local independents, some attempts were made to form a pressure group through a local appliance dealers association, but these proved ineffective.

Changes in the integrated channel between Manila and Dagupan had to await policy changes by Manila enterprises. In 1970 GE dropped DRB as its exclusive distributor. The local DRB franchise remained in operation, but the change enabled it to carry items other than GE products. Ysmael Steel, the assembler and distributor of Admiral, encountered fatal financial difficulties and was bought by another company (DMG, Inc.) in 1973. Because the new owners tightened the agreement and held on to brand exclusivity, the original franchise holder in Dagupan went independent and multiline. About the same time Philacor (distributor of Westinghouse) decided to sell not only to its franchise, but also to several independent appliance merchants in Dagupan. The Dagupeño dealer kept the contract, which now allowed him to handle different brands. Madis, finally, was bought by its principal (Liberty Commodities Corporation), and the former franchisee in Dagupan has gone independent. The relation to Manila of Dagupeño appliance traders began to lose much of its former rigidity.

The growing complexity of the Dagupan market increased in 1971 when two wholesale branches of Japanese-controlled distributors, Precision Electronics Corporation and Radiola-Toshiba Philippines, Inc., opened their doors. They began to serve much of northern Luzon through their warehousing facilities, finance services, and perambulating dealer coordinators. Their presence contributed heavily to the total appliance sales volume in Dagupan, which started to go beyond ₱10 million in 1972—within a setting in which 8 percent of all Dagupeño households in 1970 had a TV and 13 percent a refrigerator. In Pangasinan the respective percentages were only 2 percent and 3 percent (Republic of the Philippines 1974).

The success of some retailers stimulated others to emulate them, and the number of autonomous retailers in the city grew. Three more independent Filipino appliance centers opened, and the two Chinese enterprises were joined by a third one in 1973. Some new businesses continued to be integrated with their suppliers. Two are branches that carry allied lines. They belong to small chains headquartered in San Fernando (La Union) and Angeles (Pampanga). The third entrant is a franchise representing Yamaha pianos and refrigerators. Up to 1977 it was the only brand-exclusive franchised retailer of a Japanese concern in Dagupan. Finally, the long-standing Singer branch was changed into a franchise to comply with the new restrictions on alien activities in retail trade. Appliance sales passing through Dagupan reached nearly ₱16 million in 1974. Five million of this was handled by Japanese-controlled wholesalers, ₱3.5 million by independent Chinese, and the rest (₱7.5 million) by Filipino franchise dealerships, branches, and independent merchants.

The appliance trade in Dagupan, like that on the national level but with a time lag, has experienced two phases and is now well within a third phase. It existed in a rudimentary form in the first phase. The second phase lasted nearly a decade and was marked first by ownership and then by contractual penetration of the Manila supplier into the retail market of Dagupan. The second half of the sixties ushered in the third phase. First Chinese, then others entered the trade as merchants without long-term commitments to a single product brand or supplier. In 1976, 19 appliance outlets were operating in Dagupan. Of these, nine were independent (three of them Chinese), six were franchise dealers (four of them brand exclusive), and four were branches (two of them brand exclusive and wholesale only).

The Model and Reality of Channel Evolution

How does the last 40 years' experience of the appliance market in the Philippines compare with the model of channel modernization that predicts channels will evolve toward tight and formal integration? Briefly, what had developed into a streamlined and fully coordinated distribution system has since been transformed into one that is complex, heterogeneous, and often nonexclusive, one in which many channel members relate to one another through pricing rather than contractual or ownership control. Trade relations and terms are subject to redefinition with each transaction. The independent family-based business has gained a prominent position, and the number of wholesale sources has multiplied.

As channel power shifted from the importer-manufacturer to the wholesaler-retailer, a fragmentation of the channel took place not only vertically, but also, with the free entry of numerous autonomous merchants, horizontally. Competition has increased, and retail margins have gone down. In many ways the opposite of what the model predicts has happened. After moving in the expected direction for 15 years, the channel "swung back" to a more traditional form. The model of market-channel development has provided a good indication of what trade leaders tried to institute, not what eventually succeeded.

Distribution via coordinated penetration has received considerable attention in the literature lately. Its spread in industrial societies is attributed to the fact that vertically integrated channels are more efficient than fragmented ones: (a) communication and material flow within the channel are encouraged; (b) redundancy of units is low; (c) scalar economies are attained; (d) innovations, once accepted, spread readily throughout the entire channel; (e) contact points are routinized and negotiation time lowered between trade levels; (f) the goal of each trade unit is set to maximize the operation of the entire system; (g) centralized and total planning is made possible (Etgar 1976; Mattson 1969).

But the picture is not entirely rosy. To repeat a point I made before, any strategy involves a trade-off between advantages and disadvantages. The negative side of coordinated penetration and channel integration includes the following characteristics: (a) the dominant member of the channel receives not only the profit but bears also the cost of distribution (this in ownership penetration); (b) consumer choice of outlets is limited, and pricing and product policy tends to be uniform; (c) failure in one part of the system will have immediate repercussions upon the other parts which lowers overall resilience; (d) basic innovations in distribution are not likely to be experimented with; (e) trade autonomy is valued by some merchants (for example, Chinese), so that controlling their decisions may lower their incentives to perform (Robicheaux and El-Ansary 1976; Stern and Reve 1980:56). Pushing the case for fragmented channels, Bucklin states that "flexibility in the distributive system . . . arises from the availability of uncommitted agencies on all stages of the distributive system. Despite all the arguments about the improved efficiency that closely coordinated channels provide, the notion that all competition should take place on this basis seems fundamentally wrong" (Bucklin 1972b:37). Why did the appliance channel in the Philippines become more fragmented after it reached the pinnacle of channel integration? It is not enough to point out which distributive system is more efficient in itself. Every channel organization has both positive and negative features and which count more depends on the social and historical context. What should be pointed out, instead, is the conditions under which particular marketing systems prove to be more competitive than others.

In the present case, as long as demand outpaced production and dominant channel members shared the goal of attaining maximum control over distribution, the integrated system worked well. Even those who did not believe in this strategy were forced to act as if they did as long as others adhered to brand exclusivity for their own channels. But when production rose above demand and when Japanese products and Chinese entrepreneurial skill entered in force, a different strategy was needed. Trade autonomy and multibrand inventories were more effective in the new situation, and the existing channel lacked the capacity to withstand their challenge. When brand exclusivity was discarded, furthermore, one of the reasons for full vertical integration was removed. The "wheel of retailing" (Hollander 1960) had moved another notch after the more fragmented and localized mode of distribution outcompeted the existing integrated one.

The explanation of this transformation into the third phase lies partly in the rigidity of the existing channel and the capital scarcity of many of its members in the face of only slowly expanding demand and temporarily relaxed import controls. For many, moreover, overcoming the commitment to a prestigious imported marketing ideology was a painful process. The explanation is also to be found in the strength of the most important newcomers, the Chinese. I have documented in the case of textiles that this strength lay both in their business acumen and in their organization.

The appliance field today, even on the wholesale level, is far less closed and homogeneous along ethnic lines than textiles, nor do the Manila sources give provincial Chinese dealers quite as liberal terms. Price lists and other forms of documentation are far more common in appliances than in textiles. Also, to receive more than 90 days' product credit from Chinese suppliers is unusual even for Chinese merchants in the provinces. One of the major favors, instead, is to be the first to be informed that new shipments are available. But the ingredients of the Chinese way are there: a preference for independent, personalized owner-operated businesses that set their own terms, and a preference, other factors being equal, for giving fellow Chinese a slight personal edge over others.

The integrated appliance channel of the early sixties could be challenged most effectively by the Chinese because they maintained a quasi-integrated form of distribution of their own together with considerable flexibility in buying and selling and ample capital. Over time they have combined two procedures in the appliance trade: first, they maintain business autonomy on each market level while giving vertical trade preferences to one another. The result is a system of trade coordination without its contractual rigidity. Features of the semipassive marketing strategy reappear here. Second, they combine this traditional channel organization with an innovative attempt to redefine appliances as mass or shopping articles rather than high-cost specialty goods.

In all of this, however, the importance of the ethnic variable should not be overrated. Without extraneous factors (such as overcapacity on the supply side) their entrance would have been less rapid and it would have had less of an impact on the channel structure. Chinese participation has not transformed integrated channels into fragmented ones in other product lines, such as cars and gasoline. Chinese are far from monopolizing the appliance trade today, nor do they form a corporate interest group. Finally, a point I elaborate when turning to the consequences of active marketing in Chapter 8, their entrance has opened the field for independent Filipino traders. Many of the Filipinos are successful because of capable management and their ability to personalize trade relations where necessary without relying on ethnic identity with their suppliers. In fact, a case could be made for the assumption that even without Chinese involvement, the appliance channel would have changed in the direction it did, although at a slower pace.

Retailing Strategy and Personal Selling

Appliance selling continues to be a decidedly ostentatious affair. It presents a modern front, symbolized by air-conditioned offices and generous display areas behind glass windows, even in provincial stores. The image of prosperity and efficiency is pushed by all, whether independent or not. The stimulus for this was provided when the channel was fully integrated and Manila suppliers could readily impose their wishes. Coordinated penetration has resulted in a construction boom, and together with banks, service stations, and car dealerships, appliance stores are responsible for much of the new urban look of many provincial communities.

Also the internal organization of appliance businesses takes on a modern image. The initial period of full integration stamped a uniform pattern on provincial outlets which most of them have adhered to even after turning independent. The basic division between manager, sales manager, store sales personnel, itinerant salesman, collector, technician, and so on is retained. These positions may or may not be filled by family members; the important point is that the division of labor is more complex than in businesses handling less capital-intensive goods and in which penetration from Manila has been less aggressive. It is as if the sophisticated physical front of appliance retailers requires commensurate personnel to impress the public and Manila suppliers.

The appliance channel has become more resilient after a wide range of channel organizations appeared alongside the integrated type of a decade ago. Coordinated penetration is now joined by various forms of sales penetration from Manila, and even the semipassive mode has grown in importance. Should one type prove inefficient or ill adapted to new circumstances, others are now available to take up the slack. Despite losing channel uniformity, however, the appliance trade continues to share certain characteristics beyond the product itself. One of them—its modern look—I have already mentioned. Two others are the ready use of finance companies and the tendency among appliance retailers to have recourse to itinerant salesmen for house-to-house sales. Both characteristics derive from the fact that in this trade merchants must finance a costly product and sell it to often reluctant customers, something encountered also in the distribution of motor vehicles, agricultural machinery, and other capital-intensive consumer goods.

Singer Sewing Machines learned a long time ago that the ability to offer installment financing is a prerequisite for successful distribution. The cost of the product handled by appliance distributors has meant that consumers need considerable backing to afford them, and the same turned out to be true for retail outlets once they became franchisees or independent. DRB and Ysmael Steel learned this in the fifties, and to support their consumer customers and (eventually) dealers, both established subsidiary finance companies. At the same time independent finance companies appeared on the scene, some of them with branches in the provinces.

Initially these institutions gave loans directly to customers wanting to buy appliances. Soon this proved too risky, and today finance companies discount sales papers to give themselves asset security; in other words, they buy at a discount the sales notes of retailers who have made an installment sale. Either alone or together with the retailer, they then take over financing and shoulder the risk of the installment sales. In practice this means that sales become subject to the finance company's approval—another way in which the autonomy of the retailer is undercut.

One of the more successful subsidiary finance companies is Radiowealth Finance Company (RFC), established in 1964 to support the installment sales of Radiowealth, Inc. (appliances) and DMG, Inc. (VW cars). Since then it has expanded its activities. It began with credit and collection for the affiliated firms, a year later it financed dealers, and in 1969 it entered into repair service of appliances in the provinces. In 1976 the company had 68 finance branches and 62 service centers in strategic places around the country. Wherever a DMG or Radiowealth dealer is, RFC can be found, and because most of these are in the provinces the company prides itself that its main "thrust . . . is . . . in areas where there are limited or practically no financing institutions in operation" (*PDE* March 1, 1976). This is stretching the point in communities like Baguio, Dagupan, and Cabanatuan; but in Alaminos, Urdaneta, and similar small centers in Pangasinan where RFC also has branches, the company propaganda is not far off the mark.

Radiowealth requires all its franchised dealers to send their notes through the company's financial arm. RFC extends installment sales financing only after it has investigated and approved the credit of the buyer, in effect taking the decision out of the dealer's hands. It also finances the dealer's purchases and thus sets the terms he receives. In 1976 this meant 60 days' consignment, after which interest is charged on the dealer price. Similar to DRB dealers some time ago, dealers of Radiowealth are little more than commissioned salesmen. The skillful use of its own finance company has allowed Radiowealth to hold on to an exclusive and tightly controlled franchise system.

Only large Manila enterprises with a network of dependent provincial outlets have the wherewithal to establish a finance company chain. Independent merchants in the provinces are at a disadvantage. Unless they can finance their own sales—as many of the Chinese do—they have to bear higher interest charges and stricter customer-selection procedures than others when they discount notes. It is extraordinarily difficult for appliance retailers to become independent in their financial operations. Hardware or grocery merchants may have problems in offering adequate credit to small retailers and consumers, but most manage to do so by relying on their own resources and on product credit their suppliers give. In appliances and similar capital-intensive lines, even if retailers receive generous advances from their suppliers, most cannot forgo having others finance their installment sales to consumers. Perhaps those who can will eventually replace those who cannot.

Related to the fancy physical front and elaborate business organization is the conviction shared by most appliance merchants that personal house-to-house retailing is the backbone of the trade. Mass advertising and fancy store display may be necessary to create demand, elaborate office help and a good installment plan may be a sine qua non if the consumer is to commit himself to a transaction, but failing to send out salesmen to beat the bushes for customers, many believe, will surely condemn a business to death. Historically, retail sales penetration directed from branches and dealers was most important when the specialized appliance channel first appeared. Demand had to be created, and the effort by salesmen, in a setting in which personalism is paramount, was greatly appreciated. Manila firms saw in the itinerant salesman a way to extend the reach of their coordinated penetration. Some also sought to introduce flexible retail pricing by telling their branches and dealers to encourage salesmen to cut into their own commission when searching for orders.

Nearly all independent appliance traders today continue to rely on itinerant salesmen. The walk-in customer is simply too rare, and potential credit sources in Manila like to see what seems to them a capable sales organization among retailers they serve. This system differs from the sales penetration described in the previous chapter. First, these salesmen engage in retailing; in groceries and similar products they wholesale. Moreover, under normal sales penetration the salesmen are salaried and commissioned by the Manila supplier; in appliances salesmen are attached to and remunerated by the local retail dealer, branch manager, or independent merchant. Finally, appliance salesmen constantly look for new customers or prospects, and rarely do they serve the same ones over and over again. The transaction speed is too slow. Through installment sales steady customers are gained, but these are more likely to recommend new customers than to repeat purchases themsleves. This is not to say that genuine sales penetration is absent in the appliance trade, as will be seen below.

Some Manila companies find that 70 to 80 percent of the sales made by their dealers are placed by itinerant fieldmen. To DRB, salesmen who are well versed in the art of mobilizing consumers are at least as important as capable and trustworthy dealers. "Salesmen establish a definite number of prospects to maintain a certain sales volume and a list of 30–50 prospects is kept in reserve. If this list falls below the magic number, the salesman drops everything else until he has rebuilt his prospect list. A good prospective list enables the salesman to pick up new customers as fast as he loses old ones. If production lags, he must step up his number of calls, interviews and follow-ups" (Magbag 1966:135–136). What are the methods used to search out the customers? They include house-to-house canvassing, asking old customers for new prospects (the chain method), contacting newlyweds and new residents, and visiting those responsible for building construction. Salesmen are expected to activate their own family and acquaintances to fill the prospect list. In short "to a salesman, a tip concerning a hot prospect is [a] new life of the best kind . . . prospects are everywhere and the salesman who is 'prospect minded' will find the potential customers" (ibid., p. 136). I need only add that the statement "prospects are everywhere" refers to households with an annual income of ₱10,000 or more.

These remarks refer to salaried salesmen, those over whom the local dealer or branch manager has some sway. The salaried salesmen are usually the most important source of orders, but they form only a minority of the fieldmen most appliance retailers depend on. When dealers boast that they have 10 or 30 salesmen, and many of them do, it means that most of these salesmen are not salaried. The only pay they receive is a commission (5–10 percent) for orders they place, with the result that control over them is minimal. They serve different suppliers and dabble in different products according to their own wishes. These are the "independent" or "international" salesmen mentioned in Chapter 5, note 2. Juan Camejon of Dagupan City (he calls himself an "unlicensed general contractor") is a good example of this breed.

Camejon worked formerly as an employed salesman for Consolidated Foods and other grocery goods companies. In the late sixties he decided to become independent and started to organize private deals. He collects orders from individuals and institutions, he contacts suppliers who are willing to consign or sell to him at a wholesale price, and he makes a profit between this price and his selling price. At times he also represents individuals who want to sell. For instance, he tells prospective customers that the party he represents asks ₱2,000 for a Singer sewing machine and, to emphasize its quality, that it is worth $400 in the States. The seller actually expects ₱1,200, and Camejon pockets the difference. In all of this haggling takes place, and he gambles upon the limited knowledge customers have of one another and the product. Even suppliers in Manila are his contacts as long as they offer dealer prices. He works with minimal capital because in most of his deals he acts merely as go-between without obtaining title to the goods. Camejon is a typical example of the "where there is a peso there is a trader" syndrome so common in the Philippines (and certainly not only there). For a period he supplied movie theaters in Dagupan with cleaning material, he has been in auto sales and insurance, and he plans to stay in appliances as long as sales are good. The role he occupies makes him a flexible catalyst of distribution. According to him, his strategy is based on developing appropriate contacts, building temporary trust, and giving and receiving favors.

There are many like Camejon, not only in appliances, but also in cars, agricultural equipment, and even groceries (especially PX goods) and other mass consumer items, though they are most prevalent in products that command a high markup. International salesmen are notorious for switching from one line to another, for playing customers off against each other, for their speculative orientation. They hang around stores with their ears open and travel from *población* to *población* in search of opportunities. Few ever reach what they dream of, namely to settle in their own office with a phone and a secretary and run a wholesale business in one particular line. More often they drift back into employment. A few months after my first meeting with Camejon, he was a salaried salesman for one of the Chinese appliance stores in Dagupan although he had previously insisted that the independent life was for him.

And finally, on the bottom of the appliance channel, there is the tipster. His relation to the provincial retailer is as informal and transient as can be. The independent salesman is at least ostensibly associated with particular retailers for a period, and he perceives himself as a full-time businessman. The tipster, in contrast, is anyone who introduces a customer to a dealer or one of his salesmen. Often they are former customers who know that a friend, or have heard that a friend's friend, is planning to buy a refrigerator or any other expensive item. If the sale is consummated, the expectation is that he (or she) receives a 2 to 5 percent commission. No formal agreement is drawn up between tipsters and the supplier, nor do tipsters make a living from this alone.

Tipsters flourish in certain lines more than in others. The costlier consumer articles are, the more likely it is that tipsters will be present, for three reasons: the time elapsing between the formation of an intention to buy and the actual purchase is likely to be enough for knowledge about the intention to become widespread; the value of each transaction is sufficiently large that any attempt to cut in seems worth the effort; and finally, retailers find themselves in stiff competition so that most of them accept the services of tipsters—it is better to lose 2 to 5 percent of the sales price than the sale itself.

Marketing through retail sales penetration is aggressive and primitive at the same time. It reminds one of the vacuum cleaner salesmen of bygone days in the United States. Some Manila and provincial dealers are doing away with itinerant retail salesmen in favor of luring customers into their stores through low prices, wide product selection, service, and credit. So far, however, the base of the appliance channel remains broad and filled with fieldmen. Much of this base is not organized directly by retail merchants, but has emerged as a result of individuals perceiving opportunities in collecting orders from consumers on behalf of retailers who have no direct access to them. Viewed differently, the appliance trade provides local entrepreneurial talent an entrance point into commerce on a scale and with a degree of sophistication only a few other products make available. In this way coordinated penetration and subsequent developments in appliance distribution have encouraged, not stifled, local commercial initiatives, a matter I return to in Chapter 8.

The Role of Sales Penetration

I have shown how the appliance channel has changed over the past 15 years from coordinated penetration to one in which vertical fragmentation is common. The reader may therefore wonder how Manila suppliers today contact independent retailers in the provinces. In some cases the semipassive strategy has replaced the integrated channel. Between wholesaler-retailers in Manila and large Chinese merchants in the provinces considerable (confidential) trust exists, and these merchants visit Manila to negotiate orders personally. Here the channel structure and trade activity resemble those of textile distribution. By far the more common substitute for formal channel integration, however, has been sales penetration. In many cases the transition from vertical integration was simple enough. Most franchise systems already included itinerant "dealer coordinators" who collected orders and served as a means to maintain personal communication between parent company and franchise retailers. If franchise dealers are changed into independent merchants, sales penetration automatically comes into being as long as the former dealer coordinators are used to collect orders from the now independent retail customers.

Sales penetration in appliances is organized in two ways, as a loose dealership system or warehouse branching. Rolling stores and jobbing for obvious reasons are not practical. Of the two, the loose dealership system is the more popular. Most Chinese wholesaler-retailers use this marketing strategy. One of these is

Abenson, Inc., which we encountered before. During the seventies it was one of the fastest growing appliance wholesale-retail businesses in Manila with a network of nearly 50 dealers in the provinces. Like Abenson itself, these dealers are nonexclusive in the brands they handle and suppliers they tap. Some of them are substantial businesses. Anybody with sufficient purchasing power and a satisfactory credit record can become a dealer, irrespective of how his business is organized, whether he has fieldmen for retail sales or not, and the like. This system differs little from what is found in groceries. No contract is involved—bulk purchases and a good reputation automatically lift provincial merchants into dealership status, after which they receive special discounts and credit from the supplier. Abenson classifies its dealers into "active" (make monthly purchases), "casual" (order every two months), and "inactive" (no purchases for a quarter of a year), and it has 18 fieldmen (for the sake of prestige it calls them "dealer coordinators") to serve them. These are grouped by territory, not function.

Positioned between this loose dealership system and coordinated penetration is warehouse branching. In this arrangement independent dealers are retained, but they are now served from provincial branches. We encountered this type in soft drinks and soaps, and more sophisticated versions of it in drugs. In appliances, Japanese-led companies have pursued wholesale branching, together with repair service, most diligently.

When penetrating a new market, Japanese companies, whether they handle appliances or other products, typically procede in two stages. First they swamp the area with low-priced products. This is followed by branch warehouses and a dense service network. Radiola-Toshiba Philippines, Inc. (RT) and Precision Electronics Corporation (PE; National brand) are well into this second stage. Both are joint Japanese-Filipino ventures and therefore are kept legally from retailing, and both concentrate on brown lines (tape recorders, stereo sets, and the like). Because of their similar background and because they are each other's immediate competitors, their distributive strategies show many parallels.

RT is the younger of the two and was formed when Radiola of the Philippines was partially sold to Toshiba in 1971 to receive technical input and cheap components from Japan. The company has repair outlets and warehouse branches for independent dealers in Davao, Cagayan de Oro, Cebu, Bacolod, Iloilo, San Pablo (southern Luzon), San Fernando (Pampanga), Baguio, and Dagupan. Each branch has two dealer coordinators, and the Dagupan branch, which takes care of all western Luzon north of Pangasinan, has five other employees. The whole network on Luzon is headed by an area manager and two supervisors, one responsible for north-central Luzon, the other for Manila and southern Luzon.

Precision Electronics is headed by a former president of DRB and is a joint venture with Matsushita Electric Industrial Company, Ltd. When the company started in 1967 it had a sales force of five which was confined to Manila. Since then it has been the most aggressive company selling brown-line appliances in the Philippines so that by the mid-seventies its National brand accounted for over half of the TV market. Almost from its inception, it established wholesale branches in order to avoid shortages in stocks as demand outpaced supply, and soon it also offered repair service—dealers were expected to provide it, but many did not. It has branches in Davao, San Fernando (Pampanga), Dagupan, San Pablo, Cebu, and Cabanatuan. These are clustered under area offices which are located in Dagupan for central and northern Luzon, in Manila, and in Cebu for the Visayas and Mindanao.

The wholesale outlets of these two companies are kept under remarkably tight rein from the center, and the Japanese touch is felt down to the provincial branches. The influence goes beyond quotas, hiring, internal organization, and pricing and includes the general atmosphere of the organization. "Each branch is like a family," in the words of one who belongs, " and all members call each other by their first name." In both Manila and Dagupan the employees practice the company code, which all have to memorize and recite in unison daily, and on all levels of the business the avowed philosophy is that each employee is equally important to the proper operation of the company.[6]

Despite its recent growth in popularity among some Manila suppliers, it is an open question whether warehouse branching will last. Large wholesaler-retailers in Manila and the provinces are once again the key. RT, PE, and other assemblers and distributors using warehouse branching allow large provincial dealers—one appliance merchant in Dagupan has this privilege—to buy directly from the Manila factory at a low price, bypassing thereby their own branch network. In a similar fashion Abenson and other large dealers in Manila receiving special discounts from producers can offer the appliance brands at the same price and better credit terms than the producers through their warehouse branches. Therefore, the avowed policy of these producers to keep direct contact with as wide a dealership pool as possible clashes with their policy of giving special privileges to large dealers. Wholesale branching may turn out to be as ephemeral as most of the retail branches and franchises turned out to be, unless the repair shops attached to an increasing portion of them can save the system.[7]

Another even more serious threat to warehouse branching seems to be developing. Earlier I made the point that Chinese wholesaler-retailers who helped fragment the appliance channel in the sixties saw no need to move into contractual or ownership penetration beyond Manila. For most that remains true, yet the temptation is always there. After all, these businesses have always been characterized by aggressive retailing (jobbing, supermarketing) and their ability to use family and ethnic connections to construct retail chains. Now that they dominate Manila, why not expand? Abenson, until recently confining itself to the loose dealership system of distribution, is one of the few that has begun to do so. It has branch retail stores in Unimart, Cubao, Makati, and Harrison Plaza in Manila, and it has an experimental outlet in San Fernando (Pampanga). The latest rumor has it that the firm plans to buy the oldest independent Filipino appliance outlet in Dagupan, Ricafort Trading. Nothing is immutable in the trade. Abenson's branches are multibrand retail stores which stand in direct competition with the dealers of Abenson and the warehouse branches of Manila producers. A new irony is appearing on the horizon. A firm that helped break the existing integrated channel created under American tutelage now seems to be on the verge of creating its own integrated marketing system.

Cases

The appliance channel between Manila and the provinces today exhibits considerable variety. There is the occasional case of the semipassive strategy in which integration is achieved through informal means; more common is sales penetration which uses wholesale branching and the loose dealership system for its ends; finally, there are the remaining franchise systems and retail branch networks. No longer is it true to say that provincial appliance stores are Filipino-operated, brand-exclusive retail branches or franchises. Today outlets differ according to ethnicity (Filipino or Chinese), sales organization (simple or complex), link to the supplier(s) (independent or dependent), brand identity (multiple or single), level of trade (wholesale or retail), and several other diacritical features. As I have stressed, the most significant of these variables typologically is the connection with the supplier. On the basis of it the appliance stores in Dagupan can be grouped in the following way:

a. Independent business
   1. Chinese
   2. Filipino
b. Full franchise with access to suppliers other than the franchisor
c. Full franchise or branch that is product but not brand exclusive (it can only handle goods obtained from the principal, but the brand selected is not specified)
d. Full franchise or branch that is brand exclusive.

The sequence of this typology describes increasing dependence of retailers on their suppliers. What set of characteristics do traders of each group have, and how do they fare as a result of these characteristics? To help answer these questions I give one illustration of each group selected from Dagupan.

A-1. Only three cases of this type are found in Dagupan. Central Luzon Furniture and General Merchandise operated by Mr. Co is the largest of them, with a turnover in 1974 of ₱2 million. In addition to the proprietor and his wife, who act as manager and bookkeeper respectively, the business has two delivery drivers, two technicians, two helpers for installations, and five persons for sales within the store. Some goods are obtained from the producers in Manila (PE, RT, Hitachi, Philacor, and the like) and most from Manila wholesaler-retailers (Action, Abenson, Automatic, and others). Co is the best friend of the proprietor of Action. He can get up to 40 percent discount and 90 days' credit on large orders, which has enabled him to subwholesale in Dagupan and Pangasinan.

In conformity with general practice, Co used to have salaried retail fieldmen. These were placed in four territories, three to four salesmen per territory headed by a supervisor. Then in a surprise move Co in 1971 scuttled the entire setup and stopped employing or otherwise using itinerant salesmen, whether salaried or commissioned. So far no other appliance merchant in Dagupan has dared go so far; at the most some have dropped salaried salesmen. In 1971 Central Luzon was already large and independent enough to challenge the expectation held by Manila suppliers that their dealers should retain a formal field force. Moreover, a force like that is of little value to Co's business because much of it is wholesale, and Co enjoys ample personal connections in the local commercial community. As a result he can save the commission and salary. It also means that Co need not worry about whether his salesmen work for someone else on the side, or whether they quote incorrect prices to pad their commission. He now sees to sales himself, only occasionally relying on tipsters for retail customers.

Co has kept prices low by another innovation. Up to the seventies he used the FNCB Finance Company for financing and sold his receivables to them at 10 percent. Now he does his own financing: 6–12-month installment plans for consumers and 30–60-day credit sales for dealers and institutional buyers. Central Luzon is well on its way to becoming the major appliance subwholesaler in the region.

A-2. When Francisco Ricafort opened his Ricafort Trading in 1969 he was the first Filipino in Dagupan to successfully enter the appliance trade as an independent store merchant. He began with car radios and expanded into TV, and now he manages one of the more prosperous general appliance stores in the city. For a period he shared with DRB-Dagupan the local distribution of GE products—he had the right to buy directly from the factory. Since 1974, however, he has had no exclusive agreement with any source. He buys from local wholesale branches and from Manila producers and wholesaler-retailers, and is a dealer of virtually all of them.

Ricafort's turnover is smaller than that of Central Luzon, but he pursues a similar sales strategy by capturing the patronage of institutions and small local traders for whom it is not worth their while to buy in Manila. Fifty percent of his turnover is now wholesale, and he keeps his net margin at a bare 4 to 5 percent. He uses a finance company (FNCB) only if he does not know the customers or otherwise doubts their reliability. The business has a payroll of 12, including himself as manager, his son as assistant manager, and four technicians who provide 24-hour repair service. This service has made Ricafort famous in Dagupan, and the new repair centers that Manila suppliers are introducing into Dagupan make him uneasy. In the early seventies Ricafort opened a display office in Villasis to capture some of the market in southern Pangasinan. Except for personnel attached to this office, he has no hired field force; instead, he uses tipsters and international sales agents.

B. In this case traders continue to depend contractually on one supplier, but are allowed to buy some of their inventory from other sources. DRB-Dagupan has a long and honorable history in the city even though its relation to Manila has changed rapidly over the years. It started as a branch in the late fifties, was turned into a franchise in 1963, then was changed into a corporate dealership five years later, and in 1975 was made a full franchise once again. Through much of this the store has been under the management of the attorney Coquia.

After the DRB Corporation in Manila lost its license agreement with GE, it began to distribute its own appliance brand, SEARS, and DRB-Dagupan is now the exclusive dealer of the new brand in Pangasinan. When he was a corporate dealer, Coquia could obtain merchandise from DRB-Manila under 60 days' consignment after which, if an item was not sold, 1 percent interest was charged per month. Now he has to *buy* the appliances from DRB which gives only 15 to 30 days' credit. He buys other products from PE in Dagupan (15 days' credit), and on his weekly visits to Manila he orders some items from Anson Emporium Corporation on 30 to 60 days' credit. Compared to Ricafort and Central Luzon, he carries a meager range of products, and he gets less advantageous terms.

The peak of Coquia's business fortunes occurred when channel integration was still intact in the appliance trade and he was the only one selling GE goods in the province. Now he lives on the distribution of the SEARS brand to consumers and small traders in

Pangasinan. Unfortunately for him, large merchants in Dagupan can obtain the same brand from wholesaler-retailers in Manila. Because Coquia needs financing from DRB-Manila, he cannot receive the lowest possible price even from this source.

Despite his exposed position, Coquia has 13 employees in his Dagupan office. In addition, he maintains an elaborate field organization which clusters into six territorial groups, with two supervisors and about three commissioned salesmen in each group. Four of these groups are assigned to Dagupan, one to Alaminos, and one to Urdaneta. In 1975 he opened a display office in these two centers, each staffed with a sales manager and a secretary-receptionist. These branches, Coquia hopes, will help him reestablish his former position in the trade.

C. Since the breakup of the integrated appliance channel between Manila and the provinces, several attempts at coordinated penetration on a more limited regional basis have been made. Manila-based national companies have not been the only ones at the game of outsmarting others by constructing branches or assigning franchises. I have noted that some Dagupan appliance merchants have lately entered into retail branching to improve their coverage of Pangasinan. Some have gone a step further and operate branches in major centers beyond the province (such as Baguio and San Fernando [La Union]). The reverse has also taken place; medium-scale enterprises headquartered in the provinces (other than Pangasinan) have opened branches in Dagupan. So far Central Plains Marketing is the most notable case of this.

The Dagupan branch of Central Plains Marketing opened its doors with much fanfare in 1975, an event lauded by speakers from Westinghouse, Sharp, and Radiola-Toshiba. It is an impressive store, brand-new with one of the largest display areas for appliances in Dagupan. But after the first few months of buoyant sales, turnover dropped below the break-even point of ₱50,000 a month. The business is headquartered in Angeles City, and all orders have to pass through it. The head office, in turn, buys from manufacturers and Chinese wholesaler-retailers. It does not have a brand of its own. It sets the prices the Dagupan branch can offer and determines the range of brands available to it. All too often the branch finds that items it handles are offered at better terms by local rivals.

The branch manager is only free to act on his own when customers place orders for out-of-stock items—then he can buy from Radiola-Toshiba or Ricafort in Dagupan from whom he receives 5 percent discount as a dealer. Even this freedom has a snag. Because of a "misunderstanding" between the president of Central Plains and the head of Precision Electronics, Central Plains-Dagupan is forbidden to sell the National brand, which is a giant gap in its inventory if it wants to be competitive. Nor is this all. The worst problem that can beset a dealer is to run out of stock constantly. It ruined the long career of Ysmael Steel and plagues most others on and off. For Central Plains-Dagupan, however, it is chronic because the head office prefers to deliver to its branch in Tarlac since it is nearer to Angeles. Also shipments to Dagupan have to pass through Tarlac, and many items are kept by the branch there if it has a use for them.

Despite these impediments the president of the company has high expectations for the Dagupan branch, and the branch manager is required to phone his daily sales and collections to the head office where accounts and records are kept. Central Plains sees personal selling in the field as the key to penetrating new markets. In addition to six employees, the branch has two sales supervisors and six unit managers who are territorially divided, work exclusively for the branch, and have a quota. Each of these, in turn, has four to five international salesmen. Financing is done through finance companies or under a plan offered by Central Plains. Collectors are sent out from the central office to check on the credit worthiness of customers and to monitor payments. To overcome stagnant sales, Central Plains has introduced an installment plan that is unique in Dagupan. It requires daily payments for 120 days and is a gimmick to attract market vendors. Others in the trade disparage it as an attempt that in the long run is bound to fail because of its high administrative expenses. So far the chances of Central Plains-Dagupan surviving seem to be slim, irrespective of the confident front it presents to the public and its sophisticated sales organization.

D. The number of Manila companies that sell their appliance products only through franchised outlets and that demand brand exclusivity among their provincial retail dealers is small. In Dagupan, Radiowealth, Singer, Yamaha, and DMG-Admiral are represented in this fashion. I dealt with Radiowealth in connection with finance companies in "Retailing Strategy and Personal Selling" (this chapter), and it is a convenient case to return to here. Today the company has more than 60 franchise stores. These are bonded, handle only the Radiowealth brand, and are required to have a retail fieldforce. Ten to 15 of these dealers are grouped under a regional manager to whom is "delegated . . . appropriate authority to decide on peculiar problems confronting their regions" (Banguis 1965:5). This gives provincial outlets some flexibility to respond to circumstances that may be unique to their area without affecting the policy of dealers in other regions.

North Point Appliances is Radiowealth's franchise in Dagupan. The store goes back to 1966, and although it has gone through several owners, it has remained the exclusive representative of Radiowealth. It has eight employees plus one supervisor and three salaried salesmen. Each of these has about 10 international salesmen working for him. In response to the suggestion of Radiowealth, the dealer (Mr. Maramba) recently opened display offices in Urdaneta and Alaminos, which are staffed with a sales manager, a secretary-cashier, and 10 commissioned salesmen. Each office has a territory, but the invoicing and accounts are taken care of by Maramba in Dagupan. The terms North Point receives are set by Radiowealth Finance and have been described earlier. Maramba specializes in retailing because selling to stores would violate the company's commitment to channel exclusivity down to where the consumer is served. Instead of selling to whomever wants to buy, Radiowealth in Manila has responded to the competition stemming from the Japanese and Chinese by broadening its product mix. Like Singer which several years ago began to offer refrigerators and other white line products under its own brand name, Radiowealth added to its brown line stoves, refrigerators, and furniture. Exclusive access to the Radiowealth brand and the increasing range of products it has available have enabled North Point to keep its position among the 10 largest appliance businesses in Dagupan.

WHAT CAN BE LEARNED from these cases? The examples cited are representative of each type of appliance outlet existing in Dagupan, and others having similar characteristics could be named.

First, given the current wide range of Manila suppliers available, to be independent is the best condition for provincial appliance merchants. Alternatively—and here the old chicken and egg problem enters—the most creative and successful traders in the business have managed to become independent (cases A-1 and 2). Independent traders can keep their sales organization simple to limit costs. Flexible prices and terms, together with their willingness to take advantage of opportunities in Manila, are the key to their success, and the fact that most of them can self-finance sales and engage in some wholesale trade helps.

Second, total dependence on a single Manila supplier continues to be a viable option for provincial traders as long as they are the only ones permitted to carry the brand of the mother company (case D). Only then can they survive the demands (for a salaried field force, bonding) and restrictions (on consumer financing) set by their principal. Leakage of the brand to other merchants can kill the exclusive dealers.

Third, establishments in Dagupan that are semiindependent (or semidependent) face the worst of two worlds (case B). To be a franchisee of a major supplier entails costs: restrictions on sales tactics and terms, an obligation to keep a hired field force, and so on. Yet the full benefit of being subject to contractual penetration is not received by the dealer because the principal also sells to other buyers, and the fact that the dealer can buy from sources other than his principal is negated by his obligations as a franchisee. Under these circumstances, a potentially profitable retail business slowly withers. Why then do so many of Dagupan's appliance traders abide by this arrangement? Why don't they break away, close up shop, or become independent? At least part of the problem is that their capital base is too small and at the same time too large. Created during the time when full channel integration ruled appliance distribution, they are today too small to stand on their own feet as independent merchants and too large to collapse totally under the present semidependent arrangement. Most of them at least manage to muddle on.

Fourth, to depend on one supplier who demands unified terms and an elaborate sales organization spells problems for dealers if the supplier fails to offer a popular brand not handled by other merchants. The weakness of case C lies not in the fact that the head office of Central Plains is located outside of Manila or that it chose ownership penetration—I have shown in "History" (this chapter) that franchise agreements can be just as binding and restrictive to the retail outlet as ownership penetration—but in the fact that the business depends on brands obtained from sources accessible to virtually any trader in Dagupan. The only way this setup could succeed is by underpricing the competition, and this can be accomplished only if very large purchases are made from producers in Manila. Firms like Abenson have done just that, but not Central Plains.

To conclude, even under conditions in which much of the appliance channel is fragmented, to depend on one supplier is not a bad thing for the provincial retailer, provided that brand exclusivity is assured. In those circumstances demands from the center for uniform pricing, elaborate sales personnel, and the like, can help, or at least need not hinder the local business. If full dependence on one supplier means for a dealer access to goods also available elsewhere, only low prices from the principal will ensure his survival. Similarly, if the principal bypasses the dealer, serious damage is done to the latter even if he can carry allied lines. To be independent, and to participate in at least some wholesale trade, constitute the best solution. The catch is that before adopting this solution a business size is essential that up to now only one-fifth of the appliance merchants in Dagupan have attained.

Chapter 7

COORDINATED PENETRATION:

EXAMPLES OF SUCCESS

THE PREVIOUS CHAPTER has shown that coordinated penetration can be unstable despite its appearance of strength and that more traditional channels can outcompete it. From this it is tempting to conclude that coordinated penetration is ill adapted to conditions in the Philippines. Perhaps one should replace the Western model of channel evolution with one that is applicable to economies, like that of the Philippines, in which subsistence agriculture still forms a mainstay of production and in which a viable middle class is expanding only slowly. Unfortunately, matters are more complicated. Even in the case of appliances, coordinated penetration did work for a considerable period in the Philippines. In addition, it continues to be viable in several product lines and is spreading in others. The present chapter explores these cases.

Motor Vehicle Distribution

Coordinated penetration had already been introduced into the distribution of motor vehicles before World War II, and the channel has remained tightly integrated ever since. Even recent changes on the production end have not changed this. In 1951 one firm assembled cars in the Philippines, and in 1968, there were 29. After this period of extreme fragmentation, the Board of Investment, in its effort to rationalize the industry and build up local production capacity, allowed only the most viable assemblers to survive. Thus, in 1975–1976 there were only five automobile assemblers, grouped under the Progressive Car Manufacturing Program (PCMP). Starting before World War II, and continuing today, imported and locally assembled motor vehicles have moved through licensed distributors to franchised dealers (or subdealers), and from these to consumers. Each level also sells to consumers.

Automobile retailing is characterized by product and brand exclusiveness, formal organization, elaborate displays, personal selling in the field, installment financing, repair service, mass advertising, and other devices adopted from the American and (later) Japanese example. In this respect the distribution of cars differs little from that of appliances or other capital-intensive consumer goods. Why look at motor vehicle distribution, therefore? The reason is that it has changed in interesting ways, though less radically than the appliance trade, and it currently shows some features that are not as clearly developed in other products. The changes are best captured by tracing briefly the history of one of the oldest still extant car distributors in the Philippines, Manila Trading and Supply Company, or Mantrade for short.

Mantrade and Dealership Fragmentation

Cars began to be imported into the Philippines in 1907 (Bachrach Motor Company was one of the earliest importers), and registrations of cars were first recorded in Dagupan in 1912. In 1918 American-owned Mantrade bought the Ford agency from McCullough and Company—at that time McCullough was selling 500 Fords a year in the Philippines. When Mantrade bought the license it was a general trade house, but in 1920 it sold off its other interests and became concerned only with the distribution of Fords. At about the same time dealers in the United States became product and brand exclusive.

Mantrade began by using resident salesmen and nonexclusive dealers in the provinces. The salesmen had a commission contract with the company and placed orders only after customers had been found. During the boom years of the mid-twenties Mantrade decided to launch into ownership penetration, the only one in the automotive trade to do so on a large scale at that time. It opened branches in San Pablo, Lucena (southern Luzon), Baguio, Tarlac, and Dagupan and in Pampanga and Bataan provinces. These were full-fledged affairs with a sales force, accounting department, and branch manager. The firm contined to have dealers and resident salesmen in the Visayas.

Mantrade's fortunes started to dwindle after the war. For reasons I turn to later, Ford split the Philippines in half and restricted Mantrade's sales to the north (including profitable Manila). The big carving up of the Mantrade territory had begun. Also farm machinery and tractors, heretofore handled by Mantrade, were assigned to another firm (G. A. Machineries, Inc.). After import controls came into effect in the fifties and after Yutivo and Sons began to assemble cars for GM in the Philippines, Mantrade established an assembly facility for Ford cars. Immediately after the war Mantrade had reopened its branches, but in 1953 it changed over to a franchise system. The reasons were conventional: scarce capital and the proven utility of the system in the United States. For Mantrade the phase of ownership penetration had begun two decades before it appeared in appliances. During the next 20 years exclusive franchise dealers represented the company in the provinces.

In 1967 matters came to a head. Mantrade was sharing the fate of several other American companies: "Filipinos, with the assistance of American banks, began the takeovers of the wealthier and more successful American companies. In nearly every case, the new owners contributed little or no capital, confidently expecting to pay for the companies out of future profits" (Gleek 1975:163). Anticipating that the special legal rights Americans enjoyed in the Philippines would soon be terminated and having been frightened by the Manila mayor's office, which forbade it to retail in the city for a period until Malacañang (the president's palace) intervened, the owners of Mantrade sold out to Filipino interests. Probably for similar reasons, but ostensibly in order to rejuvenate sales and offset the limited capacity of Mantrade to expand production, Ford in 1968 bought the assembly facility from Mantrade, and worse, canceled the company's status as distributor in northern Luzon. Mantrade had no encroachment agreement with its principal so that Ford could restrict the territory of Mantrade at will and take over its dealers. Some of these were dropped, some became direct dealers of Ford; either way, they were lost to Mantrade. From this time on Mantrade was just another franchise outlet of Ford confined, together with three other dealers, to Greater Manila.

Several other large American car assemblers in the Philippines have split up their formerly consolidated distribution networks. Having relied on one distributor who covered the entire country, Ford now has 20 direct dealers instead. General Motors Philippines, Inc. had two distributors (Northern and Southern Motors), and now it has 14 direct dealers. Chrysler Philippine Corporation remains conservative with only six. All three operate their own production facilities in the country. VWs and Toyotas, on the other hand, are produced by licensed assemblers. These either supply dealers directly (24 in the case of DMG, Inc. for VW) or through a subsidiary distributor (from Delta Motor Corporation Toyota cars move to Delta Motor Sales Corporation and from there to 14 dealers). Despite the reduction in assemblers in the Philippines, the number of car dealers in the country rose from 27 to 80 between 1961 and 1972 (Republic of the Philippines 1964–1965; 1975).

One cause of this proliferation was an increasing call from the assemblers for aggressive marketing. "One has to be there to sell," and to do so effectively, financial and organizational resources were needed on a scale only the overseas manufacturer, not aged and unwieldly distributors, could provide. Distributors like Mantrade and their local representatives proved to be too overgrown and sluggish. In Dagupan the Mantrade dealership, Dagupan Trading, was managed by an American who had little interest in the business and even less managerial know-how. But he remained the choice of the company because of his position in the community as an American and because of personal ties forged between a former manager of Mantrade and the dealer's family. This worked well as long as competition stayed away, which it did until the mid-sixties. Other than Mantrade, only Northern Motors (GM) was represented in the city. International Harvester already had a dealership, but it sold agricultural vehicles, not cars. Then in 1967 the avalanche began. That year a franchise of DMG opened (T. G. Borja, Inc.), in 1968 Chrysler began to be represented by Geryal Marketing, and in 1969 Mercedes Benz started to be sold by

Calasiao Motors. Two years later, 1971, was a very fertile year: Delta entered through Urduja Motor Court, and both GM and Ford came to be represented by two new franchises (Pan Ilocos Motors, Inc. and Pangasinan Auto Mart). In 1975 a new franchise of Chrysler opened its showroom (Springfield Motor Sales Corporation). By 1977 eight car retailers did business in the city, some of them direct dealers of Manila producers, others franchisees of major distributors.

Most older dealers, like Dagupan Trading, did not survive this onslaught. Manila companies did not shy away from opening new dealerships in the territory of established ones, and eventually the more successful dealers—almost invariably the newcomers—were given the territory. New dealers were chosen on the basis of financial resources, proven business acumen, and contacts in the community. For example, Pangasinan Auto Mart is backed by several local families prominent in education and the medical field, Pan Ilocos is owned by Chinese commercial interests closely allied to the owners of its Manila principal (Supercars, Inc.), and Urduja Motors is owned by the head of the Dagupan Electric Corporation, a valuable position for contacts with the local government. In those cases in which capital is there but not managerial skill, as in Pangasinan Auto Mart, a manager is hired from the outside.

Competition between producers undoubtedly did play a role in the fragmentation of the automotive dealership system. In fact, this is the explanation favored by the producers. Yet there is more to it than that. Fragmentation does not mean only the proliferation of distributors and dealers; it also implies that no one dealer can maintain a position that might threaten the power of the manufacturer. As I have already shown with respect to Ford and Mantrade, the issue of Filipinization is also important. It is one thing for an American company to enter into an agreement with a large Filipino distributor; it is another for the company to see its long-standing, powerful, and trusted American-owned distributorship forced to pass into Filipino hands because of political pressure. At that point, rather than leaving most of its business in the hands of one or two distributors, the American company deems it wise to fragment the system into smaller units. The chairman of the Council for Economic Development, David SyCip, has complained that foreign suppliers are "breaking up established Filipino distributor organizations, who had built up the markets in the first place, into small dealerships, so that the Filipinos will no longer have bargaining strength" (*BD* November 5, 1975). True enough. What he does not mention is that in many cases these "established Filipino distributor organizations" were once foreign (that is, American) owned.

Whatever the cause of fragmentation, more manageable automobile dealers have been created without sacrificing coverage. If anything, market coverage has been improved, and competition between dealers has intensified. Since the late sixties producers and large distributors of motor vehicles have adopted the old trick of squeezing additional sales out of their dealers by pitting them against each other, or by threatening to add rival outlets in their territory if sales are low. The same game is played with even more gusto by gasoline companies (see "Gasoline Distribution," this chapter), whereas in appliances this tactic lost its importance because most dealers are now nonexclusive.

The car manufacturers' policy may have improved market coverage, but relations between the manufacturers and the dealers are far more fragile now than was true some time ago. Mantrade used to have differences with Ford, and its arrangement with the company was modified from time to time, but between 1918 and 1967, its status as a major distributor remained unchallenged. The same can be said of the GM and Chrysler distributors, although the relationships were of shorter duration. In contrast, here are the events that occurred in 1974 alone: Carmasters, Inc. separated from GM and joined Ford because it could not obtain as many units from GM as it had hoped. For the same reason Fortune Motors (Phil.) Corporation, then the largest outlet for Chrysler, began to talk with Delta Motors about a dealership. Two former dealers of Chrysler were looking for an agreement with GM because Chrysler decided to maintain only two dealers in Manila. A fight was also developing over who should distribute utility vehicles. Chrysler divides its dealers not only territorially but also according to the brand they sell. Union Motor Corporation specializes in Minicas and because of its limited success was bidding hard for the sole franchise of the company utility vehicle, whereas

Chrysler was contemplating whether it would not be in its own interest to appoint a new dealer.

Comparison with the Appliance Trade

What has happened in the distribution of cars recalls developments in appliances. In both cases fragmentation of distribution has taken place, and in both—this I have not yet mentioned for cars—Chinese have appeared on the scene. How deep does this convergence go?

To begin with the last point, many Manila dealerships are today under ethnic Chinese control: Commercial Motors Corporation, Universal Motors Corporation, Supercars, Inc., Fortune Motors (Phil.) Corporation, Northern Motor Corporation, and so on. In Dagupan the role of Chinese among car dealerships is more subdued. Only Springfield and Pan Ilocos, both latecomers in the field, are Chinese operated.

Chinese have always participated in the automobile trade in the Philippines, but until the fifties not as exclusive franchisees. What was true in appliances also applied to motor vehicles: Chinese avoided exclusive ties with non-Chinese suppliers. Why is it then that Chinese appliance merchants have retained their independence, while those in cars have accepted franchising with all its restrictions? The reason appears to be, first, that motor vehicle producers never became as weak as appliance manufacturers and, second, that automobiles are more brand specific.

In the mid- and late sixties car assemblers were tempted to sell wholesale to whomever would buy. Overcapacity was endemic, and the stage was set for the same pattern to appear in cars that had appeared in appliances. But exclusive channels were never discarded. The nature of the product itself made it unlikely that the strategy followed by Abenson and others in appliances would succeed. The identification of cars with the producer is exceedingly strong, so that to engage in "car supermarketing" seemed an unpromising venture. Moreover, in 1971 the BOI saved the day by imposing restrictions on who could and could not assemble automobiles in the Philippines. Owing to this intervention the remaining manufacturers retained sufficient strength to keep distribution brand exclusive and integrated. That meant Chinese had to submit to exclusive agreements if they wanted to participate at all in the lucrative car trade. As in appliances, the role of Chinese in the distribution of cars has increased, but their role in changing the structure of the channel has been far more modest.[1]

What about the other area of overlap between motor vehicles and appliances, namely that in both cases the late sixties witnessed the fragmentation of the channel? Once again the difference turns out to be just as important as the similarity. The distributors who first built the integrated channel in appliances and cars are smaller today than they used to be, at least insofar as their territory is concerned, and they have been joined by many more. Products now move to the retail level along a greater number of routes. Beyond this, however, the similarity stops. In contrast to that of appliances, the distribution of automobiles continues to take place through exclusive and tightly controlled channels. No equivalent of the independent wholesaler or retailer has appeared (or was permitted to appear), and contractual penetration has survived the perturbations of the sixties.

In the previous chapter I made the point that personal house-to-house selling is regarded by appliance suppliers as a major factor that will ensure success. Car distributors are even more convinced of this. Customers have to be personally enticed to favor particular brands and businesses. Walk-in customers for cars are very rare, and subwholesaling in the provinces, which would reduce the need for fieldmen, is nonexistent. All car dealers in Dagupan have salaried or commissioned salesmen, and all rely also on international salesmen and tipsters. The system resembles that found in appliances, and there is no reason, therefore, to repeat the description here.[2]

Gasoline Distribution

According to the material I have presented so far, retail sales penetration supplements tight channel integration. It seems that coordinated penetration is not enough for those in Manila who follow an aggresive marketing strategy. This is true in cars and appliances and is true also in the distribution of farm equipment and motorcycles. But this association is not universal. In some sectors provincial dealerships and branches are not expected to use fieldmen to expand retail sales. One example of this is tire distribution,[3] another and better one is gasoline.

Gasoline dealers are fully franchised, brand-exclusive retailers who rarely, if ever, retain a field force. There is no mystery to this. The immediate consuming unit (car, truck, motorcycle) has to have gasoline if it is to operate. Demand for gas is created indirectly by the growing popularity and use of motor vehicles. The gasoline distributor in Manila, therefore seeks to develop brand loyalty for this commodity, not demand for the generic product. Also the consuming unit needs to buy the product at frequent, often unpredictable, intervals, so that it is easier to have the customer contact the supplier than the other way around. Under these circumstances it is a waste of effort for service station (and tire) dealers to have a sales force search for customers.

If I were asked to pick an entire product line, not just one or another company, that best exemplifies extreme vertical channel integration, gasoline would be my choice. Coordinated penetration is extensive, irrespective of what supplier of gasoline is examined. The system is capital intensive, it is consistently brand and product exclusive, it is stable over time, formal in its organization, and simple and streamlined in its operation. Rational, aggressive marketing experiences here its epitome, and it is for this reason that I choose to discuss this product channel last.

With only limited local production, the Philippines imports more than 10 million tons of oil a year and processes it in four refineries. Most processed oil is destined for the transportation sector in the form of gasoline and lubricants, with some going to industrial and household use as heating oil, liquefied gas, and kerosone. The following discussion revolves around gasoline distribution unless otherwise indicated. Company terminals for storage of the refined product are found in Pandacan (Manila), Santa Ana (Manila), Poro Point (San Fernando [La Union]), Apalit (Pampanga), Legaspi City, and Cebu City. These are stocked by the major oil companies in the Philippines: Caltex (Phil.), Inc., Petrophil Corporation (formerly Esso), Mobil Oil Philippines, Inc., Pilipinas Shell Petroleum Corporation, and Getty Oil Philippines, Inc. From there the product is withdrawn in bulk and transported to smaller storage depots, service stations, and, at times, to end users.

In 1975–1976 there were nearly 4,000 service stations in the country, probably the largest centrally controlled investment in retailing found in the Philippines. With an estimated average investment in physical plant and land of ₱100,000, the total value of gasoline stations in the Philippines is approximately ₱400 million. This does not include the investment in large and small bulking stations and the tankers that keep them supplied.

In the teens gasoline was sold in gallon cans (marketed by the Standard Company, forerunner of Socony-Vacuum, Stanvac, Esso, and Petrophil). In 1919 the first gasoline pump appeared in Manila. Prefabricated imported gas stations made their debut in 1925, followed in 1929 by the first locally constructed station, located in the Ermita district of Manila. Not until the thirties did the service station and exclusive dealership make an impact on the retail scene in the Philippines. In the fifties most service stations were still modest affairs. They had one or two gas pumps and a small office, often without extra space for repair or maintenance service. Alternatively, pumps were located in front of a store that the dealer happened to run at the same time.

Although large stations did not appear en masse in the provinces until recently—indeed the total number of stations in 1961 was only half the 1975–1976 number (Republic of the Philippines 1964–1965)—the new equipment spread rapidly in the provinces. Pumps appeared in Pangasinan in 1923, and during the thirties Dagupan had at least three Socony stations (or pumps), one Shell, and one Caltex station. The next change began in the late fifties and lasted through the sixties. Major gas companies opened many new service stations and renovated old ones to conform to a "new look." Ample space, three to six pumps with storage tanks, full lubrication service, displays for tires and other accessories, rest rooms, and a spacious office now became standard. Each station was run by a franchise dealer with five to 10 employees who would devote all their time to the business (at least in theory).

Today there are 12 large and slick stations in Dagupan and four franchised bulking depots. These outlets and thousands like them have been a factor creating the standard modern appearance of most medium and large urban centers in the Philippines. Even smaller communities have not been spared. Nearly all municipalities in Pangasinan have at least one, more often two or three stations in their *población*. To these must be added outlets located along important interprovincial routes and those clustered next to major intersections. Largely because zoning laws are lax and local officials easily manipulated, nothing stood in the way of the oligopolistically fueled competitive expansion of fancy gas stations taking its full course in the Philippines. It continued until every major producer had a station virtually next to that of every other major one, each more glamorous than the last. Only after the market was more than saturated did restraint enter the trade. In the mid-seventies the gas companies observed a moratorium on the construction of new stations since the economic returns no longer justified the high investment costs.

Retailing of gasoline has been the direct concern of Manila suppliers since the introduction of pumps and service stations in the twenties. Since that early date the channel has been brand exclusive and integrated, showing an extraordinary degree of stability. In the United States most gas stations were owned by the producers until independent distributors started to crowd the field in the thirties. These could adjust prices and sales tactics to local conditions far more effectively than the branches of the large producers. In response to this the companies began to lease their stations to managers who operated them "independently" while the rest of the station personnel continued to be in the employ of the companies. This complicated scheme did not survive long. In the thirties new government regulations required the companies to pay social security and overtime to their employees, and rather than shoulder these costs themselves, the suppliers adopted full contractual penetration, retaining ownership only over the physical plant of the stations. They found that this strategy reduced costs and that "personal attention to the customers by the dealers was greater than it had been under salaried managers" (Vaugh 1974:14). Franchising has been adhered to in the gasoline trade ever since.

By the thirties franchising also typified gasoline retailing in the Philippines, and in most cases the physical structure of the station was owned by the company and leased to the dealer. This combination of ownership and contractual penetration still exists. There are two types of service stations today, company owned and dealer owned (cf. Valenciano 1974). In the first type the major facilities are built and owned by the company, including the building, paved yard and driveway, truck hoist, dispensing pumps, and underground tanks. The dealer supplies the minor items (air compressor, gear oil dispenser, tire changer, tools) and has to pay rent for the station, which is usually pegged at 30 to 40 percent of what the company pays to lease the land. The physical plant of dealer-owned stations is the property of the dealer, and the land is rented or owned by him. Only the company sign, dispensing pumps, and storage tanks are owned by the company. Various combinations of these two types exist, but the basic division is clear, and currently a rough numerical balance exists between them in the Philippines: 1,600 company-owned stations versus 1,700 dealer-owned ones. This balance, however, is more apparent than real because company-owned stations on the average are larger and better located than dealer-owned ones. In other words, a greater amount of investment has flowed into company-owned stations than into the other type, which suggests that company investments have captured most of the market.

The Acme of Coordinated Penetration

Nearly everything having to do with the distribution of gasoline is extreme: the number of franchised retail outlets, the stability of the channel over time, the fragmentation of dealerships, the large capital investment in each outlet. This is also true of the standardized procedure for organizing the business and displaying the product, the intense competition between dealers who carry the same brand, the duplication of services offered in the same location, and so on. Some of these conditions are apparent in the elaborate procedures for opening new stations. They are also reflected in the formalities involved in recruiting and training dealers and in the suppliers' generous contractual rights, which result in frequent conflict between suppliers and dealers.

Site selection of company-owned service stations has become a complicated affair during the past two decades. The size and cost of stations have grown and so also the risk of misjudging their location. Producers of cars and appliances still follow the old rule of having one to three retail outlets per province and locating them near or within the urban center of the major commercial munici- palities. Such a rule of thumb has long since ceased to be relevant in the gasoline field where the method of siting new stations is now highly rationalized. A lengthy sequence of steps and decisions is involved, the highlights of which are as follows:

a. The company sales representative (or dealer coordinator) in charge of a territory recommends a new site for a station; the recommendation is passed on to the supervisor and then to the district sales manager.

b. If all three support the recommendation, a formal site pro- posal is handed to the department responsible for retail market development. It estimates the market potential and the performance of existing company and competing sta- tions, and it checks with the appropriate municipal offices for zoning regulations, permission for road widening, and re- lated matters.

c. If this body gives its tentative approval (in some instances the project development and site acquisition managers are also included in this decision), the sales representative obtains an option to lease the grounds in question.

d. The layout and design engineer in consultation with the district sales manager and project development manager designs the layout and physical appearance of the station, which is then submitted to the local Bureau of Public High- ways and the District Engineer Office for building permits. At the same time the sales representative prepares a final report justifying the station and showing the location and business character of competitors.

e. When this is approved by management, the lease agreement between the owner of the land and the company is signed and construction begins.

From the inception of the idea until the beginning of construction more than a year can elapse. Shortcuts in the sequence can take place, decisions can be speeded up or delayed, and self-interest of one or another party in the affair can lead to an unfortunate choice. It remains remarkable, however, how much care is taken in planning, in double checking and keeping a number of options open, and in carefully estimating the strength of competitors.

The same care is taken with the selection criteria for dealers and with their training, although here actual practice more often fails to be congruent with the ideal. The following list of criteria is distilled from the policies of several companies.

a. The potential dealer must be a responsible and active community member and show some competitive aggressiveness.
b. He should be 30 to 40 years old, married, and have children.
c. He should be financially able to weather the break-in period at the beginning. He should be able to raise ₱20,000–40,000. He should not already earn more each month than he could by running a station.
d. The service station should be the dealer's primary interest, not merely a sideline. The dealer is expected to be present when the station is open and to act as a dealer-operator.
e. The dealer should be financially responsible. He should devote his capital to the station and not dissipate his resources in nonproductive channels.
f. Those who have had some previous experience in retailing are preferred.

In short, the ideal dealer is a middle-aged married person (male or female) who is locally popular and has financial resources that are just sufficient to launch and operate a station.

It cannot be denied that this scheme possesses a certain degree of sophistication. The companies are not looking for wealthy individuals who can afford to buy and (therefore) sell, a practice that was once common in automobile distribution. Rather, they seek those who are likely to find the operation of a service station one of the most appealing investments around, given the resources they have. Commitment to the business is generated by the companies through mobilizing the self-interest of the potential dealer.

The theory on which these selection criteria are based probably is sound, but actual selection usually falls short of the criteria. In Dagupan nearly half the dealers (both Filipino and Chinese) have major business interests other than their station, which means that the operation of the station is delegated to some family member or friend. The trouble is that when companies cannot find appropriate persons of middle-range financial strength, they tend to select members of the wealthy business community who acquire the dealership for profit alone, not for profit and subsistence. When they discover that operating a station leads to lower returns than those obtainable elsewhere, they lose interest and eventually leave. This is one of the reasons why there is a high turnover of gasoline dealers in Dagupan. In this respect the distribution of gasoline is exactly the opposite of appliances: the channel structure of gasoline has remained stable over time while retail outlets have changed hands frequently, whereas in appliances the channel has changed drastically but most franchise dealers are long-term operators.

Another practice interfering with the "rational" selection criteria just outlined is that dealers seek franchises for their sons and daughters. Petrophil has no formal policy on this matter, and when one of its stations in Dagupan lost its dealer, Mrs. Tandoc managed to secure the dealership for her eldest son. She has been with the company since 1938 when it was still Stanvac and today operates one of the oldest and most successful stations in the city. Her pull in the marketing division of the company is not insignificant, and she is now hoping to obtain the dealership of a new station the company is planning in Dagupan for her second son. In her words, "as long as the quota is met, Petron does not care."

This is not entirely true, at least according to unofficial company selection procedures. Most majors avoid allocating dealerships to close kin of existing dealers for fear that such dealers could thereby improve their bargaining power. Moreover, to allow a string of dealerships to fall into the hands of one family would hardly be conducive to the goodwill the companies seek to foster—bitterness over not being selected as a dealer because others have special relations with the company is not unheard of in Dagupan. Nor do kin connections stimulate competition between dealers. In this connection it is noteworthy that all but two of the gasoline firms avoid hiring kin of their employees. In the most extreme case this means anyone related up to the fourth degree of consanguinity (see Catre 1974). Obviously the companies are greatly concerned about nepotism undermining their rational operations, and the same concern, though less openly admitted, extends into the relations between their dealers. In Dagupan only two families control more than one station, each of them two.

What about favoritism and nepotism in the selection of dealers by the Manila firms? Most companies assign dealer coordinators to look for new dealers, and "prospects are usually recommendees of friends or relatives of the sales representative" (Valenciano 1974:73), which means the selection procedure is open to abuse. One way to avoid this is to advertise the position that needs filling and to accept unsolicited applications. A more common procedure tries to retain personalism during the initial period of selection, and then proceeds to find the best choice among the candidates on grounds of merit alone. In one typical case the sales representative is expected to select at least three candidates for an open position, and all three have to fill out an application. Their references are then checked by the credit department, which hires an independent investigatory agency to do so. The candidates are then interviewed by the dealer coordinator, supervisor, district sales manager, credit manager, and at times even the vice president for marketing. The collected materials and reports are then discussed by a committee, usually composed of the same individuals who interviewed the candidates; and it is they who make the final decision. As one report has put it, "It is significant to know that the six oil companies have graduated from the 'one man rule' style of selecting service station operators" (ibid.:35).

Through this procedure companies hope to gain two things: to guarantee that the best candidate receives the franchise and to make sure that the dealer coordinator in the field has some personal interest in the candidate. Good personal relations between sales representatives and the dealers are very important to the suppliers because they create trust and a buffer zone between the interests of the franchise holder and whatever the company policy may be. Dealer coordinators of gas companies do not just take orders from retailers; they act as marketing counselors, technical advisers, and confidants. The harsher, more restrictive, and rationalized the company policy is, the more important this personalized link between the company and the retailer becomes.

The managements of Caltex, Shell, Getty, and the rest regard dealers as independent businessmen and so explain their success or failure largely on the basis of the dealer's ability to run a business. The fact that the policy of the supplier, or inroads of other dealers, can destroy a dealership is (officially) recognized as only of secondary importance. From this position it logically follows that all companies have training programs to upgrade the management abilities of their dealers. Prospective dealers are brought to Manila for about a week of theoretical and practical instruction. How dealers perform during this training is supposedly included in the calculation of whether or not to retain them, although it is rare to find a person rejected on these grounds and at this late date. All companies also offer refresher and retraining courses for established dealers which usually take place every six months or every year; but only one company actually carries this out consistently. Official company policy regarding training and follow-ups is even more an ideal not fully attained in reality than the other procedures I have reviewed. Gasoline companies (and other franchisors) offer follow-up training, but admit that enforcement is spotty and that the most important training takes place in the day-to-day operation of the dealership.

Control over Station Operators

The gasoline industry provides an extreme illustration of another aspect inherent in contractual penetration: the ambivalence existing between the company's desire to control its retail outlets and its desire to perpetuate the notion that franchise dealers are independent merchants. The interests of both parties do overlap, must overlap to some degree or no agreement can prevail, but in the gasoline trade they all too often diverge sufficiently to undermine mutual goodwill. The restrictive conditions in most dealership contracts remind one of those that prevailed in the appliance field two decades ago. They include the following:

a. All contracts stipulate minimal sales quotas which differ according to market potential—only during periods of oil shortages are they done away with.
b. Strict product exclusivity is insisted upon; the company sets the wholesale prices and rebates at will.
c. The supplier company has the right to enter and inspect the premises of its dealers whenever it wants to.

d. The dealer can use the premises of the station only for the dealership.
e. Dealers may not transfer any right in the station to anyone else without prior written consent of the company.
f. Dealers are responsible for all government taxes.
g. Marketing and advertising strategy is determined by the company.
h. Most contracts include an escape clause, which exempts companies from responsibility for delays in delivery or damaged products.
i. Most lease and dealership agreements run for one year, a few for six months, and only one for four years; either party can terminate the dealership with (usually) 90 days of written notice.
j. A bond security may be required of the dealer to ensure compliance.
k. The company has the right to open additional dealerships near existing ones.

No territorial monopoly is guaranteed to the dealers, no credit extension or discount assured, and until recently company terms could change drastically with only minimal consultation with the dealers. Before the oil crisis in 1973 service station operators received 15 to 30 days' credit and various volume discounts, some of which were specials to encourage the competitive position of selected dealers and coerce (or punish) recalcitrant ones. During the Quirino administration (1949–1953) the majors tried to stimulate sales in order to maximize dollar allocations by showing that demand was insatiable. They gave discounts of up to 30 percent and even sold at a loss. In the late sixties the typical station received an allowance (discount) of 5 centavos per liter when it fulfilled the quota. The wholesale price per liter of 30 centavos was thereby reduced to 25, and the pump price that listed 32 to 33 centavos per liter was lowered by the dealer for good customers to 29 to 30 centavos per liter.

Then came the oil crisis and the companies, without consulting the dealers, made an about-face in their policy. Now no credit was allowed, no minimal sales quota demanded, no discounts given— all disincentives for dealers to buy and sell the product. The government fixed the gasoline retail price and allowed a 5 to 6 centavos per liter margin for retailers if they sold without discount and gave a 10 percent discount to public utility vehicles through a coupon program.

The oil crisis and the active interference of the government intensified the jockeying between dealers and their suppliers, and dealers finally started to play a more active role in setting company terms. The contenders in the struggle to dominate industry policy now include the Federation of Petroleum Dealers Association of the Philippines (FPDAP), the petroleum companies, and the government's Oil Industry Commission (OIC). For an example of the issues involved, let us look at what happened in early 1976.[4]

In January 1976 four oil companies (Mobil, Getty, Caltex, and Petrophil) petitioned the OIC for a 12 centavos a liter price hike. While the OIC considered the case, the FPDAP handed in its own request for a 7 to 10 centavos per liter increase on top of that asked for by the oil companies to improve what it considered to be a very low margin allowed to dealers. When this became public two of the largest overseas companies objected, through confidential channels, that the "dealers themselves are raking in huge amounts of profit in marketing fuel products." Some marketing executives of oil companies have resigned, so they argued, and turned to operating filling stations and, to clinch their point, "at least five of them . . . have made good" (*PDE* January 7, 1976).

What are the figures? The national average for sales of a gas station is 100,000 liters a month (this is also true for Dagupan). With a gross margin of about 6 centavos a liter, the monthly gross for the dealer is ₱6,000. Subtracting rentals, wages, taxes, and other expenses, the oil companies argue, should leave a net of ₱2,500. This is fine on paper, but does not take into account the discounts that dealers have to offer their customers if they want to stay in business. These might consume from one-half to two-thirds of their net margin. Consequently dealers end up with a realistic figure of ₱1,000 earnings per month or less. This amount, of course, does not include sales of accessories and mechanical services.

To operate a service station is no guarantee of success, and failures are not caused only by lack of managerial expertise as company officials like to argue. The heavy hand of the supplier is ever present, and dealers cannot seek alternative sources (except for local depots—see below). To be sure, terms of trade also change drastically in other product lines, but most low-margin products are not distributed through contractually fixed exclusive channels. Gasoline retailers handle a low-margin mass commodity, yet they cannot play many sources off against each other. At the time of the research short-term credit (seven days' postdated checks) was once again made available to Dagupan's service stations, minimum quotas had been reintroduced, and at least in one case (Shell) brackets were made part of the package. Good news for the dealers, but how long this would last was anyone's guess.

Of equal concern for the established dealers is the Manila companies' practice of locating more than one service station in the same town or even at the same intersection. We have come across a milder form of this practice in automobile distribution where inefficient dealers can be challenged by new ones in their own territory. As long as car dealers do well, however, they enjoy territorial integrity. Gasoline franchisees have no monopoly over territories. New dealerships can be established literally next door to existing ones, and the companies have the right to retail petroleum products directly to fleets and other large customers in the areas in which their dealers operate.

Although it is not openly admitted, this policy appears to be part of a strategy to encourage dealers handling the same brand to compete against one another. On the refinery and wholesale level, price competition between companies is of minor importance; there oligopolistic relations reign supreme. Prices offered to dealers tend to be equivalent across companies except during periods of transition from scarcity to oversupply or the reverse. The majors compete for the retail market by financing mass advertising, organizing promotional events, and copying each other's market network. Price competition, if it takes place at all in the gasoline trade, is confined to, and encouraged among, dealers who are expected to cut into their own margins in the process.

To attract good customers, such as lumber companies, construction firms, transportation teams (fleets of minibuses used for public transportation), and government offices, it is imperative for the station manager to offer discounts from the official pump price, *and* to be good at public relations, *and* to allow some, usually 30 days', credit. Together with a good location, prudent management, and a measure of luck, this can lead to success. I have mentioned that dealer coordinators are supposed to inject a personal touch into the basically impersonal and lopsided relation between dealers and oil companies. Dealers, in turn, are supposed to be flexible with customers, to offer personalized terms in a trade that is rational and standardized to the utmost. Even here aspects of the semipassive strategy are not entirely absent. Similar conditions prevail in appliances and cars, but the position of gasoline station operators is especially precarious because they have no opportunity to shift some of the burden of public relations and discounts onto the shoulders of field salesmen or smaller retailers.

The fact that there are so many service stations in places like Dagupan does not make it easy to be a dealer. Appropriate connections with potential customers are among the most important requisites for a healthy business. Mr. Ong runs a Getty Oil station in Dagupan. Virtually all of his important *suki* customers patronize him because of some preexisting acquaintance. He is very active in the Chinese Chamber. This leads him to interact frequently with personnel of the BIR and the Bureau of Commerce, with the result that vehicles of both bureaus tank up at Getty. The trucks of the largest lumber and biscuit companies in Dagupan get gas from his station because the proprietors of both are old friends of Ong. Nawasa (the city water system) vehicles are served by Ong because he and the head of the system have collaborated in real estate transactions. This list could be extended. Mrs. Tandoc of the old Petrophil station I mentioned before is locally regarded as one of the most able at public relations. Anyone buying more than ₱500 worth a month receives a discount and credit. This is not all. She counts among her good customers the Coca Cola Bottling Plant in Calasiao which buys ₱40,000–50,000 worth a month (she is a close friend of the plant manager's wife), the Overland Bus Company (owned by one of her children), and Goyena Lumber Company which buys ₱30,000 worth a month (a compadre). With these and 50 other credit customers, some of them as large as the ones mentioned, Mrs. Tandoc has a turnover of nearly ₱400,000 a month, making her the largest dealer in town.

Without proper connections, a dealer's business cannot become large. Typical of someone in this situation is Mrs. Carvajal, a

Mobil dealer. She sells ₱40,000–50,000 worth of gasoline a month and usually buys from the local bulk plant because it offers 15 days' credit (the Mobil source in Poro Point allows only seven days), even if it means a price that is higher by 1.5 centavos per liter. Her customers consist of private car owners and jeepney (converted army jeeps used for public transportation) and tricycle drivers, who buy from her for reasons of location, parking space, and her willingness to make small repairs. Lacking suitable social links with government and large business, she has been unable to attract substantial customers.

Dealers today do have at least some choice in suppliers they can tap. Carvajal obtains her gas from a local bulk plant, and so do many other station operators. Each oil company (except Getty) has a wholesale depot under franchise in Dagupan. These were established in the late fifties to cope with the expanding number of service stations in the provinces, which the facilities at Poro Point were not capable of handling. Most dealers prefer to buy directly from their principal in Poro because the price is lower—bulk dealers in Dagupan charge for transportation. However, the credit policy of bulk plants is more flexible and their delivery is prompt, so that even well run stations receive some of their gas from them.

The intent of the foregoing discussion is not to argue that gasoline dealers in all cases suffer excessive exploitation, are squeezed out of business, are unduly pressured by customers and companies alike, and barely, if at all, survive. Conditions are patently not so dismal. What I argue instead is that there are factors that have undermined the position of gasoline dealers in their relation to suppliers (and customers) to an extent unusual in contractual penetration. Basic to their weakness is the small size of each gasoline dealer compared to his principal. Car producers tried their best to carve up the territory of their distributors and dealers, yet large ones, especially in Manila, still command strong bargaining power. In appliances, large wholesaler-retailers with their own branches are ascendant, and small dealers have turned independent. This development is not likely to occur in the distribution of gasoline. The oil companies demand brand exclusivity and see to it that each station is operated by an "independent" dealer. There is no room for subchains; and, therefore, the attempt by Tandoc to have a second child of hers operate a station is unlikely to succeed. Under these conditions the only thing that can help the dealers is a trade association, which today exists in the FPDAP.

Because of the FPDAP and the negative image that has become attached to multinationals in the Philippines, the legal position of service station dealers has been slightly improved recently. This is shown by several rulings announced by the OIC during the seventies (Oil Industry Commission 1972):

a. Both parties have the right to renegotiate the terms and conditions of their contract after due notice.
b. Dealers can decide what kind of petroleum products (diesel, gasoline, and so on) they want to handle, and companies shall not discriminate against dealers in prices and supplies.
c. Perhaps most important of all, no petroleum products retail outlet of the same oil company shall be constructed at a distance of less than one kilometer from an existing one, unless it is shown that there is need therof. The last part of the sentence leaves a giant loophole, but at least this ruling addresses itself to a major problem endemic to gasoline distribution.
d. All dealership agreements have to be registered with the commission (OIC); establishing new dealerships is now subject to public hearings, and the commission gives a one-year license to each dealer. The license can be revoked only if the operator clearly violates the agreement.

These rulings are more likely to prove cosmetic than to alter the position of dealers fundamentally. Also, in the Philippines it is easier to formulate regulations than to implement them. But at least a beginning has been made.

Chinese

The dealer of the Petron (Petrophil) bulk plant in Dagupan is Chinese, as are those who manage the bulk plants of Shell and Mobil, and three service stations are operated by Chinese (Shell, Mobil, and Getty). Recollecting once again the point I made under appliances (see "History," Chapter 6) that Chinese avoid product-exclusive contracts with (especially non-Chinese) Manila suppliers, how does one explain their participation in gasoline distribution? The reasons are slightly different from those that account for their role in the automobile trade.

Before the war Tan Co Co (hardware) was a dealer for Shell in Dagupan, the original proprietor of City Grocery had a hand pump for Shell in the back of his store, and a Tan family, which eventually settled in Dagupan, had a Stanvac station in Tayug. None of these arrangements violated the aversion of Chinese to full franchises because their trade in gas was in each case decidedly secondary to their main line of business. This has changed. Chinese in the provinces have signed exclusive distributorship agreements even more readily with gasoline than with automobile companies.

Beginning in the fifties, both cars and gasoline could only be retailed by those willing to accept exclusive franchises. The difference between these products lay in the matter of wholesaling. Car wholesaling in the provinces is not well developed, except in the sense of Manila dealers selling units to their provincial subdealers. As a result, Chinese participation in the trade is centered in Manila. Gas companies, by contrast, assigned wholesale franchises over provincial depots during the period of rapid expansion of service stations, and it is these wholesale dealerships that have become the prime target for Chinese. To run a depot is more profitable than running a service station, and it does not conflict with the Filipinization policies of the government. Companies, in turn, have been glad to hand these dealerships to Chinese because the companies believe the Chinese to be more financially resourceful and commercially astute than Filipinos.

Among Chinese in Dagupan some association exists between being a wholesale dealer and having a background in gasoline distribution. The Shell bulk plant is operated by the brother of Jimmy Lim, who manages City Grocery; the Petron plant is managed by an offspring of a Tan family who used to have a Socony station in the thirties; and the grandson of the owner of Tan Co Co is involved in the Mobil bulk station. Only one wholesale dealership is in Filipino hands—the wife of a former congressman of Pangasinan manages the Caltex storage facility. The fact that one-third of Dagupan's stations get their gas from local bulk stations and another third buy from them occasionally shows how important these dealers (and therefore the Chinese) are in the trade.

Chinese play a far less important role in retailing. Two of the three that have service stations in Dagupan combine the business with other activities, one with appliances, the other with trucking. The third station is run by a kin of the City Grocery manager. Over the years several other Chinese have held retail dealerships, but they eventually gave them up because of constraints imposed from Manila and the constant favors they were expected to give to relatives, local officials, and others. Because of their visibility and the fact that they represent wealth in the eyes of many, Chinese service station managers are especially prone to being squeezed by customers.

The oil industry in the Philippines has been in Euro-American hands from the beginning. This tradition was not broken until 1973 when the government acquired Esso (now Petrophil). Filipinos have always been prominent among service station operators, whereas the contribution of the Chinese has been only marginal. It is in the middle-range wholesale level that Chinese have had some say. In other words, the product, which more than any other is distributed by means of a streamlined system of contractual penetration, ironically continues to show ethnic plurality of the traditional sort. Filipinos are on the bottom level, Chinese in between, and occidental foreigners in control of the top.

Recent Developments

Manila suppliers are ever ready to try new modes of distribution if an opportunity arises. As long as marketing is seen as one of the key means through which a company can carve out a larger share of a consumer pool (or at least maintain its share), this is bound to remain the case. The result has been a movement into sales and coordinated penetration on a scale not foreseen two or three decades ago. Products most affected by retail branching and franchising—items that have a large capital content and are brand specific in character—naturally have been most amenable to this system of distribution.[5] However, attempts are increasingly being made to go beyond these product lines.

Floro Photo

I have discussed the largely unsuccessful experience of active marketing in textiles, and so far grocery and hardware retail chains have confined themselves to Manila. Photographic equipment and drugs are another story. Kodak Philippines, Ltd. continues to dominate film sales and, to a lesser extent, photo processing. It used to be very aggressive in retailing with branches in Dagupan, Cebu, Iloilo, Baguio, and Naga (southern Luzon), and two in Manila. By the mid-seventies it had only one branch left outside of Manila (in Cebu)—another company that retrenched because the special privileges allowed Americans in the Philippines were threatened. Now it distributes via sales penetration to 207 dealers (one in Dagupan)[6] who need not be exclusive in the film brand they carry.

The largest of these dealers is Floro Blue Printing, Inc. (Floro Photo) of Manila which handles some 40 percent of the film and cameras sold by Kodak in the Philippines. What Kodak is terminating, Floro is busily building up. This Filipino company began in 1954 as a blueprinting and architectural supplies business. Over the years it added whiteprinting, microfilm equipment, and film processing, and in 1965 it made its big coup by obtaining the sole distributorship in the Philippines of Polaroid products (eyeglasses and cameras). By then it had 10 retail branches in the Manila area and a nonexclusive dealership network in the provinces which it supplied through fieldmen. In 1976 it had 35 branch stores in the Manila area, the Tagalog provinces, and Cebu. Floro's expansion of ownership penetration has been slow, but so far irresistible.

In 1971 it introduced a type of retail outlet that had become quite successful in the States under the sponsorship of Fotomat Corporation. These are tiny photo shops located in parking lots and other open spaces accessible by car, which serve those who drive or otherwise pass by. In 1972 Floro had 15 of these branches in Manila. Each is 2.5 by 1.3 by 3.3 meters, has a copier, cash register, and air conditioner, and is staffed by a woman. "These compact booths are designed to broaden the outlet network of photo finishing at maximum effectivity and minimum cost" (*MH* March 1976:25). Their small size allows each to be profitable at ₱500 a day in average sales, which most of them attain, given the mass advertising and liberal promotions (for example, one free roll of film for every roll developed) that back them up. In 1973 the firm had 28 of these outlets in Manila; in 1976 there were 66, many of them in provincial areas close to Manila, such as Bulacan and Pampanga. Before entering directly into Dagupan—the company has a dealer for the Polaroid line in the city—Floro hopes to fill in the intervening area between Manila and Pangasinan. Geographical overextension is not one of the weaknesses of the firm, nor reliance on one marketing strategy. In each region Floro has three supervisors, one responsible for branches, one attending to the photo shops, and the last one overseeing fieldmen who contact dealers.

Mercury Drug

Compared to Dagupeño photo dealers who up to now have been spared direct competition from Manila retail branches or franchises, drugstore operators in the city have not been so fortunate. For more than a decade they fretted over such a possibility, and in 1976 it became true. If the appliance trade illustrates that a fully integrated channel is not safe against forces leading to fragmentation, the recent experience of the trade in pharmaceuticals suggests that channels in which sales penetration and loose dealerships are well entrenched are not immune from forces leading to greater integration. In both instances the forces originated in Manila, and in both local resistance to the change proved ineffective over the long run.

For more than half a century drugs have moved through channels that are national, specialized, well organized, and largely in Filipino hands (see Chapter 5). Until the early sixties it seemed the drug trade would be based on sales penetration and independent, nonexclusive dealers forever. But then clouds started to gather for the independent retailers.

As early as 1966 representatives of independent drugstores in Manila complained vehemently to the Philippine Pharmaceutical Association about the growing threat to their existence posed by the multiplication of retail outlets that were part of chains. Mercury Drug Corporation was already the largest, followed by Commander Drug, Merced Company, Inc., and Casman Drug Company. The cries of the independents became more desperate and were taken up by independents in the provinces after one chain broke out of the confines of Manila. This was Mercury Drug, which over the years has succeeded in widening the gap between itself and other chains until the gap has become an unbridgeable chasm.

The origin and current operations of Mercury are shrouded in mystery. It is one of the few firms run along modern and sophisticated management principles that has been able to keep much of its background and marketing strategy to itself, and it is the only one that categorically refused us an interview. The fact that it is Chinese and embroiled in a battle to dominate the Philippine drugstore scene no doubt accounts for this. Mercury first appeared as a drugstore in 1945, helped along by those who later organized United Laboratories, Inc. It appears to be a renamed version of the United Drug Company, which in 1953 became the distributor of its sister company, United Lab. In 1961 Mercury took over the retail end of United Lab as well as the pharmaceutical lines that United Drug represented. By 1970 the company had 19 branches in Manila, all with the same decor and same efficient service, and all linked to a centralized purchasing and delivery organization. It built up a reputation with the public for low prices and full stocks, and wherever a branch opened, established drugstores lost out.

Mercury's active penetration of the provinces at the beginning of the seventies was accompanied by a changeover from ownership to contractual penetration. In Manila it continued to use branches, but in the provinces it turned to franchising. This move lessened the sting of the criticism coming from independent drug merchants who charged that an alien (even if naturalized) enterprise was pushing them to the wall. It enabled the company to show that independent Filipino dealers, not merely Filipino branch managers, represent Mercury Drug, and it also co-opted those who might be the most ferocious opponents of the newcomer—local pharmacists, drugstore owners, and medical doctors. The idea was to involve them financially by encouraging them to contribute to the capitalization of the franchise in their community and perhaps even have one of their own kind manage it.

Up to 1977 Mercury was alone in its foray into the provinces. The second largest chain, Commander Drug, has 13 branches in GMA (1975), compared to Mercury's 20. Outside of Manila, Commander has none, and Mercury has 15 spread over most provinces in Luzon and under a different name (Botica Pacific, Inc.) in Cebu. Early in 1976, after a long drawn-out battle, another franchise was added, this one in Dagupan.

The first bid by Mercury to open a franchise in Dagupan came in 1970. I have already noted the important position of Dagupan as a center in the regional drug trade, so it was only to be expected that the firm would choose the city as a prime target. Judging by its previous experience in Tarlac, San Fernando (Pampanga), Olongapo City (Zambales), Angeles, Cabanatuan, and Baguio, the company expected to succeed. But it underestimated the strength and opposition of the drugstore operators in Dagupan. The fact is, not only are there 23 of them, but several have over the past two decades elevated themselves into the wholesale trade and operate a large network of sales penetration via trucks in Pangasinan and further afield. By the late sixties they had attained a position strong enough not to be easily dislodged by Mercury Drug or ignored by the city government.

Mercury was able to rally drug company representatives and doctors to its cause, but it failed to win over the local government and the independent dealers. Late in 1970 it had interested some Dagupeño MDs in investing in a franchise, and it had mobilized the support of a powerful family in real estate that owned the building in which the new store was to be located. Manila company fieldmen interested in simplifying and boosting sales in the meanwhile had presented Mercury's case to doctors and to those dealers who would listen.[7] In spring 1971 the new franchise was all but opened; the Mercury sign even gazed ominously across the street at Farmacia Flor, the busiest drugstore in Dagupan. Everyone expected the new store to open soon. Nothing happened, though. Then a few weeks later the sign vanished, and after a few months the space was leased out to accommodate a bank.

What had happened? Local drug merchants had joined forces in the Dagupan Drug Association and begun to put pressure on the city government to deny a permit to Mercury. The mayor regarded the drug merchants as an important constituency and supported them. Pressure was also applied on the provincial level through the Pharmaceutical Association of Pangasinan and nationwide through the National Drug Association. This agitation stopped when martial law was declared in 1972. By then, however, dealers in Dagupan had convinced the city to block the license temporarily on the grounds that Mercury engaged in unfair price competition and that drug distribution should be kept in the hands of native-born Filipino citizens. This was not a total victory, only a temporary reprieve. Mercury agreed not to enter Dagupan for another three years and then to seek a location that did not immediately threaten the livelihood of any of the major independents. In return, there would be no significant local opposition to such a move.

Whether or not Dagupan's drug merchants meant to abide by this arrangement matters little, for when the new franchise opened early in 1976 martial law was in force and local opposition was emasculated. The new store is located near the plaza, well removed from the center of the city's retail business, and the franchisee is the wife of a landowner from Pampanga who has now moved to Dagupan. I know of no financial participation by Dagupeños in the dealership. It is ironic that the opposition of local traders resulted in the absence of any contribution by Dagupeños to the management and capital of the business once it did enter the city. The dealer's husband raised the ₱250,000 bond required for the dealership.

Franchise dealers are usually advertised as being independent merchants who happen to rely on a major source for their supplies and advice. Beyond the fact that they hold title to the goods they sell, there is some truth in this as long as retail prices and other terms to consumers are set by the dealers. Even gasoline dealers have that privilege, although the motivation of the oil companies in allowing them this freedom is not to enhance dealer autonomy but to encourage competition among them. Mercury Drug forbids even such limited autonomy. In return for territorial protection and the right to use the Mercury name, franchisees are required to adhere to strictly defined company terms, including fixed prices. This is not all. The store in Dagupan (as well as others in the system) has to keep a central record book in which all sales and purchases of the day are recorded, and each week inventory is taken and used as the basis for determining purchasing needs. The store orders stock for only two to three weeks in advance (from a selection of 10,000 items); anything more would tie down capital unnecessarily. In this the Mercury outlet is unique: other retailers in the city order on the basis of rough estimates, rely on their memory, and if they take inventory at all, do so only once a year.

Mercury monitors the stock and financial flow of its franchisees, and these have to obtain all their supplies from the Manila office, enabling the company to place large orders with its suppliers at very favorable terms. Dealerships are grouped under regional managers whose responsibility it is to nurse new dealers until they can stand on their own feet. Resident franchise representatives are assigned to dealerships to examine the books, check on the payables and purchases, and "calculate the money." The company figures 25 to 30 employees for each store in Manila. The Dagupan franchise has a staff of 16 (two pharmacists, two cashiers, one accountant, eight sales clerks, a utility man, one clerk, and a supervisor), virtually all of whom are local residents. In the first few months Mercury personnel took care of all important matters, and the dealer stood on the side and learned while watching. Mercury, in turn, receives 5 percent of gross sales for allowing its name to be used and 2 percent for the services it extends.

The secret of Mercury's success is a centralized sales structure which is rationalized down to the white uniforms without pockets (to inhibit pilferage) worn by the clerks in all stores, and a low-price policy based on a strategy that relentlessly takes advantage of scale. Another important ingredient in its success is the public image the chain has managed to create for itself. Independent drugstores hardly ever match the open, spacious, clean, and orderly display of Mercury outlets. Efficiency and service to the public are played up by the company. A typical story goes as follows: "When a flu epidemic broke out years ago, [the] Mercury sales force rendered round-the-clock service, as long as there was a single patron to serve. It was discovered later that this unselfish service brought to bed more than half the total number of the retailers, all afflicted with flu caused by the exacting job they had to do to serve the people continuously during the epidemic" (*MT* March 1, 1971). Whatever Mercury does, whether offering 24-hour service in Quiapo or opening a new franchise in a province (which creates employment for those in need), it is "for the public good."

The final ingredient in its success may be one of the most important and, paradoxically, also the most embarrasing to deal with. Many customers are convinced that Mercury's outlets are the cheapest in town, not only because of its obvious size and efficient image and its (stated) policy of keeping provincial prices aligned to those in Manila, but also because it is a Chinese enterprise. Filipinos may complain about the Chinese position in commerce, especially if they have a stake in it themselves, but it remains true even today that given the choice and other factors being equal, a Filipino will prefer to buy from a Chinese rather than a Filipino trader. Chinese can be subjected to stronger demands, and the Chinese business sense and their connections, it is believed, result in lower prices than those offered by Filipinos. Mercury retailers do not respond to haggling and are impervious to demands for personalized services—impersonalism and fixed prices are built into its efficient image, and *suki* customers officially receive no special privilege on the retail level. Here the American way has replaced the Chinese way. Nevertheless, the fact that ultimate control of the business is in Chinese hands has its attraction for many customers.

By introducing an effective and aggressive system of coordinated penetration, Mercury is posing a serious challenge to the existing structure of the drug trade; and not only there, because Mercury's success may encourage similar attempts in groceries and other products. The company is committed to expanding its franchise program further, and, as if this were not enough, it has embarked on a course of horizontal integration to broaden its strength. In 1972 the firm bought itself into Philusa Drug Distributors, Inc., a large pharmaceutical company, and some time before it acquired a supermarket chain in Manila, Tropical Hut Food Marketing, Inc. Many observers believe that Mercury is becoming the Philippine version of Rexall Drug of the United States. There are now 12 subsidiaries of the Mercury Group of Companies (Taza de Oro, Inc., the famed restaurant-coffee shop in Manila, is one of them) in which Mercury Drug Corporation still retains the top position. With such backing and with its special relation to United Lab, this chain is solidly established in the Philippine drugstore scene.

Will the independent *botica* or pharmacy disappear as chains spread? Mariano Que, president of Mercury, has clear and comforting words on this subject. Although blaming the failure of small *boticas* on the excessive margins they set to keep profits high, he is nevertheless convinced that most will survive. "The old Filipino tradition of buying things only needed for that particular moment hasn't changed. And the botica is where this little need is usually found." They are similar to *sari-sari* stores, just as resilient and tied to local needs, so that "their role in the total pharmaceutical market will be long felt and needed" (*MH* June 1968:40). These words may be soothing for Que himself, but hardly for those independent merchants who are facing the challenge of his evermore widespread chain.

Yet, unless the economic structure of the Philippines changes more radically than it has in the last quarter of a century, the gist of his statement is true. Low purchasing power and limits to the mobility of customers call for local traders who provide small-scale services together with personalized credit and flexible prices. Mercury can offer the first if the customer has access to its stores; the latter two it does not. What might evolve with time is that franchises similar to the Mercury outlet in Dagupan will begin sub-wholesaling to smaller drugstores in the region. This would spell difficult times ahead for present-day independent merchants in the city who perform that function, but the small drugstore operator will be preserved.

What will actually happen is anybody's guess. In an interval of four months I made two price comparisons between Dagupan's new dealership and several other drugstores in the city, and I could not find any appreciable difference. But the Mercury store was far more busy at the end of the period than when it first opened. Perhaps more telling for the future was the opening in 1977 of another Mercury dealership in Pangasinan, this one in Urdaneta.

FLORO PHOTO and especially Mercury are unusual because they are trying to replace an already entrenched system of distribution (sales penetration) with coordinated penetration. Until recently retail branching and franchising worked best when they could be applied to products (such as cars or gasoline) around which no other channel had yet formed. The current efforts of Floro and Mercury, therefore, may have far-reaching consequences.

Chapters 5–7 described the types of active marketing strategies that firms employ in the Manila-Dagupan trade and indicated how each has developed over time. Now I turn to the consequences these strategies have had for Dagupan.

Chapter 8

LOCAL CONSEQUENCES
OF ACTIVE DISTRIBUTION

DAGUPAN HAS ALWAYS EXCHANGED products and personnel with Manila.[1] Once it was an important bulking point for produce destined for the Manila market; now it is the distribution point of Manila-derived goods in north-central Luzon. Its merchants, whether Chinese or Filipino, keep in close touch with their counterparts in Manila, and there has been an easy movement of entrepreneurs and employees from one center to the other. What has happened during the past half-century is not that Dagupan (or even Pangasinan) has been opened to outside trade, but that its commercial ties with Manila have expanded. The organization of many of these ties, moreover, has changed from one based on conservative marketing strategies to one in which active distribution is the guiding principle. With this in mind, I turn to the following questions: what have sales and coordinated penetration from Manila meant to the trade community in Dagupan? What have been the consequences for the provincial channel and its attached entrepreneurs of active marketing strategies emanating from Manila?

This touches a broader issue that has been part of the development literature ever since the fate of colonial and postcolonial societies became the subject of scientific inquiry shortly after World War II. The issue relates to what happens to a peripheral region, society, town, or ethnic group when strong commercial interests located in a center (industrial country, primary city, metropolis) start to penetrate it? Will its social and economic conditions be improved or not as a result of this contact? The economic repercussions in Java and Sumatra of the Dutch economic entrance in the islands in the nineteenth century are an example; so also is the local effect of multinational companies opening South America to mass consumer goods, or the consequences to its hinterland of the economic expansion of Bangkok.

Evaluating nearly anything in the social sciences is a difficult task, yet that certainly has not diminished the temptation among scholars to do so. This is especially true for the "dependency issue"—the name this subject is often given. Judging the effects of market penetration from a center on a periphery is complicated by factors that do not always relate easily to the empirical data. From whose perspective should the consequences be evaluated—that of local consumers, local traders, the supplying firms in the center? Emotion often becomes an important part of the debate because the peripheral region, colony, small town in the hinterland of a large city, or whatever, is seen as weak and the underdog needing help. Through this door the matter of good and evil enters. Furthermore, the role of multinational companies is likely to be important. This adds the issue of national autonomy to that of regional independence and turns the problem into a political one with the result that the rhetoric ends up more akin to political pamphleteering than social science writing.

Because Dagupan has experienced considerable input from Manila in the form of new commercial institutions and because these institutions have been either directly managed by overseas concerns or inspired by them, this quagmire of opinion cannot be entirely avoided. Instead of devoting the next pages to an exhaustive review of the literature, I outline the major arguments that repeatedly crop up. Then I turn to the case of Manila and Dagupan and examine what has happened insofar as the data allow me to do so.

Theoretical Positions

First, to summarize the predictions made: the position of dependency maintains that free commercial interaction between center and periphery will be detrimental to the periphery.[2]

    a. Local trade channels and entrepreneurial talent in the periphery will be destroyed by capital-strong outsiders.

    b. The relationship of outside institutions with the periphery is exploitative. Penetrating firms extract more than they invest and transfer their profits out of the region. The periphery is left without capital, and its population is impoverished.

    c. Cheap and standardized products will swamp the local market and replace indigenously produced items. Cottage industry collapses, and the local economy is simplified as people are pressed into agriculture and services.

    d. Promotions, advertising, elaborate sales organizations, and similar techniques tempt the poor to consume unessential and even harmful products.

    e. Commercial penetration of a region from a powerful center diminishes local autonomy and political self-determination.

    f. Should, despite the first point above, local capital formation and entrepreneurial talent be encouraged in the periphery as a result of commercial contact with the center, this is a negative development because it leads to "embourgeoisement"[3] of a sector of the local population. The outcome is a new exploitative capitalistic class which wittingly or not acts in the interests of nonlocal capitalists.

These points can be collapsed into two. First, there is the conviction that trade, especially between a center and a less dynamic region, is characterized by a zero-sum relation. When one side (intruding firms) gains, the other (local enterprises, consumers) loses. On the international level a current version of this position is the belief that multinational corporations deprive developing societies of their capital, technology, and ideology and make their efforts to become strong difficult (Barnet and Müller 1974:152). Second, any development that does result in capital formation under the aegis of commercial stimulation from the outside is bad because exploitation of some by others necessarily accompanies this. If these two basically contradictory positions are combined, as some neo-Marxists have done (Frank 1969; Kay 1975), then whatever condition arises is unsatisfactory. We have here a no-win proposition.

Those who take a benign attitude toward trade penetration of peripheral regions—who hold a position of interdependence—

believe that local commercialization and capital formation feed on external links.[4] This position maintains that competitive trade, even between unequals, is not a zero-sum game, that both partners will be better off with such trade than without it, and that an entrepreneurial component is worth encouraging in the periphery to stimulate development. Center-periphery trade will prove generative to the economy of the periphery.

a. It is likely that the local commercial scene will be disrupted when new channels enter the peripheral region. But this disruption will prove more stimulating than destructive. Effective distribution will probably be enhanced and local monopolies removed, and outside firms may even take advantage of local entrepreneurial talent and traditional trade networks.

b. The degree of exploitation by outside institutions depends on their monopolistic position. This position tends to be enhanced if they control both production and distribution and if they combine economic with political power. Such a situation is encountered not only in colonial capitalism, but also in totalitarian socialism. Under competitive conditions the exploitation by outsiders is neither more nor less extreme than that generated by local entrepreneurs, and both have a tendency to invest profits where they can find the highest return. Obviously, external as well as local entrepreneurs try to make more money in the long run than they invest, but that does not necessarily result in a net capital loss for the peripheral region. Their investments in the region will have a multiplier effect by encouraging others to invest in related endeavors, and the secondary investments may add up to be more than the amount initially expended.

c. Cheap, standardized, and usually better products will replace locally manufactured ones. This is good for consumers—after all, they are the mass of the population—and may provide incentives for productive behavior. New economic opportunities will open up in which the periphery has a comparative advantage; these opportunities should be able to absorb the labor forced out of cottage industry. From an economic standpoint, self-sufficiency ought not be an end in itself.

    d. There is nothing sinister about the fact that advertisements, promotions, and sales personnel influence the consuming habits of a region's inhabitants. It is easy for those who already enjoy most amenities of industrial society to decry the tendency among the poor to spend resources on nonessentials. There is no reason why those who are economically less fortunate should not have access to the same range of products that others have. Local producers, moreover, are just as likely to distribute harmful merchandise as outsiders.

    e. Regional autonomy is less an economic than a political matter. It is highly questionable that a region's or a country's political position is strengthened through economic isolation.

    f. The capitalistic road is a viable and proven route to development. For development to be successful local capital formation and the creation of entrepreneurs are important prerequisites. Development will result in a widening economic gap between some segments of the population in relative terms; without some concentration of wealth, whether publicly or privately held, development cannot take place (Adelman and Morris 1973; Kuznets 1966; Liu and Wong 1981). Absolute poverty, however, need not increase.

It seems appropriate to assume that market penetration from a center via an active strategy and integrated channels has a greater impact upon the peripheral region than penetration based on conservative distribution. The dependency position would therefore predict that a community subject to outside suppliers following active marketing would be in a more dependent and economically more detrimental position than if penetration were of a conservative kind. Has the effect of active penetration by Manila firms on Dagupan and its traders in fact been consistent with the predictions of dependency theory?

Local Effects of Sales Penetration

How important sales penetration is in the Manila-Dagupan channel is shown by the following figures. The total reported annual value of goods flowing from Manila into Dagupan is about ₱174 million, of which 44 percent, or ₱77 million, is accounted for by Manila fieldmen contacting customers.[5] There are 2,100 wholesale and retail establishments in the city; 1,343 of these (or 64 percent) obtain most of their products by placing orders with salesmen sent out by Manila companies.[6] Compared to this, the conservative channel is of minor importance. Only 212 enterprises (10 percent) receive most of their goods through passive or semipassive distribution, and only ₱22 million worth of goods (13 percent of the total) pass through them.

If one looks at the range of retail institutions operating in Dagupan one is struck by the mix of the modern and the traditional, the new and the old. Next to appliance stores, gas stations, superettes, fancy gift shops, and boutiques, market vendors flourish, hawkers still abound, general stores and bazaars are very much in evidence, and, perhaps most notable of all, *sari-sari* stores thrive. Whether modern or traditional, large or small, most retailers trade in products they obtain directly from large Manila companies. How is this possible? Certain marketing strategies used by Manila firms are well suited to bridge the gaps that may exist between suppliers and outlets. Sales penetration has served this purpose admirably. Its deployment has allowed Manila companies to search out provincial buyers with only minor disruptions of traditional trade institutions.

To recapitulate briefly, before sales penetration was used on a massive scale, large Dagupan merchants had to travel to Manila for purchases (trading usually along semipassive principles), and it was they, in turn, who supplied smaller traders in the town and its surroundings. A two- to three-tiered channel existed in the city. Since then sales penetration has altered, but not destroyed, this arrangement.

At first this strategy was confined to the loose dealership type. Manila companies appointed as dealers Dagupan merchants who were then served by company salesmen. The contact point between Manila and Dagupan had shifted to Dagupan, but the pattern whereby large merchants in Dagupan were the only suppliers of local retailers continued. Eventually greater disruption of this arrangement took place. Once fieldmen were sent out to contact dealers, it was an easy step to have them visit small retail outlets as well. Such deep sales penetration undermined the position of large local traders, with the end result that for some products the two- to three-tiered structure was collapsed into one. This development reached its pinnacle in soft drinks distribution. Dagupan's first-order grocery stores used to act as middlemen for this commodity until bottling plants, warehouse branches, trucks, and fieldmen of Manila companies took over.

Sales penetration, therefore, need not compete with local trade institutions, but it can. In the Manila-Dagupan trade it has done so increasingly as Manila suppliers have fleshed out their own provincial facilities, and today there exists only one trade level in Dagupan for several products (soft drinks, beer, cigarettes). Even with this onslaught, however, the traditional first-order merchants survive. There are several reasons for their resilience: they still have valuable ties with those Manila suppliers who play the marketing game according to the conservative strategy; most Manila companies selling through a traveling sales force continue to use the loose dealership or jobbing system; bulk purchases enable first-order merchants to obtain discounts even from those sources selling directly to small outlets; and small traders continue to buy from first-order stores because of the liberal credit terms and delivery service they receive from them.

Sales penetration, therefore, has affected the local trade structure by establishing a direct connection between small and isolated retailers and Manila sources. It has punctured the former monopoly of first-order merchants over those who could not personally reach into Manila. Now market vendors, neighborhood store operators, and grocery and hardware merchants in remote areas of Pangasinan have a choice of buying from traditional sources (usually rolling stores) or from Manila salesmen. They have become less isolated, and information about available products and pricing reaches them with greater ease.

In all of this neighborhood stores benefited more than other retail institutions. Their extraordinary proliferation during the past 30 years has been brought about by population growth and the shortage of alternative occupations. Sales penetration, however, also played an important role, as did the way in which some of the larger Manila companies promote their products. Without the widespread demand for soft drinks, cigarettes, and detergents, many of today's neighborhood stores would have to close down; in fact, without the support provided by the promotional salesmen of Manila firms, many would not have opened in the first place. Here a modern policy of active marketing stimulated a traditional retail institution.

Two other consequences of sales penetration are worth going into. It has encouraged innovations and the adoption of modern marketing techniques, and it has enabled individuals to establish themselves in commerce who were previously excluded.

To begin with the first point, when Dagupeño traders still traveled to Manila to place orders, there was little need for written documents. The modus operandi was (and still is in textiles) to rely on personal trust and face-to-face contacts. Both parties were often Chinese, which added to the intimacy of the exchange. With the coming of sales penetration, the possibility of continuing trade in this fashion was drastically reduced. Whereas sales penetration respected the independence and continued existence of traditional trade outlets in Dagupan, it has put a big dent into conservative, especially semipassive, trading practices between merchants. Because of the new strategy, at least one of the negotiators in the exchange, the Manila salesman, could not be empowered to go beyond a very limited range of selling terms without too much risk for his employer. The rapid diffusion of sales penetration, therefore, has forced merchants to document and standardize terms. Manifestations of this are memos, formal application forms for dealerships and credit, and the wide use of checks and postdated checks.

In addition to taking orders, field salesmen are told to see to it that their customers adopt marketing practices that will help the business and thereby increase purchases from Manila. This includes such simple tasks as the proper display of the company products and advertising in the local media. More elaborate suggestions include ways to rearrange the physical layout of the store, ways to keep tabs on one's product needs, whether and how to use promotions and other active marketing procedures to reach consumers.

The vast majority of Dagupan's large and small traders are conservative, and they are reluctant to adopt even the simplest suggestions. Some of the medium-sized ones, though, have been receptive to more radical innovations urged by salesmen. The most notable example is grocers who have organized their stores as small self-service outlets, or superettes, in order to capture the flavor of the supermarket and make it work in the confines of the local economy. There are also those who have been convinced by the example of Manila firms to launch promotions with their own staff. For instance, the proprietor of Tan Hardware (an offspring of Tan Co Co) sends his promotional salesman around to contact home owners and talk them into a new paint job for their houses, offering specials on Dutch Boy paints for the job. The sales representative of the Manila company is pleased. Here sales penetration from Manila into Dagupan has spawned sales penetration from Dagupan into the city's hinterland.

Sales penetration has helped modernize Dagupan's trade community directly and indirectly. First, sales penetration requires techniques that standardize trade agreements and reduce them to written records. Whether the parties like it or not, as soon as this strategy is adopted depersonalized contacts are made necessary. In this sense the influence of sales penetration is direct. Second, this strategy has served as a useful conduit for innovations. Modern marketing and business methods inspired by American (and Japanese) examples are transmitted by Manila companies through their fieldmen to their provincial customers. The role of sales penetration is indirect in this instance; there is nothing in the logic of this strategy that demands that novelties of this kind be passed on. The decision to enter into sales penetration is merely a sign that Manila companies have accepted active marketing. Whether this strategy is then used to convince customers to copy marketing innovations is up to each individual supplier.

The other consequence of sales penetration is that it has given individuals an opportunity to enter trade who would otherwise have found it difficult to do so. Two sets of individuals are involved: those who have been helped to participate in commerce as independent traders and those who have obtained employment as fieldmen.

I alluded to the first group earlier when I argued that sales penetration has given a boost to small and medium-scale traders. In effect this has improved the chances for Filipinos of lower-class background to enter commerce and lift themselves above petty trade. This has happened most dramatically in groceries, where Filipino participation has expanded extraordinarily since the war. Filipinos always played an important role in drug retailing, and the position of the Chinese remains strong in hardware, because here a small-scale retail level is absent.

It is a traditional practice for Filipino newcomers in the *sari-sari* trade to seek and receive help from first-order merchants who offer a proper selection of products on credit (Davis 1973:191–210). The *sari-sari* traders are then obliged to buy from their creditor for a considerable period, at least until the debt is payed off. Because of sales penetration the newcomers need no longer be so dependent on any one supplier. Now they can also seek similar credit arrangements with one or more Manila companies through their field salesmen; in other words, they can tap several sources, not just one, from the time they begin their business.

On the other end of the channel, Manila companies seeking reliable and profitable retail outlets in the provinces acquired with sales penetration the ability to do their own choosing, instead of going through intermediaries in Divisoria. This has meant that the "rule" that gave preferred treatment to the Chinese in Dagupan and similar centers has been undermined, a development that has been of great importance to those Filipinos in Dagupan who have tried to enter the subwholesale trade and to challenge the entrenched position of local Chinese merchants. In a word, sales penetration has helped equalize the formerly extremely lopsided nature of the ethnic composition in trade.

Table 1 sketches the social profile of Dagupeño traders for whom sales penetration provides the most important connection with Manila.[7] Note the lower- to lower-middle-class agrarian and commercial origin of most of them and the important role played by the Chinese with a long trading tradition. Also note that the profiles of first-order Chinese and third-order Filipinos are similar to the respective profiles of Chinese and Filipino traders who are tied to Manila by means of semipassive marketing (Table 2). Aside from helping Filipinos to participate in trade, sales penetration has played only a minor role in determining the social characteristics of Dagupeño entrepreneurs.

Sales penetration also gives individuals an opportunity to become company salesmen. Manila firms employ about 250 fieldmen

TABLE I. *Dagupan Traders Linked to Suppliers via Sales Penetration*

Type of trader	Sex Ethnicity	Education	Region of origin
Grocery			
Third–order N = 252	Female Filipino	Primary	Dagupan, Pangasinan, Ilocandia
Second–order Filipino N = 20	Male and female Filipino	Secondary or college	Dagupan, Pangasinan, Ilocandia
Chinese N = 8	Male Chinese	Chinese secondary or college	Dagupan, Manila
First–order N = 9	Male Chinese	Chinese primary; if son of founder has taken over, college	Dagupan, Manila, China
Hardware N = 20	Male Chinese	Chinese secondary or college	Dagupan, Manila
Drug N = 22	Female Filipino	College	Dagupan, Manila

Parental background	Career
Lower and lower middle class: peasant, petty trade, household craft	Has had store for five years; previously engaged in part-time buy-and-sell
Lower middle class: land-owning peasant, petty official, market vendor	In the trade since the forties and fifties; either began on second-order level with parental help or traded himself or herself up
Middle class: trade	Began business in the fifties or sixties after education; received help from parents
Parents in China, peasant; parents in the Philippines, medium-scale business	In the business since pre-war years; apprenticed in Manila, turned independent in Dagupan; if son of founder, inherited the store
Middle class: hardware business in Dagupan or Manila	Inherited from or financed by parents in the fifties or sixties after education
Middle, upper class: medicine or other profession	Entered the business after degree in pharmacy in the fifties

TABLE 2. *Dagupan Traders Linked to Suppliers via Semipassive Channels*

Type of trader	Sex Ethnicity	Education	Region of origin
Textile Wholesaler-retailer N = 12	Male Chinese	Secondary or college	Dagupan, Manila, China
Retailer (market vendor) N = 30	Female Filipino	Primary or secondary	Dagupan, Pangasinan, Ilocandia

to represent them in and around Dagupan. From the perspective of employment within Dagupan this fact is less important than it might seem, because only half of them live with their families in the city, and slightly less than half are native to Dagupan. From the viewpoint of those Dagupeños who have found positions as fieldmen, however, the expansion of sales penetration has been a boon, and not only because it offers a means to make a living.

Nearly all fieldmen of Manila companies (especially the younger ones) refuse to consider their position as a lifetime commitment. Instead, they see it as a means to reach one of two ends. Many intend to lift themselves into supervisory or even managerial positions. This disposition is held mainly among those working for companies that maintain subcategorized agents: promotional, junior, senior, and so on. The other intention, which does not necessarily exclude the first, is to start their own business at some future date. I showed above that sales penetration enhances certain entrepreneurial elements in Dagupan by providing a direct link with Manila. Here this theme reappears in the guise of employment opportunities offered by sales penetration, which individuals hope to use before starting their own store.

For many the cheapest and most effective way to gather experience about the vagaries of commerce is to work as a fieldman. This is particularly important for Filipinos. They are likely to come

Parental background	Career
Lower middle class: small to medium business, often textiles	Since early fifties or pre-war years; experience in the business since childhood
Lower to lower middle class: peasant, buy-and-sell, petty government position	Began in the fifties or sixties; on and off in buy-and-sell before turning permanently to dry goods

from a family background not noted for its commercial sophistication so that the experience gained as fieldmen can be invaluable. This is especially true if they occupy several positions in sequence and work for a range of companies. It is quite common to encounter Filipino salesmen of Colgate-Palmolive, Kimberly Clark, and similar firms, whose avowed aim is to jump from job to job (in Chapter 5 we saw that the hiring practices of many companies encourage this) and to accumulate in this manner experience and capital for the eventual big day. For most, of course, this hope—as also the vision of ending up as sales supervisor or manager— remains a hope; but it is kept alive by the occasional success. There is Cirilo Tecson in the furniture business who used to be a sales representative for U.S. Tobacco, Darigold Milk Company, California Sales, and finally Cromwell Commercial before he opened his successful store on A. T. Bugallon Avenue; or Mr. Aquino, encountered in Chapter 4 with his specialized drug business in Dagupan, who 15 years ago was a senior salesmen for Richardson-Merrell and before that a salesmen for Canada Dry. To take two Chinese examples, there is Alex Ching who, before he opened Prelix Drug House on A. T. Bugallon Avenue, was a cigarette salesman, and William Chua who served as a salesman of ready-made clothes for Freeman, Inc. until he started the grocery store Cheong Sam Trading in Dagupan. My data show that altogether 10 percent of the approximately 300 independent store merchants in Dagupan were employed as sales representatives of Manila companies at one time or another during their careers. This does not include franchisees and branch managers of Manila companies, among whom such experience is even more common.[8]

Earlier I noted the resemblance between traders receiving most supplies from Manila through sales penetration and those relying on semipassive channels. Here another resemblance exists. The social profile of itinerant salesmen (Table 3) is similar to that of merchants who are tied to a passive supply network (Table 4). In both cases they are likely to be fast-moving individuals who are on the go, hoping to establish themselves in business after having tried other occupations. Some of them use employment as field salesmen in a succession of companies to further their career goals in business. Others, with the same goal in mind, tap as independent merchants whatever trade links and products are available from Manila. There are also those who have tried both avenues. All of them, however, are active in fields in which little capital is needed to enter, but considerable ability is needed to succeed.

Local Effects of Coordinated Penetration

Compared to sales penetration, coordinated penetration leads Manila firms to be far more involved in the affairs of Dagupan. What are the major consequences of this strategy to the local trade structure and to entrepreneurs? Once again, let me start with some tentative figures. We have seen that approximately 44 percent of the total value of turnover moves through Dagupan by means of Manila salesmen collecting orders in the provincial city, and that 64 percent of all establishments depend on fieldmen for most of their supplies. In contrast, although the value of products entering Dagupan by means of fully integrated channels amounts to ₱69 million a year (40 percent of the total), only 65 franchises or branches (3 percent of all trade units) are responsible for the disposition of this merchandise. Manila-dependent establishments compensate for their small number by being far more substantial than independent ones. The average annual turnover per franchise or branch in Dagupan is ₱1.1 million, compared to ₱57,000 per independent trader.[9]

How important Manila-dependent outlets are to the local economy is attested to by additional figures. These outlets employ approximately 800 individuals, an average of 12 per unit (compared to 2.5 per commercial establishment in the city). These 800 employees receive in pay ₱3.8 million per year[10] and constitute 15 percent of all Dagupeños who are permanently active in trade (the total is about 5,250)—this is a considerable percentage, when it is recalled that only 3 percent of all commercial outlets in Dagupan are legally tied to a Manila company. The market value of all commercial buildings in Dagupan was about ₱31 million in 1976. Of this an astounding 19 percent is accounted for by structures either leased or, more rarely, owned by Manila firms or local franchise dealers. In this context, it is interesting to note that if all of the net profit (computed at 15 percent of turnover) of Manila-dependent outlets were to be siphoned out of the community, ₱10.3 million would leave Dagupan annually. Full channel integration does not only mean the potential loss to Dagupan of profits that Manila firms remit to Manila—something that happens to a degree under any distributive strategy—it also means considerable investment in personnel and material pumped into Dagupan by these same firms. I return to this subject later.

How has the spread of coordinated control during the past few decades affected the established channels between Dagupan and Manila? Its impact is potentially devastating because, in contrast to sales penetration, which basically tries to use existing institutions more effectively, coordinated penetration seeks to establish its own channels. This means either that new ones are created where none previously existed, or that traditional institutions are replaced or converted (for example, by turning independent traders into franchisees). Between Manila and Dagupan no such replacement or conversion has taken place on a product-wide scale. So far the typical development has been for integrated channels to appear in relatively novel products (cars, gasoline, and the like) around which no traditional channel had yet crystallized. At the most, independent traders dabbled in these products—like hardware merchants selling appliances before the branching craze in

TABLE 3. *Company Fieldmen Engaged in Provincial Sales Penetration*

Type of trader	Sex Ethnicity	Education	Region of origin
Fieldman			
Filipino N = 20	Male Filipino	College	Dagupan, Manila, north-central Luzon
Chinese N = 5	Male Chinese	Chinese secondary or college	Manila

the fifties and sixties—and none of them was destroyed when an integrated channel eventually came into being.

Compared to sales penetration, which gets along well with little investment in the provinces other than the field staff itself, contractual or ownership penetration requires a considerable outlay. To opt for full channel integration implies a willingness by the Manila company to invest in a building or office space, office equipment, warehouse facilities, transportation, and personnel consisting of more than just a few fieldmen. To put it differently, under sales penetration Dagupan is less tightly tied to Manila and gains less from Manila than under coordinated penetration.

This picture, though basically correct, is an oversimplification. Direct investments by Manila firms are only forthcoming under ownership penetration (branching) or if franchisors hold part of the capital of their provincial dealers (usually 51 percent). Under contractual penetration most investments are typically furnished by local dealers. In this case Manila companies contribute to local wealth only by offering provincial investors potentially lucrative dealerships, thereby enticing capital to flow into buildings and employment. In other words, to say that Manila companies own 19 percent of commercial buildings in Dagupan and employ 15 percent of labor active in trade is only part of the story. Not only do most businesses (in both Dagupan and Manila) lease their store

Parental background	Career
Lower and lower middle class: trade, government, petty landlord, peasant	Five to 10 years in this position; often started after being frustrated in the field in which education was obtained
Lower middle class: small business	Ten to 15 years in this position; often frustrated former businessman

and office space, but also much investment is derived from local franchise holders. It is hard to tell how much is in Manila hands because most contracts are kept tightly under wraps. For this reason I have lumped Manila-controlled branches and franchises together.[11] My guess is that only between one-third and one-half of the investment capital of Manila-dependent establishments in Dagupan is actually derived from Manila.

It is fair to say, therefore, that the investment flow coming from Manila as a result of coordinated penetration has been less than the size and number of Manila-dependent outlets alone indicate. Having said this, it must be noted at the same time that these investments from Manila are highest when they are in greatest demand; that is, they flow most readily when active market penetration is first launched from Manila, and when bottlenecks are most likely to threaten expansion. When they first began to integrate into Dagupan, Manila companies usually raised the initial capital for the high-risk venture. In appliances company after company began its operations by branching, and only later did it turn to franchising. At that time this transformation was less an expression of long-term planning than of immediate competitive pressures; today it is part of a conscious strategy. Newcomers who seek channel integration normally plan to start provincial penetration by opening branches, which they hope to change into dealerships soon.

TABLE 4. *Dagupan Traders Linked to Suppliers via Passive Channels*

Type of trader	Sex Ethnicity	Education	Region of origin
PX goods; Aquino in drugs N = 5	Male and female Filipino	College	Dagupan, Manila

This procedure allows them to be most competitive at the beginning phase of their market penetration—they can order their branches to sell below cost if they deem it necessary—and to overcome the typical lack of enthusiasm felt by entrepreneurs when they face the prospect of taking up a dealership that has yet to prove a success. For newcomers investments pumped into branching serve as seed money to establish a reputation and eventually to attract capable dealers who can take over the financial burden. They might even be willing to incur a considerable loss during the initial period of branching, if they consider it a necessary price to pay in order to begin a successful franchise program.

Aside from generating investments from Manila firms and provincial franchises, coordinated penetration affects investments in other fields too. One of these is finance. Dagupan has witnessed over the past two decades a tremendous growth in the number of financial institutions. Consumer financing is a prerequisite to success in retailing the kind of products Manila-dependent enterprises usually handle, that is, capital-intensive consumer goods. In other words, there is a linkage between these two economic activities. If investments are made in appliance and similar retail outlets, investments in finance companies and banks are likely to follow.[12] Investment in repair service is also stimulated as is that in the insurance business. Other ramifications of coordinated penetration are the proliferation of branches or dealerships in Dagupan's hinterland, and an increase in the number of individuals who find part-time employment by collecting orders for local dealers and branches (tipsters, international salesmen).

Parental background	Career
Lower middle and middle class: profession, government, medium business	Began in the sixties or seventies; often failed in profession trained for; previous experience includes work as fieldman

Of course, the immediate factor encouraging most of these additional investments is the nature of the product, not the nature of the trade channel through which it passes. Similar investments would take place if appliances, cars, and motorcycles were distributed by fieldmen or even by a conservative marketing strategy. However, full channel integration does increase the speed of linked investments. If these products had not been distributed by Manila-dependent outlets, effective demand for them would not have diffused as quickly as it has. Independent traders in the provinces, other factors being equal, tend to have less capital strength to carry large inventories, are less aggressive in marketing, and are less prone to depend on an elaborate network of international salesmen and tipsters than Manila-dependent ones. Some Manila firms boasting a nationwide integrated channel in fact have created their own linked investment. For example, Radiowealth has its own finance company and Philacor owns a network of repair shops.

When Manila companies began in the thirties and again in the fifties to locate their contractual and fully owned offshoots in Dagupan, they were motivated by the city's location, the size of its population, and its wide economic base. These branches and franchises in turn attracted other businesses, either latecomers in the same line, or a growing flood of businesses that complemented the first ones. Today the total amount of linked investment in complementary businesses may even be greater than that pumped into Manila-dependent outlets selling industrial consumer goods. When judging coordinated penetration from Manila into Dagupan (and elsewhere), therefore, it must be kept in mind that the presence of these branches and franchises generates, nay at times requires, other services that have their own linked investments, and so on down the line.

In addition to its effect on the traditional channel and on investments, the spread of coordinated penetration has had an influence on the diffusion of innovations and the composition of entrepreneurs in Dagupan. Recall that the innovative impact of sales penetration has been concentrated on the quality of trade relations between Manila and Dagupan and on the organization of promotions and store layouts. The wide use of coordinated penetration has influenced these features in a similar manner; its main effect, however, has been on the management of local businesses.

Ever since Manila companies began opening franchises and branches in Dagupan on a large scale, Dagupeño traders have been tempted to open their own branches and draw up franchise contracts with merchants in the backwaters of Pangasinan. They have done so with the same contractual stipulations that exist in such arrangements between Dagupan and Manila, and with increasing gusto have pushed coordinated penetration from Dagupan into the city's hinterland. In addition, there have been innovations in the internal management of local businesses. A recurring example is found in Dagupeño franchise dealers who are goaded by their Manila principals into incorporating their businesses. The contract may also stipulate that they keep books and be prepared for external auditing, that they tighten inventory control (only *one* of Dagupan's first-order grocers keeps a stock list), that they assign personnel according to specified function, and so on. In effect, Manila suppliers have pressed their provincial outlets to copy their own operations in Manila. Much of this turns out to be more form than substance; drawing an organizational chart and hanging it on the wall does not in itself change the fact that a business is a family affair. Yet it cannot be denied that a chart may lead to, or reflect, a more rational allocation of responsibilities, and that such practices as keeping written records of cash and inventory flow are more than mere formalities. Branch managers and franchise dealers are often trained in these matters and must comply if the mother company insists. Independent merchants are under no such compulsion and only occasionally have innovations like these been accepted by them.

Let us now turn to the effect coordinated penetration has had on entrepreneurs and others in commerce. Who are the individuals representing Manila companies in provincial franchise stores and branch outlets? Here I am concerned with branch managers and franchise dealers; later I also say a few words about their staff.[13]

If sales penetration has been kind to small and medium-sized Filipino traders of peasant and petty bourgeois extraction, contractual or ownership penetration has helped middle-class and upper-middle-class Filipinos find substantial positions in commerce. It has been a means by which redundant entrants into the professions have been directed into entrepreneurial tasks. Take the case of appliances. Nearly two-thirds of today's 19 store operators in Dagupan came from a relatively well-to-do background, were sent to college in Manila, then struggled but failed to find a permanent position in their chosen careers (law, engineering), and through a friend, an ad in the paper, or other means, found themselves working for a Manila appliance company. A few were lucky and were trained by the firm to assume the position of provincial dealer from the start; more often, especially when the company still had branches, they were hired as salesmen, accountants, or legal advisers, and slowly worked themselves up to be branch managers—only after this experience did they become dealers.

In addition to their middle-class background, another characteristic common to franchise dealers and branch managers is their Filipino ancestry. I already made the point when discussing appliances in Chapter 6 that Chinese prefer to remain independent and that Manila companies prefer Filipinos to manage their regional retail network so as to comply with the Filipinization rules. Join this with the fact that may educated Filipinos see a dealership or the management of a branch representing a prestigious company as the gateway into large-scale trade, and this ethnic preponderance is easily understood. In addition to furthering the interests of middle-class elements in Dagupan and similar communities, therefore, coordinated penetration has enabled Filipinos to play an important role in the distribution of modern consumer durables. The largest and most prestigious Filipino merchants in Dagupan today are encountered in products that are moved through fully integrated channels. These are no mere *sari-sari* store operators. Several have gained full independence, after acquiring the necessary tools while running a Manila-dependent outlet.

The most striking example of this metamorphosis from dependent trader into independent merchant exists in appliances. Recall that the second phase of appliance distribution consisted of Manila companies extending their hold over provincial markets by branching and then franchising. The retail outlets were manned by Filipinos. Then in the third phase the integrated channel disintegrated as a saturated market succumbed to the capital strength of the Chinese. The vertical channel fragmented, and independent appliance traders spread in the provinces. Some were Chinese, but most were Filipinos who during the second phase had worked as franchise dealers or branch managers until their mother companies decided to cut the umbilical cord. By then most of them had learned the ropes and had acquired sufficient capital and access to enough alternative suppliers to make a go of it alone.

The result of the second phase, therefore, does not support the prediction that branching and franchising by large companies will squelch local entrepreneurial initiative. In this case there was nothing to squelch—no traditional channel had specialized in the appliance trade—and most of those heading the dependent outlets were from the Dagupan region. The second phase created a new local entrepreneurial group, which continued to prosper in the trade after the Chinese and others caused the rupture between Manila suppliers and their dependent outlets during the third phase. Coordinated penetration by Manila companies into Dagupan, therefore, provided the foundation out of which the subsequent development of independent Filipino entrepreneurship in appliances grew. Without coordinated penetration, it is probable that local Chinese would dominate the trade far more extensively than they do.

Similar foundations have been built in the distribution of cars, farm equipment, and gasoline. Here, too, local Filipinos have been an important constituent among dealers and branch managers for quite some time. So far, however, the next step (the third phase in appliances) has not taken place; that is, the channel has not been vertically fragmented. In this connection it should be noted that there is no general drive among Filipino branch managers or dealers to become independent from their Manila companies. Some do quite well under an exclusive arrangement—after all, it provides them with a partially captive market (gas dealers excepted)—and they would regret it if fragmentation would take place. The third phase was, to begin with, bemoaned by most appliance dealers who feared intensified competition. Only now do those who survived and flourish relish their independent status. It should also be noted that branches and dealerships serve better in some product lines than others as a training ground for would-be entrepreneurs. Gas stations, as I have already noted, are often operated by wealthy individuals as a sideline and show a high turnover of dealers. It is rare that any of them used this experience to move into new ventures.

Table 5 summarizes the social profile of those who run Manila-dependent trade outlets in Dagupan.[14] Several themes, not all of them shown in the table, are worth pointing out. (a) Parents of the entrepreneurs are decidedly middle class; they are found in the professions, government service, landholding, medium to large businesses, and the like. (b) The class background of branch managers is slightly lower than that of franchise dealers, especially if the dealer manages a large prestigious business, such as a car dealership. (c) Branch managers typically reached their present position by advancing within one company or by being promoted across companies. The career of franchisees is different. If young when they became dealers, they gained this position because of connections their family had with the firm; if older, they used their own capital resources and business reputation to bid for and obtain the dealership. In either case, dealers, in contrast to branch managers, usually entered the business without previous experience in the line. (d) Branch managers and dealers were educated for a quite different occupation from that they ended up filling. After studying law, foreign service, engineering, and the like, in Dagupan or at one of the prestige schools in Manila, they tried their hand in the occupation they were trained for, but soon quit to try more fertile ground. (e) Most operators of Manila-dependent outlets in Dagupan are native to the region. Some had emigrated

TABLE 5. *Dagupan Traders Linked to Suppliers via Coordinated Penetration*

Type of trader	Sex Ethnicity	Education	Region of origin
Appliance Filipino N = 16	Male Filipino	College	Dagupan, Pangasinan, Ilocandia
Chinese N = 3	Male Chinese	College	Dagupan
Automobile N = 8	Male Filipino	College	Dagupan, Manila
Gasoline Retail N = 10	Male and female Filipino	Secondary or college	Dagupan
Wholesale N = 4	Male Chinese	College	Dagupan
Warehouse Branch manager N = 10	Male Filipino	Secondary or college	Manila, north-central Luzon

to Manila to find work and now see themselves as returned. Those not native frequently have a spouse from the region. Managers of warehouse branches are least likely to come from Dagupan. The reasons are simple. They are employees of Manila suppliers who have a free hand in selecting managers—if in-house promotion is practiced, then almost inevitably non-Dagupeños are appointed. There is, moreover, no need for them to be part of the local culture

Parental background	Career
Middle class: profession, landlord	Since early sixties in this line; first employee, then branch manager, then dealer or independent
Upper middle class: family in large traditional business	Since late sixties in this line; began the business after college with parental help
Middle or upper class: landowner, government, profession	Since late sixties; became dealer after being well established in business or profession
Middle class: profession, business	Started late sixties; either after college or as a sideline to another occupation
Upper middle class: family in large traditional business	Began in fifties or sixties; family had previous business connections with gas company
Middle, lower middle class: medium-level profession, petty landlord	Since the fifties after initial period in occupation trained for or in army; since then worked himself up

because they act only on the wholesale level where Tagalog and English usually suffice.

Most of the other employees of Manila-dependent outlets, some 700 of them, are Filipinos from the Dagupan-Pangasinan area with roots in the lower middle to lower class.[15] This distribution is largely the result of contrasting company policies.

There is no rule shared by all Manila firms with respect to the origins and residence of their employees. Some like to staff all but the most menial positions of their provincial outlets with individuals from the home office. Others confine such preferences to upper management (assistant manager, sales manager, perhaps supervisors) to increase the main office's trust in the branch and to minimize the possibility of collusion between branch personnel and local interests (such as kin).

A slightly smaller number of firms follow exactly the opposite policy and hire natives for their outlets whenever they can. This reduces costs (except for training), assures them personnel attuned to the peculiar cultural and economic milieu of the region, and gives the head office a propaganda point against those who criticize their entrance into the local market. With the exception of the franchise holder and temporary aides from the Manila office, the entire staff of Mercury Dagupan is from the Dagupan region, a fact company representatives untiringly like to point out.

Finally there are the franchise dealers (and occasional branch managers) who are not pressured one way or another by their Manila principal about whom to hire. Among them the Filipino tendency to personalize hiring is very explicit; in some instances all employees, down to the janitor and *cargadores*, are kin of the head. Usually the connections are more diversified, though still personalized: newly hired employees are kin, fictive kin, neighbors, or friends of management or of lower-level (usually native) employees already attached to the establishment.[16] This does not exclude the possibility that some individuals (technicians, for example) are hired for their skill alone, but such instances are more the exception than the rule. It is at this point that individuals from a lower-class background have a chance.

The individual with perhaps the poorest opportunity of finding proper employment in the Philippines is the young person who has gone through provincial college, in most cases majoring in commerce or engineering, whose parents are poor and have barely managed to see one or two of their children through the diploma mill. After graduation the big problem presents itself of where to find employment commensurate with the prestige and cost of the degree. Without an upper- or middle-class background this is far from easy to solve, because proper contacts now play a crucial role.

Should some personal link exist between the poor family and personnel of any of the Manila branches or dealerships, the family will use that connection to gain entrance. The main motive of the job seeker is to find stable and acceptable employment as clerk, receptionist, secretary, itinerant salesman, and the like, and not to seek means to become independent in trade, even if the final outcome is just that.

I do not wish to argue that coordinated penetration is unusual in its capacity to facilitate the employment of lower-class Filipinos. The use of vertical personalistic contacts and intermediaries by the poor and not so poor to obtain jobs is endemic in the Philippines, and whatever business a Filipino operates, he will be obliged to employ some who can mobilize preexisting social ties with him. Contractual or ownership penetration is not unique in this capacity, but it is unusual in the composition of openings it has to offer.

The personnel needs of traditional, independent merchants are modest indeed. A first-order grocery in Dagupan needs a handful of sales people, about the same number of stock boys, or *cargadores*, and one or two drivers and salesmen. Full-time bookkeepers are not engaged by any of them. The same is the case in textiles, hardware, school supplies, bazaars, shoe stores, and the like, except that some hire people to do repair work. Manila-dependent outlets of appliances, gasoline, and cars, and branch warehouses of grocery and drug firms have a more elaborate, more sophisticated set of employment requirements. In addition to sales and warehousing personnel, they use receptionists, secretaries, bookkeepers, and general office clerks. The same is true for the businesses induced to come to Dagupan because of their linkage with the distribution of capital-intensive consumer goods, such as finance companies. Openings for *cargadores* and sales people in grocery and similar stores often go begging because they have little appeal for college or high school graduates, even those from a poor family background.[17] These positions are of low status, and there is no way to advance except by becoming independent. By accepting such a position, the graduate would in effect be wasting the investment in college. Manila branches and dealerships in Dagupan may have a greater tendency than others in commerce to import employees; and they may also rely to a greater extent on middle-class recruits than the average independent store, but they also offer a chance for the individuals from lower economic strata to gain promising positions in commerce.

Results

How do the consequences of sales and coordinated penetration of the Dagupan region by Manila companies compare with the usual criticism lodged against the entrance of large-scale commerce into peripheral regions?

   a. *Local trade channels and entrepreneurs undermined.* With respect to trade channels, sales penetration has replaced a traditional marketing strategy (the semipassive mode), without destroying existing channel levels and trade units. Contractual and ownership penetration has created new channels, without eliminating existing trade levels or market strategies. Both strategies have stimulated local innovations in distribution. With respect to entrepreneurs, sales and coordinated penetration encouraged local Filipino talents by providing ready access to Manila and by offering employment opportunities. Coordinated penetration did import entrepreneurs (especially branch managers), but a substantial number of natives also became tied to Manila in this fashion. There is no evidence that either marketing strategy has consolidated the position of "local strangers," or Chinese in Dagupan—if anything the opposite is true.

   b. *Exploitation.* There is a general and a specific side to this question. In general one would expect, according to the dependency model, a drastic impoverishment of the population over time as commercial exploitation from the outside proceeds. There is no evidence, however, that the Dagupan region, or even Pangasinan, is more impoverished now than, say, 25 or 50 years ago. During the recent years of high inflation, per capita real wages for skilled and unskilled labor have declined, but household income has remained steady. The nationwide inflation rate—the main cause of the economic slowdown in the Philippines during the seventies—can hardly be blamed on the Manila-provincial distribution links. Moreover, the expansion of infrastructure in Dagupan and Pangasinan, the rise in the revenue base, continued brisk trade, and vigorous demand in the province and city (at least up to 1978) do not convey a picture of large segments of the population sinking into poverty.[18]

Some may argue that without the trade links with Manila, local development would have been more rapid than it turned out to be. Even though the issue cannot be resolved because it is a historical "if" question, I consider this a naive position. In the first place, nearly all of the economic dynamism existing in the Dagupan region is based on trade with Manila; not much is left without it. In fact, the areas that are least accessible to Manila (the far eastern and western sections of Pangasinan) have always been the poorest. Second, to presume that without commercial links to Manila capital would have been retained in the north and invested in productive capacity, instead of being "sucked out," takes for granted that capital would have formed to the degree it has even without trade with Manila, and that local people would have preferred (or been forced) to invest in local economic ventures. I believe that because of comparative advantage, scale, and differential demand (not to mention innovations), trade with Manila has left the Dagupan region better off than it would have been without these commercial relations.

How do sales and coordinated penetration relate to all these issues? Here I leave the general effect of Manila trade on the Dagupan region and turn to the specific consequences of active marketing strategies. In Dagupan their appearance meant an economic spillover from Manila into the city.

I have no figures on the total flow of investments between the Dagupan region and Manila, but I do know that the adoption of active marketing on the part of Manila firms has resulted in a considerably larger number of direct investments moving from the primary city to the north than under conservative distribution. Furthermore, this has taken place without the destruction of local channels or entrepreneurs. During the expansion of active marketing, local capital and labor resources were mobilized that would otherwise have

lain idle. Real estate and construction have benefited, and
the linkage with banking and other investments contributed
to the capital deepening of service facilities in Dagupan. To
be sure, this has meant a growing amount of value leaving the
Dagupan area for Manila—profits, savings deposited in
Manila banks, remittances of salaries. Without such prospects, however, Manila firms would not have made investments in Dagupan in the first place.

c. *Destruction of local industry.* Dagupan has never been a
major manufacturing center. Over the years it has become
less self-sufficient because a vast array of new goods from
Manila have been made available. Even with this inundation,
however, local production has not been wiped out.[19] To turn
to some approximate figures, it is true that between 1918 and
1970 the number of manufacturing, processing, and repair
establishments declined from 956 (923 of them were cottage
industries) to 270; the number of individuals active in that
sector, however, expanded slightly from 3,127 to 4,676; and
the value of output grew from ₱1.6 million to ₱45 million (or
to ₱9 to 11 million in real terms) (Philippine Islands 1920–
1921; Republic of the Philippines 1974).[20] In other words
(and keeping in mind that the population during the same
period grew from 27,400 to 83,500), the period saw an absolute decline in the number of production units, a relative
decline of workers in this sector, and a slight relative increase
in the value of output.

Sales and coordinated penetration should not be blamed
whenever local products have been displaced by imports.
Long before these marketing strategies came to dominate the
Manila-Dagupan trade, industrial consumer products were
swamping north-central Luzon. The only suggestion that
could be sustained is that active marketing has led some items
to be distributed more effectively and, therefore, more com-
petitively, than if a conservative strategy had been used. The
battle between powdered laundry detergent and provincial
bar soap I described in Chapter 5 (see "PMC, PRC, and
IOF") is a good example. Over the years several Dagupeño
merchants have ventured into medium-scale manufacturing,
and many of them have located their operations in Manila.

They have done so, however, not because active marketing was emanating from that city—in fact, coordinated penetration, through the mechanism of linkage, has promoted repair services and other processing facilities in Dagupan. They did so, instead, because the conditions in Manila have been so very favorable for such investments. Current long-term government efforts to diversify industry away from Manila are, therefore, well placed.

d. *Consumer corruption.* It is impossible to deal with this problem without being patronizing; one point is worth making, though. If potentially dangerous products (such as antibiotics) are distributed, there is no reason to believe that more damage is done by integrated channels than by fragmented ones. The fact that sales and coordinated penetration mean more effective distribution is offset by the greater likelihood that the independent trader will be ignorant about the product and its dangers.

e. *Regional and political autonomy.* To talk of political autonomy with reference to Dagupan makes little sense. It is not a nation, nor has the region enjoyed much political independence from the central government in this century. The thing to note instead is that, whereas Dagupan's political community is very beholden to the political community in Manila (it receives a considerable portion of its revenues and political support from that level), it is not tied as a group to any one commercial interest in Manila. In fact, as often as not, policies of the city mayor and the council have frustrated the wishes of Manila companies and their local representatives. The case of Mercury Drug is only one instance. Others are high license fees, which have driven several car, appliance, and gasoline dealers from the city into neighboring municipalities, and the insistence on taxing company salesmen doing business in Dagupan. Combined with the often not too benevolent treatment of local business interests, these policies lead some Dagupan merchants to wonder whether the city government is aware that commerce is the livelihood of the community.

f. *Embourgeoisement.* What dependency theory under point (a) fears will *not* happen to a periphery because of trade with the center, is here said to be bad when it *does* happen. I have argued that local trade channels in Dagupan have not been destroyed by active penetration from Manila, nor have local entrepreneurs been eliminated. Entrepreneurial activities, in fact, have been stimulated. Anyone who denounces the rise of a commercial bourgeoisie in a peasant setting would thus have a field day in Dagupan.

IN BRIEF, the experience of Dagupan is more congruent with the prediction made by the model of interdependence than with that of dependency theory. Active marketing strategies have streamlined distribution without destroying traditional channel institutions, have undermined an ethnic monopoly among subwholesalers in Dagupan, have made an increasing range of products available to local consumers, have encouraged the development of provincial entrepreneurs without impoverishing the population, and have funneled a considerable amount of investment into useful commercial and ancillary activities. Some time ago Hoselitz (1955:281) noted that colonial capitals at first "exerted an unfavorable influence on the potentialities of economic growth of the surrounding country," but that eventually "the divergent trends of economic development within these cities and outside of them in the wider countryside, had the effect of creating a situation which tended to counteract and eventually turn the parasitic impact of these cities into its opposite." With respect to the commercial sector of Dagupan, active marketing from Manila has served as a generative force of considerable importance for quite some time.

Chapter 9

CONCLUSION

The Organization of Distribution and the Wider Society

TRADE CHANNELS ARE SHAPED just as much by the social system they are part of as by the specific economic conditions from which they emerge. Compare, for example, the complexities of Japanese society and its involuted domestic distribution system with the simpler social institutions typical of America and its more streamlined market channels (Bucklin 1972a; Yoshino 1971). Philippine trade channels are also subject to these influences.

The Philippines represents in many ways a classic case of a medium-level developing country. In per capita GNP and growth rate it occupies a place between the very poor countries of the world and those that are well along the road to development. Despite the rapid expansion of urban population, the mass of the people continues to be rural. Economically the society is divided into two interdependent sectors; one is capital intensive, commercially oriented, and modern, the other labor intensive, traditional, and geared toward subsistence. As in other societies of this kind, the national goal is to transform the latter sector into the former through development. So far the experience has been disappointing. Both sectors are expanding because economic growth is occasioned just as much by rapid population growth as it is by increases in productivity. An extreme economic gap persists between the few wealthy and the many poor, which is only precariously bridged by an emerging middle class. In the words of Myrdal (1970:208), the government is soft; that is, it is liable to corruption and frequently has difficulty implementing policies on the local level. Even martial law did not correct this state of affairs. Kinship ties beyond the nuclear family continue to outweigh other social relations and heavily influence political allegiances and economic commitments. In the cultural sphere, finally, nationalism and Filipino identity are stressed.

Some characteristics of the Philippines are more particular to that society. Extreme dispersal and centralization are its mark. It is geographically scattered over many islands and divided into numerous language groups, while at the same time its cultural, political, and economic core is found in one overwhelming primary city, Manila. The American interlude helped build the country's infrastructure, provided it with an adequate bureaucracy, and supported political democracy and economic entrepreneurship. Filipinos enthusiastically adopted the American commitment to universal education. Today, despite some strain, links with the United States continue to be strong. The important role played by Chinese in the domestic economy is a characteristic the Philippines shares with other Southeast Asian nations, but it has dealt with this phenomenon less painfully than some of the others (Malaysia, Indonesia, Vietnam). Finally, there is the Latin tradition, which has affected the society over centuries through Catholicism and the Spaniards. In some areas of social life this influence has been superficial; in others it has reinforced already existing practices. It has not altered the fact that females play a more active role in public life, especially in the economic sector, than in other developing countries and in most developed ones.[1] On the other hand, the Latin tradition has supported the Filipino preference for bridging social distance by means of personalistic ties of dependence. Patron-client relations, personal factionalism, and the use of intermediaries are prevalent (J. N. Anderson 1970; Landé 1965). Fictive kinship is employed to cement bonds that might otherwise be too fragile, and patron relations with saints ensure access to those with ultimate authority in the Catholic hierarchy.

Trade channels found in the Philippines, specifically the ones described in this study, reflect some of these characteristics. The duality of the economy is mirrored in the coexistence of highly modern and very traditional commercial institutions. Manila-based supply firms face the formidable task of bridging the gap between themselves and thousands of small retail outlets scattered over the islands. The fact that most of the consuming population has few resources helps explain this fragmented retail structure, a feature the Philippines shares with many other developing countries (Wadinambiaratchi 1965). This fragmentation is intensified by an employment situation that encourages people to enter into services for want of alternative occupational opportunities (Dannhaeuser 1977).

Like many other third world countries, the Philippines uses import controls and other protective devices to encourage indigenous development of trade and industry. Since direct intruders from outside the country are held at bay, channel leaders are usually content to consider only local competitors in their strategy formulations. When occasionally competition from the outside is allowed to enter (as Japanese appliances were in the sixties), enormous pressure is put on established channels nurtured in a protected environment. A shared goal to develop also means nationalism. In a multiethnic society like the Philippines this has spawned policies supporting the economic interests of the native majority. Partly because of this, the Filipino role in trade has expanded and the market channels built up by nonnatives have been adjusted accordingly.

Another major factor is the government. The attitude of Filipino and Chinese merchants toward it is usually one of indifference or contempt. Of course, this does not keep traders from manipulating officialdom as much as possible either individually or through trade associations. The corruptibility of the government and its administrative extensions is widely recognized by members of the commercial community, and so also is the ever-present danger of damaging interference by bureaucrats if the correct palms are not sufficiently greased. When, after a period of political turmoil, President Marcos declared martial law in 1972, members of the commercial community welcomed the move. They considered it as providing security and restraining government personnel from harassing them. However, by the second half of the seventies this enthusiasm had worn off because certain developments were not reassuring. For instance, hijacking of commercial trucks and their cargos became a problem on Luzon, and provincial store owners were again expected to give "gifts" to local officials to remain in their good graces. Many of the problems of the old society have reappeared in the new as the novelty of martial law has diminished, and from the point of view of most merchants not much has changed. They continue to stress secrecy in their dealings and endeavor to keep officials at arm's length.

Market channels of industrial consumer goods are also affected by the conditions more peculiar to the Philippines. The country's dispersed geography has led to a nationally dispersed distribution system wherein many large supply firms support regional offices on the major islands that are responsible for distribution in their respective territories. The ethnolinguistic plurality of the country has reinforced this tendency. Manila, though, remains the dominant center and has so far overcome these centrifugal tendencies. Headquarters are invariably located in Manila, and important changes in marketing policy and channel organization with repercussions in far-off provinces emanate from there.

Important also is the remarkable cultural influence of America which is perpetuated by an educational system using English as the medium of instruction. Consumer tastes and what is considered chic are defined by what is current in the United States. Most new ideas about how to organize distribution and what symbols to use in promotions—in fact, the idea of considering marketing as a separate field of inquiry—are American imports. American-inspired active marketing described in this study has made greater inroads in the Philippines than in any other comparable country. This influence also comes to the fore in the enormous drive shared by Filipinos to try their hand at entrepreneurial ventures if given a chance. The time is long past when members of the upper class disdained commercial activities other than real estate.

I have mentioned that females occupy a prominent position in Philippine public life. This carries over into trade. They have always dominated petty commerce in the marketplace and in neighborhood stores. But in this century they have come to hold leading positions in substantial Manila and provincial enterprises to a degree that is unusual internationally. In some lines, such as drugs, they have a virtual monopoly. In contrast to females in most other societies, Filipinas tend not to be content with indirectly influencing the fortunes of businesses they have a stake in through their husbands. In many cases they are the operators and their husbands are bystanders.

Although it corresponds to the current call in America for parity between the sexes, the role females play in product distribution is not an import into the Philippines. It expresses a native preference for allowing equal status to males and females in many matters and for stressing bilaterality in kinship. Kinship remains the major way of organizing social relations for Filipinos. Even those strongly committed to the American way of operating firms have to recognize this fact. No wonder that large Manila concerns often have antinepotism rules, at least in the books. Many, of course, are explicitly organized as family concerns, and medium to small-scale enterprises in virtually all cases rely on kinship. Even during the most radical phase of coordinated marketing in the fifties and sixties provincial appliance branches and franchises embodied kin networks, even if they presented a facade of formal organization. There is a simple explanation for the importance of kinship in business organizations. Preexisting kin ties are the easiest way to ensure trust. The importance of kinship, however, also creates burdens for merchants. It means employing individuals who may not be suited to their jobs, and it means servicing a large number of demands from relatives and *compadres*. Many Filipino traders have discovered that these obligations prevent them from reinvesting their profits. The more successful merchants in Dagupan, therefore, tend to be immigrants.

One of the reasons for the success of the Chinese is that they are less subject to these demands. Their minority status in a hostile environment encourages them to maintain a defensive orientation toward outsiders and to seek help among those belonging to their own ethnic group—hence the large number of Chinese trade and surname associations. Also their more lineally oriented kinship system is less inclusive than the bilateral system of the Filipinos. Over the years Filipinos have learned from them and from the Chinese way of doing business. Many now delegate authority in their businesses only to immediate family members. This limits expansion, but avoids embezzlement. Some have also adopted the Chinese reluctance to become contractually dependent upon one Manila supplier unless they are given more than token autonomy in operating their business. By thus emulating those who are successful, Filipinos have entered nearly all trade positions along the Manila-Dagupan channel, and this they accomplished without riots or bloodshed. Moderate and steady government pressure also helped, as well as new ideas about distribution (such as branching) which were implemented by channel leaders in the fifties and sixties. Even though some of these innovations were only temporary, they broke open conservative channels and their ethnically exclusive enclaves.

Despite a system of stratification characterized by a small upper crust, a struggling middle class, and a mass of urban and rural poor, Filipinos have shown a considerable capacity to establish personal connections that crosscut these divisions. I have mentioned patron-client relations, fictive kinship, personal factionalism, and the wide use of personal intermediaries. Vertical trade relations are also often formed according to these principles (cf. Soriano and Nehrt 1976:97). Between large wholesale merchants in the provinces and their small retail customers, personalized long-term contacts that reach down to include consumers are common. The *suki* bond is an expression of this. Many Manila suppliers continue this tradition by using a semipassive marketing strategy or a loose dealership system. Even when the market is nationwide and they are forced to establish deep forms of penetration, many suppliers cling to the notion that there ought to be a personal touch between themselves and their provincial customers. This is made all the more difficult by the need to locate the head office in Manila and to service all major islands from there. The most readily available solution is to employ fieldmen and use them as intermediaries. Personable, gregarious, and hard-working salesmen who are familiar with local dialects and who get along with customers (remember Alex Muñoz and Fred Lo in Chapter 5) are an important component for many firms in keeping communication open and personal between the upper and lower channel levels. Even distributors relying on coordinated penetraton recognize this. This is one of the reasons they insist on personal house-to-house selling of appliances or similar products by salesmen attached to their branches or franchises. Here active marketing imported from the United States and the realities of Philippine society are inextricably intertwined.

Channel Evolution

Throughout this study the degree to which the supply side in Manila controls the outlet side below has been considered the key variable. Conservative and active marketing strategies from Manila into the provinces engender what I regard as the major means of product distribution: passive distribution, semipassive distribution, sales penetration, and contractual or ownership penetration.[2] Each has features unique to itself, others that it shares with the rest. Moreover, product lines and traders are only rarely locked entirely into one or the other of these modes without participating at least nominally in the others. These strategies often occur simultaneously (for example, sales and contractual penetration) and change with the trade level (using branches for wholesaling and dealers for retailing). Despite this overlap, the classification reflects reality, it is useful for analytical and comparative purposes, and it emphasizes strategic behavior so important in entrepreneurship. Moreover, it captures the process of channel evolution.

Virtually all models of channel evolution contain two assumptions: as an economy grows the scale of trade establishments will expand and vertical channel integration will spread. This, indeed, is happening in Europe, Japan, and other middle-range industrial countries, and has been happening in the United States for a long time. A movememt toward larger scale and integration is also apparent in developing countries with open economies, including the Philippines.[3] There trade units handling industrial consumer goods have grown in size since the prewar period, and, more important for our purpose, an increasing portion of distribution is subject to active marketing.

These general developments have taken on four characteristics specific to Manila and Dagupan. First, vertical channel integration has proceeded downward from Manila into the province. Second, by far the most successful kind of downward control has been sales penetration. It enables modern marketing techniques to interact with traditional trade institutions without destroying them, and it integrates well with the Filipino tendency to personalize trade relations. Third, only occasionally has channel integration reached successfully the logical end of contractual and ownership penetra-

tion. In a few product lines (gasoline, for example) such development has been total; in many others only a milder form of integration has been possible (sales penetration in groceries); and in
others tight integration, once achieved, proved fragile and eventually broke down (appliances). Finally, whenever channel evolution proceeded in the expected direction in the Philippines it was
the result not only of changing economic circumstances, but also of
channel leaders imposing an imported marketing ideology upon
the Philippine condition. In some cases these efforts have been
largely frustrated (for example, textiles and appliances), bespeak-
ing the fact that a marketing ideology adapted to conditions prevailing in mature consumer economies may be only partially work-
able in a setting like the Philippines.

This last point hardly invalidates the model of channel development derived from the Western industrial societies. The model has
held up well in the Western experience, and it is likely to do so also
in developing countries as long as scalar economies obtain, demand expands, and dominant channel members share an ideology
congruent with the model. But the case of Manila-Dagupan does
show that the operation of each type of channel must be judged in
relation to local conditions before it is pronounced to be the wave
of the future.

What are the reasons that downward penetration of Manila
firms has been more successful in some products than in others?
What general points can be derived from the Manila-Dagupan
case? To answer this in a summary fashion, I am assuming that the
desire by Manila entrepreneurs to expand their control over product distribution, whether they are in textiles, appliances, or any
other line, is the same. What differs are the factors encouraging or
discouraging the realization of this goal.

Coordinated penetration flourishes where nontraditional capital-intensive products lacking an established channel are pushed
by multinational and large local corporations (as in cars). It fails
where suppliers overextend their distribution network in a restricted market and have to rely on those outlets (mainly Chinese) who
prefer more flexibility (as in appliances). These outlets, of course,
may eventually impose their own program of downward integration. Sales penetration prevails where aggressive marketing has
been accepted by Manila firms (largely because of overseas ex-

amples) under conditions of distributing mass consumer items among traditional and dispersed retail customers (as in groceries). The semipassive strategy is the norm where products are not standardized and where a traditional intermediary trade level financially controls suppliers and outlets in the context of defensive ethnic identity among merchants (as in textiles). Here multinational interests are weaker than in the other cases. Passive marketing, finally, is very widespread, but dominates no major product line. It flourishes under conditions of rapidly changing products, trade contacts, or channel members.

It goes without saying that this brief statement ignores the wider historical context of the Philippine society and its relation to the outside world. I have dealt with these broad influences in Chapters 2 and 3, and to recount them here would go beyond the bounds of this summary. The following scheme gives a more detailed exposition of the proximate causes for the presence of different channel types between center and periphery.

1. Instances in which conservative distribution has retained an important position result from:
    a. The presence of a mature channel between Manila and the provinces that specialized in the product before new notions of marketing were introduced.
    b. Financial dependence of large producers and provincial merchants upon traditional distributors in Manila.
    c. Ethnic identity between members of different channel levels and defensive orientation to outsiders resulting in personalism, flexible trade terms, and secretiveness.
    d. Variable quality of the product, leading buyers to inspect the items personally before placing orders.

Points a to d apply to the semipassive marketing strategy. The passive strategy is stimulated by:

    e. Frequent changes in products and participants, causing constant shifts in commercial contacts.
2. Instances in which sales penetration has become the dominant means of market penetration result from:
    a. Same as 1a.

b. A tenuous financial hold by traditional trade houses over producers or importers and provincial outlets.
   c. A wide product range, making brand-exclusive retail outlets impractical; product consists of standardized mass consumer goods.
   d. Oligopolistic pressures for companies to follow those who first introduced marketing innovations.
   e. Participation of multinationals in production and distribution directly or through licensees.
3. Instances in which contractual or ownership penetration has evolved result from:
   a. The absence of a mature channel between Manila and the provinces that specialized in the product before new notions of marketing were introduced.
   b. The product is standardized so that inspection need not precede orders; it is capital intensive, requiring financing of retailers and consumers; it needs repair service; it lends itself to easy brand identity.
   c. Same as 2d and 2e.
4. Instances in which coordinated penetration has broken down into more conservative marketing procedures result from:
   a. A weakened position of multinational and national suppliers because of a market glutted by imports and overproduction.
   b. Competitive pressures forcing suppliers into overly costly branching and financing.
   c. Refusal of newcomers (Japanese, importers) to stick to a brand-exclusive retail network.
   d. Diminished competitive advantage of maintaining branches and dealerships after competitors have copied this strategy.
   e. Financially strong merchants (Chinese), who entice producers into selling to them and who sell to whomever can buy.

Channel Congruence

The typology of market systems used in this study is sensitive not just to channel evolution, but to the organizational congruence between upper and lower channel levels. Enterprises standing in vertical trade relations with one another may or may not be organized in a similar manner. That is, they are congruent or not depending on the degree to which the styles of their respective organizations overlap. I use the work "styles" here because the correspondence is at best rough. Manila suppliers in nearly all cases are larger and have a more elaborate internal division of labor than the firms they supply in the provinces, and they perform different functions (production, wholesaling) from their customers (subwholesaling, retailing). Yet in their organizational style they can be quite similar.

Both may be organized according to the book so that the assignment of tasks, staff and line responsibilities, internal control, and the flow of capital are handled in a formal fashion. In this sense Mercury Drug Corporation and its franchises in Dagupan are congruent, as are Manila appliance suppliers and their provincial branch outlets. Alternatively, both the supplier and the provincial customers may be organized according to an informal and more traditional style. Here the shared norms consist of a limited division of labor, individuals switching from one task to another, and a strong centralization of authority. This style of organization is also characterized by low differentiation between household and firm, domination of kinship as an organizing principle, primitive inventory and financial controls, and premises that remind one more of stores in Tondo and Binondo than gleaming offices in Makati. Textile distribution is a good example.

Finally there may be a lack of congruence or no significant overlap between organizations on either end of the channel. This condition is widespread in the Philippines owing to the dualistic nature of the country's economy. The relationship between noncongruent channel ends can be either contradictory or complementary. It is contradictory if the demands of one level cannot be satisfied by the other because of structural limitations. The often repeated experience of new supermarkets in developing settings, including the Philippines, finding it virtually impossible to be adequately supplied with fresh produce because of a fragmented supply side among peasants, is a classic illustration of such contradiction (Guerin 1964). Contradictory noncongruence is also common where a supplier finds the traditional outlets inadequate for his needs. They do not order enough or they do not allow the supplier sufficient control over distribution. This can lead to change. The supplier may find it to his advantage to replace the traditional outlets with those of his own making, which is about to happen in Mercury Drug's contractual penetration of the provinces. Another possibility is for Manila firms to open provincial warehouse branches and to start deep sales penetration on their own account. At such points of stress the process of channel evolution becomes activated.

The relation between noncongruent channel levels can also be complementary. This is exemplified by large manufacturing firms in Japan that depend successfully on cottage industry for their inputs (Dore 1973:302–303). In the trade between Manila and Dagupan the typical form complementary noncongruence takes is for large Manila producers and trade houses to deal with small and informally organized outlets in the provinces. *Sari-sari* stores buying directly from such giants as San Miguel or Procter and Gamble is an example.

Looking at the Manila-Dagupan trade axis from the perspective of congruence three points stand out:

a. In the distribution of industrial consumer goods noncongruence is confined to situations in which the Manila supplier is large and organized according to modern management procedures, whereas the provincial outlet is not. I do not know of any product line in which the opposite is true.

b. There is a consistent association between the type of congruence existing in a channel and the nature of the market strategy. If firms on the (Manila) supply and (provincial) outlet ends are modern, then it is likely that coordinated penetration is, or once was, important. This is true in gasoline, automobiles, farm machines, and appliances. High congruence between traditionally organized trade units on both channel ends implies a conservative distributive strategy on the supply side. The semipassive mode in textiles shows this best. In those instances, finally, in which congruence is absent, an elaborate system of sales penetration from Manila appears. The itinerant sales force serves to bridge the gap between large and sophisticated suppliers and small, informal, and dispersed buyers and thereby ameliorates a potentially contradictory relation.

c. The degree of congruence between the channel ends is principally the making of Manila suppliers. This is obvious with respect to contractual or ownership penetration. Here Manila firms have molded the outlets in their own image and created businesses in the provinces that are microreplicas of themselves. To put it in more dynamic terms, once noncongruence turns contradictory it is usually the Manila end that rectifies the situation by creating its own subwholesale and retail level in the provinces through franchising or branching. Where Manila suppliers have adopted less active strategies they have also had less of a hand in constructing provincial outlets; however, their influence under these conditions has by no means been negligible. In textiles, where the semipassive strategy is the order of the day, the supply side did not create the informally organized and Chinese-controlled subwholesale level in Dagupan, but it has ensured the survival of these traders by giving them preferential treatment. Nor did sales penetration, so widely encountered in the grocery, drug, and hardware trades, create the retail institutions that handle these products in the provinces. Chinese grocery and hardware stores, Filipino pharmacies, and neighborhood stores existed long before sales penetration became a popular technique. What it has done is to enhance the position of some of these retail establishments (*sari-sari* stores, for example) and undermine that of others (first-order grocers).

Channel Competition, Change, and Development

The previous chapter discussed the repercussions of Manila-derived active marketing in the Dagupan trade area. Can anything be said about the consequences of conservative marketing in these areas? What does semipassive distribution in textiles and related products imply for Dagupan? The picture is mixed. On the one hand, it means that an ethnic minority holds sway in important sectors of the Manila-Dagupan trade. Personalized terms with all the implications for corruption and unpredictability are maintained. It means that a paranoid concern about controlling information supersedes the need to disseminate it so that those without direct access to Manila are left ignorant about prices, margins, and quality. On the other hand, semipassive distribution allows credit extensions to flow from Manila to Dagupan that are far more generous than under active penetration, even if not as evenly distributed as one might wish. It encourages low margins because trade units are run as unpretentious family affairs. And a direct link with Divisoria is maintained for products that otherwise would find their way into Dagupan through an additional trade level. The truly passive strategy, in turn, serves as a catalyst, enabling novel products to reach Dagupan and adventurous traders to enter the field. This leads to an important point. The conservative strategy offers competition to sales and coordinated penetration in the same way that the latter two compete with one another.

Experience has shown that over time Manila suppliers handling the same products and following the same type of channel strategy settle into some kind of accommodation with one another. Not really a cartel, this nevertheless comes close to a live and let live agreement. This accommodation is disrupted by merchants who are tied to provincial outlets through market strategies different from the prevailing one. Each type of channel has its own drive toward expansion, which usually prevents equilibrium from emerging until one or another type becomes dominant in a product line—hence the considerable instability and competition in appliances compared to conditions in textiles and gasoline.

Even if no other favorable point can be raised in defense of conservative (or any other) distributive strategy, it can be argued that it serves a vital role in keeping Manila suppliers and their local dependent outlets alert. Conservative marketing has kept at bay extreme vertical integration with its insistence on elaborate retail organizations and brand monopoly. Active marketing has proved a check on semipassive distribution with its ethnic hierarchy and love for secrecy.

As long as such competition between channels persists, change will be intrinsic to the distributive trade between Manila and Dagupan. The present condition in appliances is in considerable flux, and a new form of market penetration, perhaps warehouse and repair-service branches, may be just around the corner. Sales penetration, though dominant and stable in several products, is challenged in drugs by Mercury; and who knows when any of the supermarket chains in Manila may decide to break out of GMA into the northern provinces. The conservative channel in textiles and related lines is under constant attack by those attempting to bridge the gap between mill and consumers. Full integration, finally, especially in automobiles, is potentially subject to the forces that undermined channel integration in appliances. The picture is bound to change, and there are many surprises to come.

It has long been recognized that the process of economic development is partly dependent on the capacity of product channels to adjust to changing circumstances (Belshaw 1965:120–122; Moyer 1972:3–12; Slater 1974). Competition between channels guarantees that flexibility and innovations in distribution persist. It is a positive sign, therefore, that such competition exists in the Philippines.

NOTES

Chapter 2

1. Comparable figures are not available for the teens.

2. Cabanatuan in Neuva Ecija took over this function from Dagupan, and an increasing portion of the rice produced in Pangasinan began to be consumed by its own residents (*ACCJ* July 1928).

3. Occasionally Chinese trade associations in Manila hired individuals to manage a member's store in Dagupan because the owner was incapacitated or indebted to the association. This practice persists today.

Chapter 3

1. The evidence is somewhat ambiguous for the period under consideration. Generally speaking, economic conditions improved for the population up to the early to mid-seventies and has stagnated since then. Between 1956 and 1971 real family and individual incomes increased at an average rate of 3 percent annually (International Labour Office 1974:10; Rodgers, Hopkins, and Wéry 1978:44–45). During the same period the distribution of wealth became more egalitarian in urban areas and less egalitarian in rural ones (World Bank 1976:95). Between 1965 and 1973 real wages declined from an index of 100 to 90 for skilled and to 83 for unskilled labor (Development Academy of the Philippines 1976), while family income increased 44 percent and the peso declined 43 percent from 1971 to 1975 (*BD* February 27, 1976; cf. Baldwin 1975:149).

More recent figures are from the *FEER* (June 1 and 29, 1979). Between 1971 and 1975 the distribution of wealth became less egalitarian nationally, between 1975 and 1978 the index of real money wages for skilled labor went up from 73 to 76 and for unskilled down from 73 to 68, and under martial law the average inflation rate in the Philippines was 15 percent annually. Between 1971 and 1975 the incidence of poverty increased from 38 percent to 45 percent of the population nationwide; since then it has probably declined to 1971 levels owing to improved agricultural output (*FEER* March 27, 1981). Up to 1962 the official exchange rate was pegged at ₱2 to $1. From 1962 to 1969 it stood at ₱3.90 to $1. Since 1970 it has been allowed to float, and the rate reached ₱7.40 to $1 in 1976.

2. The decision by overseas firms to start manufacturing in the Philippines probably would have been made even if government pressure had been absent. If the past market strategy of multinationals throughout the world is traced, it becomes clear that they follow a particular sequence in penetrating national markets. After a period of exporting to a target country, the typical overseas company gains greater control over foreign distribution by licensing a local distributor to handle its products exclusively. Eventually the distributor is replaced by a branch or subsidiary of the overseas principal. Finally, the firm licenses the production of its goods in the overseas market or moves into production itself (Wilkins 1970:78; see also Ayal and Zif 1979).

3. Since 1974 there has been a Cash and Carry outlet in Manila offering products at advantageous terms to member retailers and institutions. It is under Chinese control and a sister company of Unimart and Makati Supermarket.

4. See Palanca (1977) on the current economic role of the Chinese in the Philippine economy and the difficulty in collecting data about ethnic, rather than alien, Chinese.

5. The city government has the same negative attitude toward hawkers as administrators in Manila and Baguio (see McGee and Yeung 1977).

6. The turnover figures must be regarded with caution since underreporting is common. They are derived from license lists and personal observations by the author. In 1974, 57 commercial businesses were operated by alien Chinese in Dagupan with a turnover of ₱5 million annually.

7. Nationally, alien Chinese control 3.7 percent of all registered corporations. Palanca identifies 227 of the 1,000 largest corporations in 1973 as Chinese, and most of them are in the upper middle size category (1977:85–88).

Chapter 4

1. As used in this study the concepts "passive," "semipassive," "conservative," and "active" do not have a psychological dimension. They simply stand for behavioral patterns that manifest themselves in different marketing strategies and channel organizations.

2. This contravenes company policy, but so far companies have been unable to eliminate this practice.

3. In the late seventies many vendors turned back to buying from subwholesalers in Dagupan.

4. According to the classification used by the Chinese merchants in Dagupan, the textile channel contains the following specialists: first-degree traders (wholesalers; sell by the bale and allow no color selection to customers); second-degree traders (wholesalers; cut up bales and allow color and pattern selection); third-degree traders (wholesalers and retailers in the provinces; often also in tailoring); fourth-degree traders (retailers only).

5. There are "six large distributors that dominate distribution of textiles in the Philippines. One manufacturer estimates that three distributors account for sales of almost 200 million yards a year" (Ronquillo 1972:41). This quote refers to 1966, but conditions have not changed substantially since.

6. Frank Lynch calls it "family-centralism" (Lynch et al. 1978:7–11).

7. Litton is the only mill that has a distributor in the north, a Chinese in Pampanga.

8. On this level the credit line is usually pegged between ₱500 and ₱5,000.

9. The same can be said for hawkers and peddlers, but all of them operate on a small scale.

Chapter 5

1. Fieldmen have to pay a fixed annual license fee to the city government, and therefore they are registered.

2. In addition to company salesmen, there are independent or international salesmen. They are also known as "ten-percenters." Each does business on behalf of several companies, and their agreement with suppliers entails the right to a commission (usually 10 percent) for orders they book. No other obligation exists, including salary. Despite the fact that they work by means of impermanent opportunity transactions, their

contribution to the total trade volume between Manila and Dagupan is significant. Independent salesmen are most prevalent in the hardware and construction, appliance, and motor vehicle trade, and I turn to them when discussing contractual penetration in Chapter 6.

3. For a more detailed presentation of the grocery retail structure in Dagupan see Dannhaeuser (1977).

4. I use the term "loose" to distinguish this setup from the dealership system found under exclusive franchises.

5. Marketing costs for companies serving their retail market directly often amount to 25–30 percent of sales and more (Economic Development Foundation n.d.:42).

6. Ice cream, milk (Magnolia brand), and chemical fertilizers are some of the other commodities the company produces. The account in the text is taken in part from the San Miguel annual reports for 1948 to 1976.

7. Most Chinese in the Philippines are Hokkienese. Cantonese are a minority, often engaged in the processing and trade of bakery goods.

8. Drugstores in the Philippines are of the European variety. Like the *Apotheke* in Germany or *farmacia* in Spain, they specialize only in pharmaceuticals.

9. Some general stores in the remoter areas are licensed by the Food and Drug Administration to carry prescription drugs without an attending pharmacist. These outlets are called Household Remedies Stores.

10. Ethical pharmaceuticals are highly technical, and special personnel is needed to present their benefits and proper use to customers. To convince doctors or hospital staff that a product is worth prescribing, salesmen of a different calibre from those used in the ordinary trade with drugstore merchants are needed. Some call any salesman who handles drugs a detail man. It is prestigious to be known as such, and the temptation exists to stretch the meaning of this term. I am using the term in its original restricted meaning to refer to those who explain and promote new drugs to the medical profession.

11. Metro and Pharma also manufacture for others under license. Aside from drugs, Metro handles cosmetics and veterinarians' supplies; Pharma, agricultural chemicals.

12. Occasionally companies will label a product as ethical for marketing purposes. Only after its mystique with the public has been lost do they reclassify it as over the counter (Hagey 1979:11–12).

13. Detail men and doctors often collude. For example, they might cooperate in buying land from patients who would otherwise not have the means to pay.

Chapter 6

1. "Coordinated" distribution is taken from McCammon and Bates (1967:287). However, while they also subsume "administrative" marketing systems under the term (that is, channels integrated by virtue of one channel member dominating others because of its size or other leadership qualities), I use it only to mean ownership or contractual penetration. I place informal administrative strategies under semipassive marketing.

2. Passages of the section on home appliances were previously published in Dannhaeuser (1979; 1981b).

3. During this difficult period Ysmael Steel lost its vice president of marketing. He established the Philippine Appliance Corporation (Philacor) which became the exclusive distributor for Westinghouse. A large number of Ysmael branch managers joined the new company because of their loyalty to the former vice president and because they thereby became dealers.

4. One of the exceptions was Sun Brothers, which was run by Chinese and in the mid-fifties handled Admiral appliances for Ysmael Steel.

5. SEARS stands for Safeway Electronics, Appliances and Refrigeration Sales, and the product is handled by a subsidiary of DRB: DRB-SEARS Corporation. In 1976 Westinghouse sold its share in Philacor.

6. The same point is made by *FEER* (June 22, 1979:71): "Matsushita has brought its company style lock, stock and barrel to the Philippines—from daily morning meetings, company trips and athletic meets, to small wedding parties for employees."

7. An increasing number of suppliers rely on nonexclusive dealers and ownership penetration via a network of repair shops in the provinces for use by both dealers and consumers. Whether consciously nor not, these companies repeat a development that has taken place in the United States. Frustrated in their effort to maintain exclusive retail chains, appliance manufacturers in the fifties and sixties established repair branches in the major urban areas of the States.

Chapter 7

1. Some early car assemblers and distributors (for example, Yutivo and Sons) were Chinese controlled. They helped other Chinese to enter the trade downstream.

2. It is no accident that a few car dealers in the Philippines have recently added appliances to the products they handle.

3. The big three (Firestone, Goodyear, and Goodrich) have branch warehouses and retread plants in the provinces. These sell to regional distributors (usually Chinese hardware or auto supply merchants) who supply nonexclusive dealers as well as consumers.

4. Unfortunately I do not know the details of the eventual outcome of this dispute.

5. Farm machinery, tire, and motorcycle distribution is positioned between the loose dealership system encountered under sales penetration and coordinated penetration. Manila suppliers of these products maintain a mixture of provincial branch warehouses and exclusive franchises that serve nonexclusive dealers as well as consumers. *Gasul*, or cooking gas, is in a similar in-between category. The major gas companies and what are called "resellers" (independent wholesalers who sell this gas under their own brand name) move the product to franchised wholesaler-retailers whose responsibility it is to lease the canisters and sell the gas to subdealers and consuming households or businesses in a given territory. What makes this setup unusual is that the dealers and subdealers are brand, but not product exclusive; that is, most are merchants in their own right, whether of appliances, gasoline, or groceries, and for them the dealership is at most an important sideline.

6. In Dagupan only one store specializes in photo equipment. Other photo dealers also handle paper products and school supplies.

7. Company sales representatives were tired of playing the "grovel or you won't get an order" game with local drugstore operators in the city (Hagey 1979:16).

Chapter 8

1. This chapter is an expanded version of Dannhaeuser (1981a; 1981c).

2. The following points are not designed to describe the dependency position in its entirety; they are merely selected abstractions of the more extreme manifestations of this position. Examples of the more extreme formulations include Bacha (1978), Barnet and Müller (1974), Caperaso (1978), Frank (1969), Kahn (1978), Santos (1970), and Sau (1978). Some attempts have been made to apply this position to the Philippines (Esperitu 1977). European colonialism is blamed for one of the more pernicious forms of dependence, because it is said to have created conditions of underdevelopment in today's third world countries (Frank 1978). Recently several cross-country studies have shown some statistical association between dependence on multinational firms and low economic

income among third world countries (Bornschier 1980; Evans and Timberlake 1980; Mahler 1980). Although much of the dependency argument concerns itself with international trade, the position can also be applied to intracountry commercial relations (see, for example, Smith 1978).

3. The use of the term "embourgeoisement" in this context is taken from Weinberg and Williams (1980).

4. The interdependence model is also known as the "growth stimulus" model (Partridge 1979:506; see Mingst 1980 for a different connotation of interdependence from that used in this study). There is a vast literature in favor of open interregional trade—neoclassical economics is founded on the notion that the division of labor and exchange through competition benefit most—but it is not written specifically as a counter to the dependency literature. A selection of works that come close to doing so includes Bauer (1976), Friedman and Friedman (1980:38–54), Galbraith (1978), Helfgott (1973), H. G. Johnson (1977), Samuelson (1973:668–680), and Vernon (1977). Some also show that the impact of colonialism on peripheral countries in many cases was not as negative as *dependistas* argue (Fieldhouse 1966; Lewis 1978; Potter 1968). Increasing maturity of the dependency debate is reflected in the recent appearance of studies arguing that both sides contain valid points (see, for example, Schatz 1981).

5. Strictly speaking, of the total value of goods, 62 percent, or ₱107 million, is accounted for by sales penetration from Manila. For convenience I classify in the text warehouse branches (such as those of Pepsi, Cheng Ban Yek, and Metro) as facilities connected with coordinated penetration. After all, they are owned by Manila companies. Actually, though, products moving through them do so via sales penetration. This marketing stragety, therefore, is even more important than appears in the text.

6. These turnover figures are derived from the city license records for fiscal 1974. They underreport the true value of sales, but give a good idea of the relative importance of each economic sector. The same is true of the peso value of buildings.

7. The summary statements in Tables 1 to 5 are based on the characteristics shared by the majority of the cases in each category. The numbers in most categories represent samples; for first-order grocery traders, appliance and automobile dealers, gasoline wholesalers, and textile wholesaler-retailers, they represent censuses.

8. Nor does this include *sari-sari* store operators, market vendors, or hawkers. A. B. Bennett found that 20 percent of Filipino managers employed in Manila companies (N = 200) began their careers as sales-

men. Unfortunately it is not clear what portion of them had been field-men (1971:132).

9. If warehouse branches are excluded, the average turnover of a Manila-dependent outlet is ₱700,000.

10. Average pay is estimated at ₱400 a month.

11. I limit myself here to franchises and branches controlled from GMA.

12. The linkage, of course, could also run in the opposite direction, as when existing financial institutions encourage the opening of appliance outlets. On the concept of linkage see Hirschman (1958).

13. The profile of dealer coordinators closely resembles that of ordinary company salesmen.

14. Independent Chinese and Filipino appliance traders are included in this table because of their close historical association with integrated channels.

15. "Lower middle to lower class" refers here to landowning and tenant peasants, petty officials and clerks, market stall vendors, and the like. I have employment data for 18 Manila-dependent businesses and 30 independent ones (vendors and *sari-sari* operators are not included). The former cover 175 employees, the latter 96. Respectively 71 and 87 percent are native to Dagupan or Pangasinan, and 65 and 69 percent of lower-middle- and lower-class extraction.

16. In large Manila firms most intracompany kin links of proprietors are with management (Vicente-Wiley 1979:474). A study of Shellane (cooking gas) dealers reports, "Because they believe that relatives have some sort of obligational indebtedness known as 'may malasaki' [to have deep concern] and could, therefore, be relied on to work hard and honestly," most dealers employ relatives (Gochoco 1971:27).

17. Employment agencies thrive on placing girls from the Visayas in Dagupan as housemaids or store clerks among the Chinese.

18. The lowest incidence of rural and urban poverty in the Philippines (after GMA) is found in central Luzon, including Pangasinan (*FEER* March 27, 1981). See also Aquino (1975:42) and Magdalena (1977:76).

19. Some local products were eliminated or are now produced in very small quantities because of imports: *calesas* and *caretelas* (two-wheeled buggies), wooden shoes, bar soap, Calasiao hats (straw hats). These items could not withstand the motorized tricycle, *chenilas* (Japanese thongs), detergents, and, concerning hats, changes in international fashions. The relative importance of other local products has been eroded, but not eliminated, by imports: pottery, *nipa* wine, traditional construction material (such as shell windows), tinware, ice, leather, lime, and copra oil. Production of several traditional items continues to flour-

ish: cheap as well as expensive traditional furniture, *bijon* (rice noodles), *bolo* knives, bakery products, *banka* (dugout) and motor boats, *bagoong* (fermented fish paste), *bocayo* (coconut candy), and tailoring. Production and processing of certain items have appeared only recently, some of them because of new imports: saw milling; hollow block and tile production; modern furniture; machine tool shops; cars, motorcycle, and home appliance repair; plastic shoes; lamination; jeepney assembly; tricycle sidecar assembly; sugar and *gaw-gaw* (starch) repacking.

20. These figures have to be regarded with caution. The collection and classification of data differed between the 1918 and the 1970 censuses. I compute the value of the 1974 peso at between 20 and 25 percent of its value in 1918.

Chapter 9

1. The role of women in local politics seems to be more subdued (Neher 1980).

2. This differs from geographically oriented market studies which tend to stress the number of trade levels between producers and consumers and the regional reach of commercial contacts (see, for example, Berry 1967; E. A. G. Johnson 1970; Smith 1976).

3. See, for example, D. Anderson (1970), Andrade (1976), Beals (1975:181), Glade et al. (1970), Goldman (1974), Grub and Miele (1969:79), and Mehta (1973:203–214). Exceptions exist. Recall the breakup of the large dealerships in the automobile line that has taken place in the Philippines since World War II. But even here individual retail outlets are considerably larger today than they were 30 or 40 years ago.

BIBLIOGRAPHY

Adelman, Irma, and Morris, C. T.
  1973 *Economic Growth and Social Equity in Developing Coun-
        tries.* Stanford: Stanford University Press.
Amyot, Jacques, S.J.
  1973 *The Manila Chinese. Familism in the Philippine Environ-
        ment.* Institute of Philippine Culture, monograph 2. Quezon
        City: Ateneo de Manila University Press.
Anderson, Dole
  1970 *Marketing and Development. The Thailand Experience.* East
        Lansing: Institute for International Business and Economic
        Development Studies, Michigan State University.
Anderson, James N.
  1969 Buy-and-sell and economic personalism: Foundations for
        Philippine entrepreneurship. *Asian Survey* 69:641–668.
  1970 Personal strategies, intermediation, networks, and trans-
        actionally generated social organization in the Philippines.
        Paper read at the annual meeting of the American Anthro-
        pological Association, November 1970, San Diego.
Andrade, Rodolfo P.
  1976 Mass retailing among low-income consumers in Guatemala
        City. In *Marketing Systems for Developing Countries,* ed. D.
        Izraeli, D. N. Izraeli, and F. Meissner, pp. 172–179. To-
        ronto: John Wiley and Sons.
Aquino, B. A.
  1975 Dimensions of development in Philippine provinces, 1970.
        Journal of Public Administration 19:15–45.

Ayal, I., and Zif, J.
   1979   Market expansion strategies in multinational marketing.
           Journal of Marketing 43:84–94.
Bacha, Edmar L.
   1978   An interpretation of unequal exchange from Prebisch-Singer
           to Emmanuel. *Journal of Development Economics*
           5:318–330.
Baldwin, Robert E.
   1975   *Foreign Trade Regimes and Economic Development: The
           Philippines.* New York: National Bureau of Economic Re-
           search.
Banguis, T. C.
   1965   The marketing operations of Radiowealth Trading Corpora-
           tion. B.A. thesis, University of the Philippines.
Barnet, Richard J., and Müller, Ronald E.
   1974   *Global Reach. The Power of the Multinational Corporation.*
           New York: Simon and Schuster.
Barth, Frederick
   1966   *Models of Social Organization.* London: Royal Anthropo-
           logical Institute.
Bauer, P. T.
   1976   *Dissent and Development.* London: Weidenfeld and
           Nicolson.
Beals, Ralph
   1975   *The Peasant Marketing System of Oaxaca, Mexico.* Berkeley:
           University of California Press.
Bellairs, Edgar G.
   1902   *As It Is in the Philippines.* New York: Scribner and Co.
Belshaw, Cyril S.
   1965   *Traditional Exchange and Modern Markets.* Englewood
           Cliffs, N.J.: Prentice-Hall.
Benedict, Burton
   1968   Family firms and economic development. *Southwestern Jour-
           nal of Anthropology* 24:1–19.
Bennett, Alfred B., Jr.
   1971   Managers and entrepreneurs: A comparison of social back-
           grounds in Philippine manufacturing. *Institute of Philippine
           Culture Papers* 10:101–140.
Bennett, John W.
   1976   *The Ecological Transition. Cultural Anthropology and Hu-
           man Adaptation.* New York: Pergamon Press.

Berry, Brian J. L.
   1967   *Geography of Market Centers and Retail Distribution.* Engle-
          wood Cliffs, N.J.: Prentice-Hall.

Bonacich, Edna
   1973   A theory of middleman minorities. *American Sociological*
          Review 38:583–595.

Bornschier, Volker
   1980   Multinational corporations and economic growth. A cross-
          national test of the decapitalization thesis. *Journal of De-*
          velopment Economics 7:191–210.

Botica Boie Drug Company
   n.d.   *Centennial Memorial Botica Boie Philippine American Drug*
          Co. 1830–1930. Manila.

Bucklin, Louis P.
   1972a *Competition and Evolution in the Distributive Trade.* Engle-
          wood Cliffs, N.J.: Prentice-Hall.
   1972b Marketing channels and structures: A macro view. *Com-*
          bined Proceedings of the American Marketing Association
          34:28–40.

Business Day
   1975   *Business Day's 1,000 Top Corporations in the Philippines.*
          Quezon City.

Caperaso, James A.
   1978   Dependence, dependency and power in the global system: A
          structural and behavioral analysis. *International Organization*
          32:13–43.

Carroll, John J., S.J.
   1965   *The Filipino Manufacturing Entrepreneur. Agent and Product*
          of Change. Ithaca, N. Y.: Cornell University Press.

Catre, M.
   1974   Hiring policies and training programs of petroleum market-
          ing companies of the Philippines. M.B.A. thesis, Ateneo de
          Manila University.

Dannhaeuser, Norbert
   1977   Distribution and the structure of retail trade in a Philippine
          commercial town. *Economic Development and Cultural*
          Change 25:471–507.
   1979   Development of a distribution channel in the Philippines:
          From channel integration to channel fragmentation. *Human*
          Organization 38:74–78.
   1980   The role of the neighborhood store in developing econo-

mies: The case of Dagupan City, Philippines. *Journal of Developing Areas* 14:157–174.

1981a Commercial relations between center and periphery in north-central Luzon. Detrimental dependence or generative interdependence? *Philippine Studies* 29:144–169.

1981b Evolution and devolution of downward channel integration in the Philippines. *Economic Development and Cultural Change* 29:577–595.

1981c Modernization of distribution channels and the dependency issue: Consequences of interregional commerce in north-central Luzon, Philippines. *Journal of Anthropological Research* 37:130–147.

Davis, William G.
1973 *Social Relations in a Philippine Market Place. Self-Interest and Subjectivity.* Berkeley: University of California Press.

Development Academy of the Philippines
1976 *Study of Poverty.* Manila: DAP.

Doeppers, Daniel F.
1971 Ethnicity and class in the structure of Philippine cities. Ph.D. thesis, Syracuse University.

Dore, Ronald
1973 *British Factory–Japanese Factory. The Origins of National Diversity in Industrial Relations.* Berkeley: University of California Press.

Economic Development Foundation
n.d. *Special Report on Philippine Marketing. One Perspective.* Manila.

Epstein, T. Scarlett
1975 The ideal marriage between the economist's macroapproach and the social anthropologist's microapproach to development studies. *Economic Development and Cultural Change* 24:29–46.

Espiritu, A. C.
1977 Multinational corporations and Philippine national development. *Philippine Political Science Journal* June-July:137–152.

Etgar, Michael
1975 Structure and performance of distributive systems: A case study. *Combined Proceedings of the American Marketing Association* 37:397–401.

1976 Effects of administrative control on efficiency of vertical marketing systems. *Journal of Marketing Research* 13:12–24.

Evans, P. B., and Timberlake, M.
1980 Dependence, inequality, and the growth of the tertiary: A

comparative analysis of less developed countries. *American Sociological Review* 45:531–552.

Fieldhouse, D. K.
  1966 *The Colonial Empires. A Comparative Survey from the Eighteenth Century.* New York: Dell Publishing Co.

Flormata, Gregorio
  1901 *Memoria Sobre la Provincia de Pangasinan.* Manila: La Democracia.

Frank, Andre Gunder
  1969 *Capitalism and Underdevelopment in Latin America.* New York: Monthly Review Press.
  1978 *Dependent Accumulation and Underdevelopment.* London: Macmillan Press.

Friedman, Milton, and Friedman, Rose
  1980 *Free to Choose. A Personal Statement.* New York: Harcourt Brace Jovanovich.

Galbraith, John Kenneth
  1978 The defense of the multinational companies. *Harvard Business Review* 56:83–93.

Geertz, Clifford
  1963 *Peddlers and Princes. Social Development and Economic Change in Two Indonesian Towns.* Chicago: University of Chicago Press.
  1978 The bazaar economy: Information and search in peasant marketing. *American Economic Review* 68:28–32.

Gist, R. R.
  1974 *Marketing and Society.* Hinsdale, Ill.: Dryden Press.

Glade, W. P. et al.
  1970 *Marketing in a Developing Nation. The Competitive Behavior of Peruvian Industry.* Lexington, Mass.: Heath and Co.

Gleek, Lewis E., Jr.
  1975 *American Business and Philippine Development.* Manila: Carmelo and Bauermann.
  1977 *The Manila Americans (1901–1964).* Manila: Carmelo and Bauermann.

Gochoco
  1971 A study of the marketing operations of Shellane dealers. M.B.A. thesis, Ateneo de Manila University.

Goldman, Arieh
  1974 Growth of large food stores in developing countries. *Journal of Retailing* 50:50–60.

Grub, Philipp D., and Miele, A. R.
  1969 The changing marketing structure in the industrial develop-

ment of Venezuela. Pt. 2. *Journal of Developing Areas* 3:69–80.

Guerin, Joseph
   1964   Limitations of supermarkets in Spain. *Journal of Marketing* 28:22–26.

Gultinan, Joseph P.
   1974   Planned and evolutionary changes in distribution channels. *Journal of Retailing* 50:79–91; 103.

Hagey, Rebecca
   1979   Distribution of pharmaceuticals in the Philippines: Changing economics and ideologies. Paper read at the Canadian Council for Southeast Asian Studies, November 8–11, 1979, Vancouver, British Columbia.

Hartendorp, A. V. H.
   1952   A short history of industry and trade in the Philippines. *American Chamber of Commerce Journal.* November.
   1958   *History of Industry and Trade of the Philippines. From Pre-Spanish Times to the End of the Quirino Administration.* Manila: American Chamber of Commerce of the Philippines.

Heath, Anthony
   1976   *Rational Choice and Social Exchange. A Critique of Exchange Theory.* London: Cambridge University Press.

Helfgott, Roy B.
   1973   Multinational corporations and manpower utilization in developing nations. *Journal of Developing Areas* 7:235–246.

Hirschman, Albert O.
   1958   *Strategy of Economic Development.* New Haven: Yale University Press.

Hollander, Stanley
   1960   The wheel of retailing. *Journal of Marketing* 24:37–42.

Hollnsteiner, Mary B.
   1965   A note to management on traditional Filipino values in business enterprise: The lumber company as a case study. *Philippine Studies* 13:350–354.

Hoselitz, Bert F.
   1955   Generative and parasitic cities. *Economic Development and Cultural Change* 3:278–294.

International Labour Office
   1974   *Sharing in Development. A Program of Employment, Equity and Growth for the Philippines.* Geneva: ILO.

Jack, Andrew B.
  1957 The channels of distribution for an innovation: The sewing-machine industry in America, 1860–1865. *Explorations in Entrepreneurial History* 9:113–141.
Johnson, E. A. J.
  1970 *The Organization of Space in Developing Countries.* Cambridge, Mass.: Harvard University Press.
Johnson, Harry G.
  1977 Changing views on trade and development: Some reflections. *Economic Development and Cultural Change* 25 (Supp.): 363–375.
Kahn, J. S.
  1978 Marxist anthropology and peasant economics: A study of the social structure of underdevelopment. In *The New Economic Anthropology,* ed. J. Clammer, pp. 110–137. New York: St. Martin's Press.
Kaut, Charles R.
  1961 Utang na loob: A system of contractual obligation among Tagalogs. *Southwestern Journal of Anthropology* 17:256–272.
Kay, G.
  1975 *Development and Underdevelopment. A Marxist Analysis.* New York: Macmillan.
Kotler, Philip
  1980 *Marketing Management. Analysis, Planning, and Control.* Englewood Cliffs, N.J.: Prentice-Hall.
Kuznets, Simon
  1966 *Modern Economic Growth. Rate, Structure and Spread.* New Haven: Yale University Press.
Landé, Robert
  1965 *Leaders, Factions, and Parties. The Structure of Philippine Politics.* Yale University Southeast Asia Studies, monograph series 6. New Haven: Yale University Press.
Lewis, W. Arthur
  1978 *Growth and Fluctuations, 1870–1913.* London: Allen and Unwin.
Liu, Pak-wai, and Wong, Yue-chim
  1981 Human capital and inequality in Singapore. *Economic Development and Cultural Change* 29:275–293.
Lynch, Frank, S.J.
  1963 Social acceptance. *Institute of Philippine Culture Papers* 2:1–23.

Lynch, Frank, S.J. et al.
  1978   Some social anthropologists look at Philippine banking.
         PSSC Social Science Information 6:7–11.
McCammon, Bert C., Jr., and Bates, A. D.
  1967   The emergence and growth of contractually integrated chan-
         nels in the American economy. In *The Marketing Channel.
         A Conceptual Viewpoint*, ed. B. Mallen, pp. 287–298. New
         York: John Wiley and Sons.
McGee, T. G., and Yeung, Y.
  1977   *Hawkers in Southeast Asian Cities. Planning for the Bazaar
         Economy*. Ottawa: International Development Research
         Centre.
McIntyre, W. F.
  1955   Retail patterns of Manila. *Geographic Review* 45:66–80.
Magbag, Wenceslao A., Jr.
  1966   A study of home appliance marketing through franchise
         dealership organizations. B.A. thesis, De La Salle Uni-
         versity.
Magdalena, F. V.
  1977   Multidimensional scalogram analysis of Philippine cities,
         1960–70: A typological approach to community moderniza-
         tion. *Developing Economies* 15:166–181.
Mahler, Vincent A.
  1980   *Dependency Approaches to International Political Economy.
         A Cross-National Study*. New York: Columbia University
         Press.
Mattson, Lars-Gunnar
  1969   *Integration and Efficiency in Marketing Systems*. Stockholm:
         Stockholm School of Economics.
Mehta, Subhash C.
  1973   *Indian Consumers. Studies and Cases for Marketing Deci-
         sions*. Bombay: Tata McGraw-Hill Publishing Co.
Miller, Hugo
  1911   *Commercial Geography*. Manila: Bureau of Printing.
Mingst, Karen A.
  1980   An interdependency perspective: Agricultural trade between
         the United States and developing areas. *Journal of Develop-
         ing Areas* 14:501–512.
Mintz, Sidney W.
  1961   Pratik: Haitian personal economic relations. *Proceedings of
         the 1961 Annual Spring Meeting of the American Ethnologi-
         cal Society*, pp. 54–63. Seattle: University of Washington
         Press.

Montanez, M.
   1971   Survey of sales promotion activities among leading competitors in the laundry detergent industry. B.S. thesis, University of the Philippines.
Moyer, Reed
   1972   *Macro Marketing. A Social Perspective.* New York: John Wiley and Sons.
Myrdal, Gunnar
   1970   *The Challenge of World Poverty.* New York: Pantheon.
Nam, Rosa L. Sau
   1971   Marketing mix for an appliance business. *University of Santo Tomas Commerce Journal* 20:148–154.
Neher, Clark D.
   1980   The political status and role of Philippine women in Cebu province. *Philippine Quarterly of Culture and Society* 8:108–124.
Oil Industry Commission
   1972   *Rules and Regulations Governing the Establishment, Construction, Operations, Remodeling and/or Refurbishing of Petroleum Products Retail Outlets.* Manila: OIC.
Omohundro, John T.
   1974   The Chinese merchant community of Iloilo City, Philippines. Ph.D. thesis, University of Michigan.
   1978   Trading patterns of Philippine Chinese: Strategies of sojourning middlemen. In *Economic Exchange and Social Interaction in Southeast Asia*, ed. Karl Hutterer, pp. 113–136. University of Michigan Center for South and Southeast Asian Studies. Ann Arbor: University of Michigan Press.
Ortiz, Sutti
   1979   Expectation and forecasts in the face of uncertainty. *Man* 14:64–80.
Palamountain, Joseph C.
   1955   *The Politics of Distribution.* Cambridge, Mass.: Harvard University Press.
Palanca, Ellen H.
   1977   The economic position of the Chinese in the Philippines. *Philippine Studies* 25:80–94.
Partridge, William L.
   1979   Banana county in the wake of United Fruit: Social and economic linkages. *American Ethnologist* 6:491–509.
Philippine Commonwealth
   1936   *Fact Finding Report.* Manila: Secretary of Labor.

1940– *Census of the Philippines, 1939.* Manila: Printing Office.
1943

Philippine Islands
1920– *Census of the Philippine Islands, 1918.* Manila: Census
1921 Office of the Philippine Islands.
1924 *Commercial Handbook of the Philippine Islands.* Manila:
Bureau of Commerce and Industry.

Philippine Journal of Commerce
1937 Pioneer footwear factory expands. *Philippine Journal of
Commerce* 13:7–8.

Potter, Jack M.
1968 *Capitalism and the Chinese Peasant. Social and Economic
Change in a Hong Kong Village.* Berkeley: University of
California Press.

Preparatory Commission for Philippine Independence
1943 *Report of the Sub-Committee on Natural Resources and
Businesses to the Committee on Research and Planning.*
Manila.

Reed, Robert R.
1976 *City of Pines. The Origins of Baguio as a Colonial Hill Station and Regional Capital.* University of California Center
for South and Southeast Asia Studies, research monograph
13. Berkeley: University of California Press.

Republic of the Philippines
1964– *Economic Census of the Philippines, 1961. Commerce.*
1965 Manila: Bureau of the Census and Statistics.
1973 *Annual Survey of Wholesale and Retail Establishments, 1969.*
Manila: Bureau of the Census and Statistics.
1974 *1970 Census of Population and Housing.* Vol. 1. *Pangasinan.*
Manila: National Census and Statistics Office.
1975 *1972 Listings of Establishments.* Manila: National Census
and Statistics Office.

Revzan, David A.
1967 Marketing organization through the channel. In *The Marketing Channel. A Conceptual Viewpoint*, ed. B. Mallen,
pp. 3–19. New York: John Wiley and Sons.

Robicheaux, R., and El-Ansary, A.
1976 A general model for understanding channel member behavior. *Journal of Retailing* 52:13–30; 92–93.

Rodgers, Gerry; Hopkins, Mike; and Wéry, René
1978 *Population, Employment and Inequality. BACHU—Philippines.* Hants, Eng.: Saxon House.

Ronquillo, R.
1972   A study of advertising policies and strategies of major textile mills in the Philippines. M.B.A. thesis, Ateneo de Manila University.

Roxas, N.
1968   Organization and management of IBM Philippines, Inc. and Erlanger and Galinger, Inc. B.A. thesis, University of the Philippines.

Samuelson, Paul A.
1973   *Economics.* New York: McGraw-Hill.

San Miguel
1954   *San Miguel Annual Report.* Manila.

Santos, T. dos
1970   The structure of dependence. *American Economic Review* 60:231–236.

Sau, R.
1978   *Unequal Exchange. Imperialism and Underdevelopment.* New York: Oxford University Press.

Schatz, Sayre P.
1981   Assertive pragmatism and the multinational enterprise. *World Development* 9:93–105.

Schneider, Harold K.
1974   *Economic Man. The Anthropology of Economics.* New York: Free Press.

Silin, Robert H.
1972   Marketing and credit in a Hong Kong wholesale market. In *Economic Organization in Chinese Society*, ed. W. E. Willmott, pp. 327–352. Stanford: Stanford University Press.

Slater, Charles C.
1974   Marketing—a catalyst for development. In *Marketing Systems for Developing Countries*, ed. D. Izraeli; D. N. Izraeli; and F. Meissner, pp. 3–17. Toronto: John Wiley and Sons.

Smith, Carol A., ed.
1976   *Regional Analysis.* Vol. 1. *Economic Systems.* New York: Academic Press.

Smith, Carol A.
1978   Beyond dependency theory: National and regional patterns of underdevelopment in Guatemala. *American Ethnologist* 5:574–617.

Soriano, Emanuel V., and Nehrt, Lee C.
1976   *Business Policy in an Asian Context.* Rizal, Phil.: Sinag-Tala Publishers.

Stern, Louis W., and Reve, Torger
  1980   Distribution channels as political economies: A framework
         for comparative analysis. *Journal of Marketing* 44:52–64.
Stiefel, Laurence
  1963   *The Textile Industry—A Case Study of Industrial Develop-
         ment in the Philippines.* Cornell University Southeast Asia
         Program, data paper 49. Ithaca, N. Y.: Cornell University
         Press.
Studies on Philippine Industry
  1974a *Drug Industry.* Makati: Private Development Corporation of
         the Philippines.
  1974b *The Textile Industry.* Makati: Private Development Corpora-
         tion of the Philippines.
Takeuchi, H., and Bucklin, Louis P.
  1977   Productivity in retailing: Retail structure and public policy.
         Journal of Retailing 53:35–46; 94–95.
U.S. Bureau of the Census
  1905   *Census of the Philippine Islands, 1903.* Washington, D.C.:
         Government Printing Office.
U.S. Department of Commerce
  1927   *The Philippine Islands.* Washington, D.C.
  1965   *Philippines. A Market for U.S. Products.* Washington, D.C.:
         U.S. Government Printing Office.
U.S. Department of International Reference Service
  1948   *Republic of the Philippines. Summary of Current Economic
         Information.* Washington, D.C.
Valenciano, A. Q.
  1974   Selection practice and development of service station oper-
         ators by petroleum marketing companies. M.B.A. thesis,
         Ateneo de Manila University.
Vaugh, Charles L.
  1974   *Franchising.* Lexington, Mass.: D. C. Heath and Co.
Vernon, Raymond
  1977   *Storm over the Multinationals. The Real Issues.* Cambridge,
         Mass.: Harvard University Press.
Vicente-Wiley, Leticia
  1979   Achievement values of Filipino entrepreneurs and politi-
         cians. *Economic Development and Cultural Change*
         27:467–483.
Wadinambiaratchi, George
  1965   Channels of distribution in developing economies. *Business
         Quarterly* 30:74–82.

Ward, Barbara E.
  1972   A small factory in Hong Kong. Some aspects of its internal
         organization. In *Economic Organization in Chinese Society*,
         ed. W. E. Willmott, pp. 353–386. Stanford: Stanford Uni-
         versity Press.
Weinberg, M. S., and Williams, C. J.
  1980   Sexual embourgeoisement—social class and sexual activity:
         1938–70. *American Sociological Review* 45:33–48.
Wickberg, Edgar
  1965   *The Chinese in Philippine Life, 1850–1898*. New Haven:
         Yale University Press.
Wilkins, M.
  1970   *The Emergence of Multinational Enterprise. American Busi-
         ness Abroad from the Colonial Era to 1914*. Cambridge,
         Mass.: Harvard University Press.
World Bank
  1976   *The Philippines. Priorities and Prospects for Development*.
         Washington, D.C.: International Bank for Reconstruction
         and Development.
Yambot, Efrem
  1975   *Philippine Almanac and Handbook of Facts for 1975*.
         Quezon City: Almanac Printers.
Yoshino, M. Y.
  1971   *The Japanese Marketing System. Adaptations and Innova-
         tions*. Cambridge, Mass.: MIT Press.

INDEX

Abenson, Inc., 135, 150, 152
Active marketing strategy, 26,
   193, 230, 239; coordinated
   penetration and, 123; drugs
   and, 115; informal, 47; manufacturing sector and, 26; organizational classification of
   channels and, 43–46; peripheral region and, 198, 223–224,
   226; sales penetration as, 46,
   72, 120, 122; textiles and,
   61–68
Advertisements, 13, 22, 49;
   cigarette, 109–110; dependency
   issue and, 196, 198; detergent,
   100, 101–102, 105; drug, 118,
   120; Floro Photo, 186–187;
   gasoline, 180; PCC and, 11;
   popularity of (Dagupan), 36;
   soft drink, 94–95, 98–99; textiles and, 62, 63, 65. *See also*
   Promotions
Agriculture, 5, 6, 16, 17
Alhambra Industries, Inc., 81–82
Allied Textiles, 64–65
Americans, 33, 35, 38; Commonwealth period and, 8–13; in

Dagupan (American period),
   18; early period of, 5–7; food
   processing and, 74–75; historic
   influence of, 228, 230; marketing in Philippines and, 26, 202,
   230
Amon Trading Corporation,
   86
Ang Tibay (footwear company),
   12
Appliances. *See* Home appliances
Arson, 50
Assembly plants (auto), 161–162,
   163, 164, 167
Automatic Electrical Appliances,
   133–134
Automobile distribution. *See*
   Motor vehicle distribution

Bacnotan Consolidated Indus-
   tries, Inc., 79
Baguio (construction of), 16
Banks, 55, 224; in Dagupan,
   37–38
Beer, 49, 91
Board of Investment (BOI), 27,
   33, 161, 167

and, 220–221; Manila-Dagupan channel effects and, 209, 210

Entrepreneurs: coordinated penetration and, 212, 215; dependency issue and, 197, 222; manufacturing and Filipino, 27; neighborhood (*sari-sari*) stores and, 9; retailing and Filipino, 32–33

Envy, preferred treatment and, 96–97, 99

Erlanger and Galinger, Inc., 23

Ethnic composition: Commonwealth period, 8–9; Dagupan in American period and, 17–18, 19; Dagupan after independence and, 38–40; early American period, 6–7; in Philippines after independence, 31–34; textiles and, 70. *See also* Americans; Chinese; Europeans; Filipinos; Indian families in Dagupan; Japanese

Europeans, 6, 8, 16, 18, 38

Evertex Sales, 62

Exploitation, Manila-Dagupan channel analysis and, 196, 197, 222–224

Exports: Commonwealth period and, 7–8; early American period and, 6; incentives for, 27; of rice from Dagupan, 16, 17

Families: gas station franchises and, 175–176; groceries and centralized, 98; social profile of entrepreneurs and, 217–218; textiles and centralized, 59–61, 70. *See also* Kinship

Farm machinery, 163, 169

Federation of Petroleum Dealers

Association of the Philippines (FPDAP), 179, 183

Females, role of, 228, 230–231

Fieldmen. *See* Sales force; Salesmen

Filipinization, 39, 75, 215, 229; auto dealerships and, 165–166; gasoline dealers and, 184; Japanese and, 32; law (1954) for, 33; milk industry and, 77

Filipinos: American period ethnic cleavage and, 6–7, 18–19; auto dealerships and, 163; Commonwealth period and, 8, 9; coordinated penetration and change in social class of, 215–222; cultural sphere and, 228, 230–232; in Dagupan (trade and), 38–40; drug stores and, 113, 187, 190, 192; as entrepreneurs, 9, 27; as fieldmen (salesmen), 206–207; gasoline dealerships and, 185; groceries and, 74; hardware and, 75; home appliances and, 125, 136, 138, 139, 142, 154–155; Japanese occupation and, 32; kinship relations and, 231; Manila-Dagupan channel (sales penetration) and, 202–203; milk industry and, 77–79; retailing and, 32–33; *suki* relations and, 52; textiles and, 50–51, 54, 59, 60, 61, 64, 68

Finance companies (subsidiary, appliance businesses), 143–145, 158

Financial institutions, coordinated penetration and, 212

Fishpond industry, 17, 35

Floro Photo, 186–187, 193

Foreign exchange, 26

Pepsi-Cola, 91, 92, 93–95
Personalized business relations,
232, 233; Filipinos and *suki* relationships and, 52; tradition
of, 228
Pharmaceuticals, 241; distribution
(sales penetration) and, 114–
120; Mercury Drug coordi-
nated penetration and, 187–
193; passive marketing and,
47–48; production and, 111–
112; retailing history of, 112–
114
Pharma Industries, Inc.,
115–116
Philippine Manufacturing Company (PMC) (groceries), 12
Philippine Packing Corporation
(PPC), 84–85
Philippine Pharmaceutical Association, 187
Philippine Refining Company
(PRC), 100–102, 103, 104, 106
Philippines: Dagupan and American period in, 13–23; ethnic
plurality in, 31–34; geographic
and cultural aspects of, 228–
229, 230–232; government corruption and, 229–230; historical sketch of American period
in, 5–13; as medium-level developing country, 227–228;
organization of distribution in,
25–31. *See also* Government of
Philippines
PMC. *See* Philippine Manufacturing Company (PMC); Procter
and Gamble Philippine Manufacturing Corporation (PMC)
Political issues, 225
Population: of Dagupan, 35;
growth of, 5; in 1980, 25

PPC. *See* Philippine Packing Cor-
poration (PPC)
PRC. *See* Philippine Refining
Company (PRC)
Precision Electronics Corpora-
tion, 150, 151
Procter and Gamble Philippine
Manufacturing Corporation
(PMC), 100–102, 103, 104,
105–106
Produce, 39
Product specialization, 8
Profits, Manila-Dagupan channel
effects and, 209
Progressive Car Manufacturing
Program, 162
Promotions: dependency issue
and, 198; detergents and, 101–
102, 105, 106; drug, 118; drug
(passive marketing), 47–48;
Manila-Dagupan channel and,
196, 202; soft drink, 95, 98–99.
See also Advertisements
Pure Foods Corporation,
79–81
PX goods, 48–49

Radiola-Toshiba Philippines,
Inc., 150
Radiowealth, Inc., 129; finance
company of, 144–145, 158
Railroad (Manila-Dagupan), 22;
construction of (1894), 13–16;
transportation of rice and,
16–17
Regional issues: dependency and,
198; Manila-Dagupan channel
analysis and, 225
Republic Glass Corporation,
78–79
Restaurants, 73

appliances and branch, 150–152; branching and, 79; detergents and, 101; drug and branch, 115–116; of Manila companies in Dagupan, 37; sales penetration and, 73, 84, 88–89

Warner-Chilcott Laboratories (Phils.), Inc., 115, 116–117

Wholesale outlets (appliances), 151, 153

Wholesaler-retailer, 19, 33; appliance, 135, 136, 139, 149–150, 152; drug, 115, 118; grocery, 74; textiles and, 54–55, 59

Wholesalers, 38; appliance, 137; branches and, 23, 29; Chinese, 12, 33–34, 39, 40, 74, 75; Commonwealth period and, 7; distributive channel after independence and, 29; distributors acting as, 107–111; drug, 113–114; gasoline, 182, 184; number of, 199; passive marketing and Chinese drug, 47–48; textiles and, 54–55, 57, 61

Women. *See* Females

World Bank, 26

Ysmael Steel Manufacturing Corporation, 128–131, 134, 138